Understanding Racism

To all the scholars and activists who have invested in me.

Sara Miller McCune founded SAGE Publishing in 1965 to support the dissemination of usable knowledge and educate a global community. SAGE publishes more than 1000 journals and over 800 new books each year, spanning a wide range of subject areas. Our growing selection of library products includes archives, data, case studies and video. SAGE remains majority owned by our founder and after her lifetime will become owned by a charitable trust that secures the company's continued independence.

Los Angeles | London | New Delhi | Singapore | Washington DC | Melbourne

Understanding Racism

Theories of Oppression and Discrimination

hephzibah v. strmic-pawl

Manhattanville College

Los Angeles | London | New Delhi
Singapore | Washington DC | Boston

For information:

SAGE Publications, Inc.
2455 Teller Road
Thousand Oaks, California 91320
E-mail: order@sagepub.com

SAGE Publications Ltd.
1 Oliver's Yard
55 City Road
London, EC1Y 1SP
United Kingdom

SAGE Publications India Pvt. Ltd.
B 1/I 1 Mohan Cooperative Industrial Area
Mathura Road, New Delhi 110 044
India

SAGE Publications Asia-Pacific Pte. Ltd.
18 Cross Street #10-10/11/12
China Square Central
Singapore 048423

Printed in the United States of America

ISBN: 9781506387789

RECYCLED
Paper made from
recycled material
FSC® C008955

Acquisitions Editor: Jeff Lasser
Editorial Assistant: Tiara Beatty
Production Editor: Bennie Clark Allen
Copy Editor: Laureen Gleason
Typesetter: Cenveo Publisher Services
Proofreader: Sue Schon
Indexer: Integra
Cover Designer: Dally Verghese
Marketing Manager: Will Waters

This book is printed on acid-free paper.

20 21 22 23 24 10 9 8 7 6 5 4 3 2 1

Brief Contents

Detailed Contents

PART II   MICRO-LEVEL THEORIES

Chapter 4   Implicit Bias: Mahzarin Banaji | Anthony Greenwald | Brian Nosek

PART III MACRO-LEVEL THEORIES

PART IV   FROM "OLD RACISM" TO "NEW RACISM"

Chapter 9   Laissez-Faire Racism:
Lawrence Bobo | James Kluegel | Ryan Smith

Preface

● ●

As a young student, when I heard the word *theory*, I thought of grand, incomprehensible language and faced an impending headache from trying to see the connection between theory and real life. I often resorted to the idea that theorists should not be lauded because they don't put into practice what they put into words. Such thoughts scared me away from theory and made me believe I would never seriously engage with it. These ideas faded, however, when both my scholarship and my activism progressed, until I realized the truism of "theory plus praxis, praxis plus theory," or, in other words, theory and action need each other. Theory provides the guidance and the conceptual framework for understanding social facts. Thus, theory is necessary for scholarship and activism to progress. This point is particularly true when addressing the nature of oppression, or, in the case of this book specifically, racism. This revelation led to an appreciation for and a grappling with theory and eventually the writing of this book on major theories of racism.

In this book, I have three general aims: (1) to make theory accessible, (2) to summarize major bodies of work by important scholars of racism and communicate them as theories, and (3) to further our conversations on racism. To the first point, I do not primarily identify as a theorist, although my research on multiracialism, contemporary racism, and pedagogy heavily engages with theory. But not being a theory specialist has led me to discover ways to distill theory in a manner that is widely accessible. Particularly in the classroom, I have learned to communicate theories in ways that "non-theorists" can understand, appreciate, and utilize. I have likewise endeavored to do the same in this book.

The second aim is to provide a guide to theories of racism. As it currently stands, if one wants a grasp of various means of understanding contemporary racism, the options are somewhat limited: read numerous books and articles, read blogs that are somewhat inadequate, or take a class. This book offers another option through providing overviews of major theories on racism.

The third aim is to further our conversations on racism. In the recent decade, there has been both a rise in overt racism and new discussions on how covert racism operates. In order to confront this racism, we need to understand it, and it is my hope that this book is useful not only for undergraduates and graduate students but also for policy makers, social workers, community organizations, and individuals who are yearning to learn more. Each theory's summary is succinct and purposeful in its inclusion of multiple quotes by the theorist and supplemented with Reflect and Discuss questions, Key Terms, Diagrams, Key People biographies, and Further Reading. This book is both a tool to learn and a call to action, as theory and praxis must coexist.

Understanding Theory

Studying theory is a difficult endeavor, particularly because there is not one unambiguous, distinct definition of what constitutes theory—or what does not constitute theory. This point may seem remarkable, considering the breadth and depth of classes and books devoted to discussing theory, as though the definition of it is a given and understood. In reality, sociology and other social science disciplines have multiple research traditions that lead to different utilizations and definitions of theory.[1] Gabriel Abend interrogates "the meaning of theory" and suggests that there are seven main ways sociologists use theory, including a proposition between variables, an explanation of a social phenomenon, or an overall perspective that provides "conceptual equipment."[2] Thus, sociologists, and specifically theorists, often use theory in different, and sometimes contrasting, manners. In a move to provide a basic conceptualization, the noted social theorist Jeffrey Alexander states that "theory is a generalization separated from particulars, an abstraction separated from a concrete case,"[3] and similarly Hans Joas and Wolfgang Knöbl in their book *Social Theory* note that "theories should be understood as generalizations."[4] In this sense, any analysis that goes from the specifics of one case to making a claim about how conditions might operate generally can be construed as (moving toward) theory.

We are constantly engaging with theory. On a daily basis, we interpret our social worlds and make generalizations about them in order to understand those social worlds. For example, you might have a theory that car salespeople are dishonest, so you visit multiple car lots to ensure that the best price is attained. Or you have a theory that you pick up good habits from friends, so you make a point to socialize with people who work hard. Joas and Knöbl remark that "theory is as necessary as unavoidable. Without it, it would be impossible to learn or to act in a consistent fashion; without generalizations and abstractions, the world would exist for us only as a chaotic patchwork of discrete, disconnected experiences and sensory impressions."[5] Theory guides behavior, and behaviors lead to amended or new theories.

It is important to grasp the fundamental necessity of theory. Theories guide us in how to understand and interpret social problems. For instance, take the two major sociological theories of conflict theory and symbolic interactionism. Conflict theory pays attention to how society is largely divided into "the haves," who have resources and power, and the "have-nots," who do not have resources and power. Symbolic interactionism pays attention to how people interact with each other and develop meaning through symbols. Now, take the social problem of teen pregnancy. Proponents of conflict theory would analyze this problem as one of haves and have-nots, wherein have-nots are more likely to experience teen pregnancy because they have less access to healthcare information and resources. Thus, the conflict theory solution would be to provide these resources. Proponents of symbolic interactionism will interpret the same data differently, as they will pay attention to symbols and meaning making. Symbolic interactionists would look at how sex is marketed to teenagers and how condoms are seen as not sexy. A symbolic interactionist solution would be to change the meaning around teen sex and condoms. These examples provide two important lessons about the necessity of theory: (1) Theory guides how one interprets data, and (2) theory and action must be connected. To the first point, theory helps explain observations and therefore frames interpretation and analysis of data. However, one theory is not always necessarily better than another, as seen in the example of conflict theory and symbolic interactionism. It is likely correct that teen pregnancy is affected by resources (conflict theory) *and* meanings around sex and condoms (symbolic interactionism), so multiple theories can coexist, rather than one being right and the other wrong. To the second point, theory and practice need each other. In the preceding example, the theoretical analysis of teen pregnancy means little if a solution is not provided. Theory is useless without action, but action needs effective theory to be most beneficial. Thus, it is understandable when Alexander argues that "theory is crucial, indeed that it is the heart of science."[6]

Understanding Race and Racism

Race and racism are in an ugly mutual engagement and cannot exist without each other. Racism birthed racial categories and our contemporary understanding of "races." However, before further discussion about racism, it is imperative to know that race is a social construction and is without any biological reality. Race is the assignment of a categorical label to a group of people who are perceived to share a set of physical features. For example, Whites are often described as sharing the features of light skin tone, straight hair, blue or green eyes, narrow nose, and thin lips. Of course, there are some people who are deemed "White" who fit this description but many who do not. There are "White" people who have curly hair, a wide nose, brown eyes, and/or brown skin. A perceived set of physical features helps guide our day-to-day social classification of people into races, but there is no unifying set of features that would encompass all Whites, all Asians, all Blacks, all Latinxs, all Native Americans, or any racial group. Moreover, research shows that humans are 99.9% identical in their genetic makeup, and there is no set of genetic markers that is distinctly shared by racial groups.[7] In fact, people who are of different races can have more genetically in common with one another than people who are deemed of the same race.[8] Thus, race is not biological and is instead a social construction—that is, a construct created and maintained by society.

Racial groups, to reiterate, were created by and are maintained through society's practice of racism. Racism is a form of oppression based on race. The word *oppression* comes from the Latin and French words that mean "state of being overcome" or "constriction," which is revealing of the nature of oppression.[9] Any social oppression is identified by an ideological belief that there is a classification of people who are at the top of a hierarchy and who are superior and that consequently there is systemic (of the system) and systematic (of a pattern) provision of resources, opportunities, and benefits to those at the top of the hierarchy, along with the simultaneous denial of resources, opportunities, and benefits to those at the bottom of the hierarchy. Oppression can operate through the micro level of individual engagement and at the macro level of institutions and structures. Oppression can be based on any type of social categorization that society deems important enough to assign value to.[10] For example, classism is a form of oppression based on money and sustained by capitalism, and sexism is a form of oppression based on gender and sustained by patriarchy. Racism is a form of oppression based on race and sustained by White supremacy. White supremacy is fundamentally the valuing of people deemed White and the disvaluing of people deemed non-White. White colonialism and imperialism led to the creation of a racial hierarchy and racial categories wherein people with light skin and of European ancestry were categorized as "White" and were placed at the top of the racial hierarchy. Who is considered "White" has fluctuated throughout time, but the valuing of people deemed White has been consistent.[11] The continuing operation and ramifications of racism are addressed by the theories of racism in this book.

A Note on Capitalization

Because racial groups are significant categories of classification, I choose to capitalize all racial groups, such as "Black" and "White." In the case of quotations used in the book, racial groups may or may not be capitalized, depending on the theorist's perspective on capitalization. For further discussion on why to capitalize the names of racial groups, see Race Forward's "Race Reporting Guide"[12] and the Brookings Institution report "Not Just a Typographical Change: Why Brookings Is Capitalizing Black."[13] Regarding the use of "Latino" and "Hispanic," I follow the author's use of the term when applicable and otherwise use the term "Latinx." The use of the "x" at the end signifies the effort to avoid gendering the term.[14]

Understanding Theories of Racism
· ·

White supremacy is often, in contemporary terms, understood within the confined ideas of White supremacy groups such as the Ku Klux Klan and Les Identitaires. White supremacy is apparent through the existence of such groups, but it can also operate on a level that appears more covert to some through means such as incarceration, immigration, and even access to good schools. As society has generally moved away from overt racism to more covert racism, theories of how racism persists have burgeoned. The theories addressed in this book are primarily from the sociological discipline, as sociology is the study of society, but also included are theories from philosophy, psychology, and law.

There are 13 theories covered in this book: prejudice and discrimination, White privilege, White supremacy, implicit bias, microaggressions, racial formation, systemic racism, critical race theory, laissez-faire racism, structure and culture, color-blind racism, colorism, and intersectionality. Some of these theories are largely undisputedly understood *as theories*, such as racial formation, systemic racism, and laissez-faire racism. Yet there has been debate, which will likely continue, about whether all 13 theories covered in this book actually constitute *theory*. Some might instead label them as "frameworks," "approaches," or even "concepts." Tanya Golash-Boza engages in a similar conversation in her article "A Critical and Comprehensive Sociological Theory of Race and Racism," wherein she contests the idea that a sociological theory of race and racism does not exist. Yet in her article, the comprehensive theory of racism offered relies on a synthesis of works by multiple scholars.[15] I do not contest Golash-Boza's conclusion, but I do suggest that each of the 13 works covered in this book can be and should be understood distinctly as a theory in its own right. As outlined previously, the most fundamental characterization of a theory is an abstraction or generalization. The 13 chapters in this book meet this definition. For example, work on implicit bias describes how people generally have biases that they are unaware of, and scholarship on colorism describes the general effects of one's placement on a skin-tone continuum from light to dark. In this sense, I think that scholars of race and racism have done a disservice by not seeing how these "frameworks" or "approaches" are theories (albeit at various stages of theoretical development).

Why These Theories and Scholars?

This book has 13 chapters, but it could have had more, or it could have had fewer. I chose these 13 theories because they provide a fundamental grounding in the primary approaches to racism. The book is divided into five parts that provide a guiding organization: "Foundational Theories," "Micro-Level Theories," "Macro-Level Theories," "From 'Old Racism' to 'New Racism,'" and "More Than Race." The organizational structure of the book is further discussed in the "Features" section of this preface, but here I address the choice of the scholars used to represent each theory. I chose scholars and bodies of work based on a combination of several interrelated factors: (1) the degree to which a theoretical map and concepts are provided; (2) the scholar's depth of work with the theory, thereby signifying a committed and sophisticated dedication; and (3) the number of citations and general recognition of the work that would indicate the significance of and importance to know it.

Based on these three factors, the choice of scholar is sometimes clear, as in the cases of Michael Omi and Howard Winant, who developed racial formation, or Lawrence Bobo, James Kluegel, and Ryan Smith, who conceived of laissez-faire racism. In a couple of instances, scholarship was culled from multiple researchers who contributed to the theory's formation, as in the case of the chapter on White privilege, which relies on work by Robert Amico, Peggy McIntosh, Paula Rothenberg, and Tim Wise, and the chapter on colorism, which synthesizes work by Evelyn Nakano Glenn, Ronald Hall, Margaret Hunter, Kimberly Norwood, and others. In two instances, the prejudice and discrimination chapter and the White supremacy chapter, an "Additional Contributions" section, which briefly summarizes another theorist's perspective, is included after the primary theorist's work. This section is incorporated because the "additional contribution" was significant and distinct enough from the primary theorist covered that it needed to be included. Yet in many cases, I certainly recognize that other scholars and/or scholarship could have been chosen to represent a particular theory. For example, the chapter on critical race theory is largely based on Derrick Bell and his book *Faces at the Bottom of the Well*, but there are, of course, many other critical race theorists and other books and articles. However, I also contend that Bell and this book are a good and valuable representation of this theory. Bell is often recognized as the founder of critical race theory; he has numerous books and articles using this theory; and *Faces at the Bottom of the Well*, according to Google Scholar, had more than 3,400 citations as of January 2020. Every work and theorist used in this book fit a similar bill. Moreover, the point of this book is not to be exhaustive but to provide brief and accessible summaries that represent the heart of each theory.

Theory Building

It must be said that each of the scholars represented in this book built on prior research and practice of other scholars. For instance, intersectional analysis in this book is based on work by Kimberlé Crenshaw, yet the work of intersectionality, though not always conceptualized in that term, is visible in Sojourner Truth's (1797–1883) "Ain't I a Woman," Ida B. Wells' (1862–1931) reporting on lynching, and Gloria Anzaldúa's (1942–2004) work on feminism, queer theory, and cultural theory. White abolitionists such as William Lloyd Garrison (1805–1879) and Sarah Moore Grimke (1792–1873), along with her sister, Angelina Grimke (1805–1879), articulated the dynamics of White privilege long ago. Native American leaders such as Crazy Horse (ca. 1842–1877), Sitting Bull (1831–1890), and Tecumseh (1768–1813) spoke of the horrors of White supremacy. Similarly, W. E. B. Du Bois' (1868–1963) scholarship provides a foundation for much of our contemporary theory on race and racism, as has been detailed in Du Boisian scholarship such as Aldon Morris' *The Scholar Denied: W. E. B. Du Bois and the Birth of Modern Sociology* and Phil Zuckerman's edited collection of Du Bois' work in *The Social Theory of W. E. B. Du Bois*. The chapters in this book do not discuss these contributions or numerous other preceding scholars, but that is not to imply that they are not important. It is just not within the scope of this book to address previous work, though if one chooses to engage further with any of these theories, reading the work that inspired them is recommended.

Features of *Understanding Racism*

Understanding Racism is divided into five parts that aid in organizing the 13 theories through a shared contribution and/or orientation. Part I is "Foundational Theories," which consists of prejudice and discrimination, White privilege, and White supremacy. Each of these theories addresses overarching dynamics of racism. They are important theories in and of themselves, while they also provide pivotal concepts that are used in other theories. For example, White privilege is a critical theory that describes how Whites receive the benefits of racism, while the concept of White privilege is also utilized in many other theories of racism. Part II is "Micro-Level Theories," which covers implicit bias and microaggressions. Both of these theories critically explore how individuals participate in racism, intentionally or not. Part III is "Macro-Level Theories," which includes racial formation, systemic racism, and critical race theory. These three theories focus on how institutions and the social system created and maintain racism. Part IV, "From 'Old Racism' to 'New Racism,'" consists of laissez-faire racism, structure and culture, and color-blind racism, all of which describe how racism evolved from overt, discriminatory laws and practices to the contemporary era where racism, though still active, can be harder to recognize. Part IV, the last part of the book, is "More Than Race," where the theories of colorism and intersectionality detail how other factors such as skin tone, class, and gender work with racism in the oppression of people of color. Although this organizational structure of five parts is used, it should be noted that some theories could be organized under more than one of these headings. As previously detailed, each of the theories is represented through work by a key scholar or scholars. Throughout each chapter, a point was made to incorporate multiple quotes and to cite important passages in order to give the reader a sense of the theorist's voice and language.

Each chapter is organized by the same primary headings: "Why This Theory," "Description of the Theory," "How to Challenge Racism," "By the Numbers," "Evaluation" (with "Methodological Benefits," "Methodological Limitations," "Theoretical Benefits," and "Theoretical Limitations"), "Conclusion," "Reflect and Discuss," "Diagram," "Key Terms," "Key People," and "Works Cited and Further Reading." "Why This Theory" provides the context for the emergence of the theory and the problem it addresses. "Description of the Theory" details the primary facets and concepts of the theory. "How to Challenge Racism" covers how the theory frames a solution, or at least a challenge, to racism, and this section reflects the goal to connect theory to practice. The "Evaluation" section gives a few key methodological and theoretical benefits and limitations of the theory.

There are six special pedagogical features to help the reader reach a more in-depth understanding of the theory. "By the Numbers" provides contemporary statistics on racial inequality that align with that theory's perspective. These data help the reader connect theory to observations. "Reflect and Discuss" offers three questions to encourage dialogue and learning retention. For those for whom an illustration assists comprehension, a "Diagram" is included that proposes the basic relationships between the theory's components. The "Key Terms" section gives the definition of key concepts used in the theory, and, whenever available, the terms are in the form of a quote from the theorist. In many cases, theories share key terms, so it is important to recognize how the definitions of these terms vary across theory. "Key People" is a brief biography of the theorist or theorists and where applicable includes the theorist's personal website and/or Twitter account. "Works Cited and Further Reading" includes the scholarship cited in the chapter and related sources that can be consulted in further investigation. This systematic organization, which is used in every chapter, will aid the reader in learning how to analyze theory and make it easier to compare and contrast the theories.

A Note on Reflexivity

I write this book as a White woman born and academically trained in the United States. As a White woman, I recognize my privileged status, both in society and specifically in academia. This privilege has helped me secure a position as a tenured professor and teach about the horrors of White supremacy without the degree of pushback that my colleagues of color experience. In addition, not intentional, but apparent, this book reflects my orientation as a researcher in the United States, as most of the theorists used in this book are also from the United States. Yet the theories themselves often speak to issues that cross national lines, and therefore I hope they remain of use to those not working in the United States. In writing this book, I aimed to be critically reflexive on how my social position informs my thinking and writing, to be aware of the opportunities given to me, and to remain committed to pushing our conversations and our activism on racism forward.

WORKS CITED

Abend, Gabriel. 2008. "The Meaning of 'Theory.'" *Sociological Theory* 26(2): 173–99.

Alexander, Jeffrey C. 1987. *Twenty Lectures: Sociological Theory since World War II*. New York: Columbia University Press.

Bonilla-Silva, Eduardo. 2003. *Racism without Racists: Color-Blind Racism and the Persistence of Racial Inequality in*

America. Lanham, MD: Rowman and Littlefield.

Feagin, Joe. 2006. *Systemic Racism: A Theory of Oppression.* New York: Routledge.

Gannon, Megan. 2016. "Race Is a Social Construct, Scientists Argue." *Scientific American,* February 5. Retrieved January 2, 2020 (https://www.scientific american.com/article/race-is-a-social-construct-scientists-argue).

Golash-Boza, Tanya. 2016. "A Critical and Comprehensive Sociological Theory of Race and Racism." *Sociology of Race and Ethnicity* 2(2):129–41.

Joas, Hans and Wolfgang Knöbl. 2009. *Social Theory: Twenty Introductory Lectures.* Cambridge, UK: Cambridge University Press.

Lanham, David and Amy Liu. 2019. "Not Just a Typographical Change: Why Brookings Is Capitalizing Black." Washington, DC: The Brookings Institution, September 23. Retrieved January 2, 2020 (https://www.brookings.edu/research/brookingscapitalizesblack).

Mills, Charles W. 1997. *The Racial Contract.* Ithaca, NY: Cornell University Press.

National Human Genome Research Institute. 2018. "Genetics vs. Genomics Fact Sheet." Retrieved January 2, 2020 (https://www.genome.gov/about-genomics/fact-sheets/Genetics-vs-Genomics).

Oxford English Dictionary. 2019. "Oppression, n." Retrieved January 2, 2020 (https://www-oed-com.librda.mville.edu/view/Entry/132008?redirectedFrom=oppression&).

Race Forward. 2015. "Race Forward's Race Reporting Guide." New York: Author.

Simón, Yara. 2018. "Hispanic vs. Latino vs. Latinx: A Brief History of How These Words Originated." Brooklyn, NY: Remezcla, September 14. Retrieved January 9, 2020 (https://remezcla.com/about-us).

Steinmetz, Katy. 2018. "Why 'Latinx' Is Succeeding while Other Gender-Neutral Terms Fail to Catch On." *Time,* April 2. Retrieved January 9, 2020 (https://time.com/5191804/latinx-definition-meaning-latino-hispanic-gender-neutral).

Turner, Bryan S. 2016. "Introduction: A New Agenda for Social Theory?" Pp. 1–16 in *The New Blackwell Companion to Social Theory*, edited by B. S. Turner. Malden, MA: Wiley Blackwell.

NOTES

1. Abend (2008); Turner (2016).
2. Abend (2008:179).
3. Alexander (1987:3).
4. Joas and Knöbl (2009:4).
5. Ibid. (5).
6. Alexander (1987:3).
7. National Human Genome Research Institute (2018).
8. Gannon (2016).
9. Oxford English Dictionary (2019).

10. Bonilla-Silva (2006); Feagin (2006); Golash-Boza (2016); Mills (1997).
11. Mills (1997).
12. Race Forward (2015).
13. Lanham and Liu (2019).
14. Simón (2018); Steinmetz (2018).
15. Golash-Boza (2016).

Acknowledgments

This book, like most, has been a long process, and many people have helped and encouraged me along the way. I am incredibly lucky to be surrounded by a large group of supportive students, colleagues, friends, and family.

As a professor at a liberal arts college, I am heavily invested in teaching and have been afforded the opportunity to teach several courses on race and racism. It is in these classes that students often push me to be clearer and engage me in nuanced dialogue, for which I am very grateful. Thank you to all the students in African American Communities, Race and Ethnicity, Race and Housing, and Social Inequality classes. A special shout-out to students who read chapter drafts and provided their insightful feedback. Thank you Ariel Abdul-Mateen, Lia Garcia Berrido (who read multiple chapters), Monica Keel (who also helped with editing), and Moriah McDuffie.

Many colleagues have helped with this book by talking with me through this process, providing critical feedback, and reading chapter drafts; I could not have written this book without their assistance. A huge thank-you to David Brunsma, Erica Chito Childs, Woody Doane, Corey Dolgon, David Embrick, Chip Gallagher, Amanda Koontz, Cameron Lippard, Emalee Quickel, Saher Selod, James Thomas, Milton Vickerman, Johnny Williams, Beth Williford, and George Wilson. I am fortunate to say that many of these colleagues are also very good friends, and they have supported this process in more ways than one.

I also have a significant group of friends who keep me propped up in so many ways; I send a special thanks to Psusennes Nurisha Bey, Ben Carrington, Garfield Charles, Clay Clark, Ali Cohen, Laura Coleman, Danielle Dirks, Alicia Escott, Jessi Frazier, Anthony Freeman, James Gantt, Drea Jacobs, Meghan Johnston, Mary Beth Lineberry, Manouchehr Mohajeri, Anthony Peguero, Debbie Perkins, Louise Rasmussen, and Damien Tillman. To Teddy Adolphe, whose friendship brought me so much and whom I miss greatly, I keep close these words you gave me: "When it comes to living life, live each new day doing something worth living more."

I am grateful to my family for keeping me grounded while also believing in my goals. I particularly appreciate the persistent question that now has become a joke: Are you finished writing that book yet? I'm so very thankful for my siblings, who are always there for me; thank you Matthew, Mark, Gabriel, and Gudrun. A special recognition to my nieces and nephews, who bring me silliness and smiles, because that's important: thank you Annabelle, Cypri, Essie, Hailey, Mila, Parker, Peyton, River, Sam, and Vera. And I especially thank my parents, Mildred Strmic and Charles Pawl, who are unwavering in their encouragement and support, which are reflected in so many ways. A particularly massive thank-you has to go to my mother, who read and edited every page of this book. She is a serious critic and grammarian, and I don't know how I could write anything without her. My mom's ability to be simultaneously a critical editor and a supportive mother reflects her infinite patience, incredible dedication, and immeasurable love.

And finally, this book would not have come to fruition without the encouragement of acquisitions editor, Jeff Lasser, and the team at SAGE. Since the initial conversation about this project, Jeff has been supportive, and I sincerely thank him for believing in me and in this book.

About the Author

hephzibah v. strmic-pawl is Associate Professor of Sociology at Manhattanville College in New York, where she researches and teaches in the areas of race, racism, multiracialism, and history of activism. She is the author of *Multiracialism and Its Discontents: A Comparative Analysis of Asian-White and Black-White Multiracials* (Lexington Books) and coeditor with Milton Vickerman of *Race and Ethnicity: Constancy in Change* (Cognella). She is the founding pedagogy editor of the journal *Sociology of Race and Ethnicity*. She is also a recipient of the Joseph B. Gittler Award from the Society for the Study of Social Problems. strmic-pawl is the founder and director of the campaign Support Ella Baker Day, which aims to create a holiday in honor of the civil rights movement activist Ella Baker. See www.hephzibahvsp.com for more on her work.

Foundational Theories

Prejudice and Discrimination

Gordon W. Allport | Robert Merton

Prejudice is one of the early foundational concepts examined in relation to racism. Prejudice is most often studied as the irrational negative beliefs that individuals hold against groups and is usually observed as the precursor to discrimination, which is prejudice put into action. This chapter is based on *The Nature of Prejudice* by Gordon W. Allport, who was known for his work on personality psychology. Although this work was published in the 1950s, it continues to influence contemporary conversation. This chapter also includes a brief description of the often-referenced prejudice-discrimination typology written by the notable sociologist Robert Merton.*

---

*Photos of Allport and Merton unavailable.

Why This Theory

In the 1950s, when the book *The Nature of Prejudice* by Gordon W. Allport was published, the United States had recently confronted the atrocities of World War II and was facing difficult racial, ethnic, and religious tensions at home. The United States, like many other postindustrial nations, was experiencing success in advancing technology and growing national wealth but was not achieving similar successes in combating prejudice. Moreover, the increasingly global nature of capitalism was bringing disparate groups closer together, and as Allport states, "nations once safely separated by barricades of water or mountains are exposed to each other by air ... products of the modern age have thrown human groups into each others' [sic] laps. We have not yet learned how to adjust to our new mental and moral proximity."[1] Given these intersecting social landscapes and the prevalence of group animosities, an explanation was needed for the persistence of prejudice.

Allport culled together wide-ranging scholarship on prejudice and discrimination to propose a framework for understanding prejudice and to set a foundation for future work. While in his book, Allport states that bias can have a positive or negative connotation, his focus is on negative bias, with particular attention paid to religious and ethnic prejudice. He then explores discrimination, which is prejudice manifested in action.

Description of the Theory

Allport notes the difficulty of examining prejudice, particularly with a scientific analysis. First, prejudice is difficult to address because of the belief that prejudice is in the "eye of the beholder"; a cultural pluralistic approach often suggests that bias is based on one's cultural viewpoint, so that what is considered bias to one is not to another. A second difficulty in studying prejudice is that it can be seen as burdened by emotional bias and as a creation of "angry liberals," who believe they see bias everywhere, even where it does not exist. However, Allport unequivocally states that prejudice "is not 'the invention of liberal intellectuals.' It is simply an aspect of mental life that can be studied as objectively as any other."[2] Allport thus takes a highly systematic and scientific approach to his exploration and explanation of prejudice. *The Nature of Prejudice* is more than 500 pages, with eight main sections. This chapter does not follow the same outline of Allport's book but instead synthesizes the information into five areas: (1) the definition of prejudice, (2) the nature of categorization, (3) in-groups and out-groups, (4) why prejudice exists and persists, and (5) prejudice in action.

The Definition of Prejudice

The definition of *prejudice* is not as straightforward as one might think. There are several components or facets of prejudice. Allport begins his definition by noting that "hate prejudice" comes out of "love prejudice." Love prejudice is the bias toward and favoritism for one's own primary group, and hate prejudice is the *secondary* prejudice that develops from defending one's primary group.[3] This conceptualization helps clarify that perceptions of in-groups and out-groups are at the center of the problem of prejudice. Next is the tendency for people to form concepts, categories, and generalizations, all of which lead to oversimplification and prejudgments. A prejudice can be based on a number of categories: race, sex, age, ethnicity, language, region, religion, nation, class, and more.[4] People erroneously use these categories to classify people and then assume ideas about them that may or may not be correct. Another facet of prejudice is the distinction between attitude and belief. An attitude is expressed as a disfavor that is related to an overgeneralization of a group; an attitude can then lead to false beliefs about an individual or group.[5] For example, the attitude of "I don't like Latinxs" can then translate to a belief of "Latinxs are criminals." A culminating and basic facet of prejudice is hostility and rejection, which results in condemnation of individuals based on their group membership.[6] Thus, Allport comes to define **ethnic prejudice** as "an antipathy based upon a faulty and inflexible generalization. It may be felt or expressed. It may be directed toward a group or as a whole, or toward an individual because he is a member of that group."[7]

Yet it's important to remember that not all prejudgments or generalizations are prejudice. If a person rejects a prejudgment after being presented with alternative information and evidence, there is rational thought involved. **Prejudice**, on the other hand, is emotional and rejects countering information:

> *Prejudgments become prejudices only if they are not reversible when exposed to new knowledge.* A prejudice, unlike a simple misconception, is actively resistant to all evidence that would unseat it. Emotion tends to elevate when a prejudice is threatened with contradiction. Thus, the difference between ordinary prejudgments and prejudice is that one can discuss and rectify a prejudgment without emotional resistance.[8]

Central to this process of prejudgment is the nature of categorization.

The Nature of Categorization

Categorization is a human imperative because it makes daily activities more efficient and helpful for ordinary living. For example, categorizing types of cups can distinguish between a juice glass and a coffee mug, and such categorization can help one navigate a morning routine. A basic definition of a **category** is "an accessible cluster of associated ideas which as a whole has the property of guiding daily adjustments."[9] Thus, categorization is not necessarily negative or irrational, and there is valuable use in a "differentiated category," which has allowance for variation and subdivision rather than an irrational overgeneralization.[10]

An important part of the categorization process, which is often then associated with prejudice, is how people come to *see difference.* "Difference" is often assigned by society rather than inherent, and there is a process of coming to see certain groups of people as distinguishable from one another. First, there needs to be some easily identifiable feature to which "difference" is attached. This marker of difference then becomes easily identifiable by prejudiced people. For example, in the case of race, skin color is marked as different. Yet skin color itself is *not* the reason for the prejudice but instead is the aid for determining the target of the prejudice.[11] Difference serves as a "condensing rod" for grouping people together and perpetually seeing them unfavorably.[12]

The use of particular terms and labels is also significant in the categorization process. Prejudiced labels are embedded with negative emotion, such as the difference between calling a teacher a "schoolteacher" versus the prejudiced label of "school marm," which imagines teachers as single women who are too strict and proper.[13] Labels also serve to create cohesion between a category and a symbol. This cohesion is clearly seen with the range of labels used to symbolize racial groups, particularly those often assigned to Black communities, such as "thugs" or "ghetto." The cohesion between a category and a symbol can become so strong that the label can act independently to represent a racial group; in the example of "ghetto," the word can be used without context to provoke negative images of Black communities. These racialized terms are intended to reference only one aspect assigned to a group, thereby distracting attention from any concrete reality or evidence that would serve to the contrary.[14]

Categorization is sometimes reduced to or mistaken as the same process as stereotyping. A stereotype is not a category but an idea that accompanies categorization and prevents differentiated thinking; a **stereotype** is "*an exaggerated belief associated with a category,*" and "*its function is to justify (rationalize) our conduct in relation to that category.*"[15] Examples of stereotypes are that all Latinxs are foreigners or that all Asians do well in school. Stereotypes are useful for prejudiced people, as they assign whole sets of beliefs to a group that justify their thoughts and behaviors toward that group.

In-Groups and Out-Groups

A critical component of prejudice is the solidification of one's in-group and the creation of out-groups. A **group** is "any cluster of people who can use the term 'we' with the same significance."[16] An *in-group* is the group of one's primary membership and belonging, and an *out-group* consists of those who do not belong to the in-group. Membership in an in-group is based on the needs of the individuals in the group, and it is possible to have concentric in-groups, such as family, neighborhood, city, state, and nation. In this sense, belonging to a nation does not negate a simultaneous membership in one's family. A particular type of in-group is a *reference group*, or the group that one "refers to" in guiding personal behavior and aspirations.

In the case of race and prejudice, in-groups and out-groups serve as organizing tools. It is assumed that all the individual members of a group have the characteristics of that group—for instance, beliefs that all Blacks are prone to violence or that all Jewish people are penny-pinching. Such beliefs about out-groups may be rooted in a "kernel of truth," in that some individuals may have these traits, but prejudice is feelings of difference about a whole group, even when these feelings are imaginary.[17] As Allport states, "there is probably not a single instance where every member of a group has all the characteristics ascribed to his group, nor is there a single characteristic that is typical of every single member of one group and of no other group."[18] Moreover, no person knows *every* member of a group, so "any negative judgment of these groups *as a whole* is, strictly speaking, an instance of thinking ill without sufficient warrant."[19] In other words, beliefs about individuals because of their group membership result in prejudice based on irrational bias rather than rational, logical thought.

A group can also assert itself as the primary group. Whites proclaim themselves as the dominant reference group for all races and thereby assume that people of color should aspire to White norms. When Whites perceive themselves to be threatened by people of color, the White in-group becomes heavily solidified, and Whites construct people of color as inferior. If the needs of Whites become strongly aggressive, their definition of themselves is formed in relation to the hatred of out-groups—that is, people of color.

Why Prejudice Exists and Persists

Allport examines two overarching explanations for the existence of prejudice. The structural view looks to social factors because prejudice is most often rooted in the needs and habits of groups. The psychological view looks to individual behavior and personal development. Allport strongly states that it is a "both/and" situation, wherein prejudice is a problem of the structure and of the individual.

Structural Explanations

Structural reasons for prejudice are related to group dynamics and interactions. When groups face social pressures, prejudice is more likely. Allport outlines nine general contexts when groups are more likely to develop prejudice: (1) Significant diversity among groups (physically or culturally) can lead to an emphasis on group difference, which can then lead to the formation of strong in-groups and therefore strong out-groups. Examples of physical prejudice are often connected to race or ethnicity, whereas cultural prejudice is frequently rooted in religious differences. (2) When vertical mobility is permitted, tension and strain often develop as some groups do much better than others. For example, when some are very wealthy and others are low-income with access to few resources, animosity grows. (3) When rapid social change is in progress, there can be conflict about the direction of society and disagreement over group rights, as was seen with the advance of industrialization and women's rights in the labor force. (4) A demographic increase in the size of a minority group can lead to the majority group's feeling threatened. This situation commonly occurs with immigration, such as Northern African immigrants in France or Mexican immigrants in the United States. (5) The existence of direct group competition can cultivate a group desire to do better than another group. For instance, animosity can grow when groups compete for entry-level jobs or housing in dense cities. (6) When exploitation is sustaining one group's interests, there is an inducement to support prejudice against the exploited group. This situation often exists in capitalist societies, where wealthy barons seek to use and control low-income laborers; for example, U.S. railroad tycoons exploited prejudice against Irish and Chinese workers when they used them to build the railroad. (7) When a society's customs are more favorable to bigotry and do not limit aggression, there is a cultural context for prejudice. This situation occurs when there is state-sanctioned prejudice, such as racial or religious segregation, or if the state and society do little to curb prejudice. (8) Places where neither assimilation nor cultural pluralism is welcomed leave few options for out-groups to fit in, as they are neither welcomed into the fold, nor are their differences permitted. (9) If there are traditional justifications for ethnocentrism, perhaps ones that originate in cultural or religious rituals, prejudice is likely to have a preexisting hold. For example, societies with a White supremacy framework usually develop because of Whites' deliberate group move for this ethnocentric viewpoint to be a vital, embedded part of society's culture. Sometimes religion is also involved because of the ways in which it is used as a rationale for one group to have power over another, as was seen with Hitler's aggression against Judaism or as seen with hostile Islamic states. Religion, however, is more of a tool and not a determinant of prejudice. Each one of the nine structural contexts can singularly support a prejudiced society, or the contexts may act in concert with one another to cultivate a society where prejudice exists and persists.[20]

Psychological Explanations

Prejudice can also be a psychological trait and is often studied via questionnaires that inquire into individual beliefs. In fact, at one point, Allport notes:

> Studies constitute a very strong argument for saying that prejudice is basically a *trait of personality*. When it takes root in a life it grows like a unit. The specific object of prejudice is more or less immaterial. What happens is that the whole inner life is affected; the hostility and fear are systematic.[21]

There are several psychological explanations for how an individual comes to be prejudiced, including acquiring prejudice through the adoption of one's family or reference group, participating in processes of projection, and developing a prejudiced personality. These explanations are not necessarily mutually exclusive, but each has a different focus.

Individuals are often prejudiced because they have learned this prejudice from their family or other immediate reference group. Parents can foster an atmosphere of prejudice by emphasizing power and authority rather than trust and tolerance. Studies suggest that children as young as 2 and a half learn racial differences and labels before they quite understand them.[22] At the first stage of prejudice development, a child learns how to generalize people into groups. Next, the child practices rejection of individuals based on group membership but may not understand this behavior. At the third stage, the child learns how to make prejudice sound rational and acceptable to society. At the last stage, around the age of 12, a child knows how to use language that sounds acceptable while practicing rejection in behavior. The irony of learning prejudice is that a young child often speaks in prejudicial terms but doesn't believe these ideas, due to a lack of comprehension, while an older child knows how to practice discrimination while deferring to social graces. As adults, people learn to mold their prejudices to their life experiences and fit their biases to their particular needs.[23]

Prejudice also develops out of a psychological desire to project one's personal problems onto someone else. This desire can arise from frustration with one's personal life, community, or broader conditions of living; it can arise from aggression and hatred that an individual generally feels; and/or it can come from anxiety or guilt associated with fear, economic insecurity, or low self-esteem. Generally, **projection** emerges "whenever, and in whatever way, a correct-appraisal of one's own emotional life fails and gives way to an incorrect judgment of other people."[24] Allport notes three types of projection: (1) direct, (2) mote-beam, and (3) complementary. Direct projection helps solve one's own inner conflict by ascribing it to another group and then directly blaming the out-group members for it. Mote-beam projection is when a person exaggerates qualities in others, which both the out-group and the prejudiced person hold but go unrecognized within the prejudiced person. Complementary projection is the process of explaining one's own state of mind by projecting imaginary intentions and behaviors onto others. A particular type of projection is scapegoating—that is, when one assigns to a group one's own negative characteristics. Scapegoating is a common form of projection because it allows the individual not to accept responsibility or guilt for personal issues because it is assigned to others.[25]

A third psychological explanation for prejudice is the prejudiced personality. Allport outlines eight general characteristics of a prejudiced personality: (1) The person has underlying insecurity and buried feelings; (2) the person has ambivalence toward his/her/zir parents; (3) the person has rigid moralistic views, such as an irrational allegiance to manners and conventions; (4) the person has strong dichotomized thinking, with a clear line set between good and bad people; (5) the person has little tolerance for ambiguity; (6) the person is extropunitive, in that the person assigns blame to others, rather than taking internal stock of personal faults or limitations; (7) the person strongly adheres to social order and is devoted to institutions and organizational memberships; and (8) the person prefers an authoritarian type of power.[26] Of course, prejudiced people may have all or some of these characteristics, and some may be more or less present, but these eight characteristics are typical of prejudiced personalities. On an extreme level, demagogues, as leaders who appeal to prejudiced people rather than logic, cater to this prejudiced personality by emphasizing broad sweeping narratives, such as the people have been cheated, there is a conspiracy against the people, the government is corrupt, and the people cannot trust foreigners. Demagogues and fascists, as seen with Hitler, often exhibit a high level of paranoia, a characteristic that commonly belongs to those with extreme prejudice.[27]

Prejudice in Action

Understanding how or why someone has come to be prejudiced is important, but Allport also looks at how prejudice manifests. All prejudiced people do not translate their beliefs into action, and the level of discrimination varies. There are five general manifestations of prejudice: (1) anti-locution, (2) avoidance, (3) discrimination, (4) physical attack, and (5) extermination. Anti-locution is the verbal expression of prejudice, usually by talking about one's bias with others, but the target is not directly addressed. For example, a person talks to friends about their dislike for a group but doesn't openly share this information. Avoidance is when prejudiced people take active measures to avoid the target of their prejudice. In this case, a person will choose their important locations, such as home, school, and house of worship, based on their likelihood of coming into contact with the target of their prejudice. Discrimination is the typical manifestation of prejudice, such as rejecting employment or housing. People often do not practice discrimination if there is a challenge to doing so but will discriminate if they can do so without confronting the target. Physical attack is the forceful removal of the target from communities or general intergroup violence. The most extreme prejudice results in extermination, such as measures taken by Whites to lynch Blacks or massacre indigenous people. Physical violence is more likely in certain contexts, including when there is a long period of categorical prejudgment or a long period of verbal complaint, when there is growing discrimination in society, when prejudiced people feel some strain upon them (real or imagined), when people tire of their inhibitions, when organizations create a culture and structure for malcontents, when individuals find that their wrath is sanctioned by organizations, when there is some precipitating event or riot, and when others participate in the violence.[28]

How to Challenge Racism
· ·

Throughout *The Nature of Prejudice,* Allport suggests opportunities for challenging prejudice, both on the structural level and on the individual level. On the structural level, Allport looks to studies that suggest increased contact between groups can lessen bias if authentic relationships occur. Residential integration, where communities of color occupy equal status and common goals with Whites, can be an effective route.[29] Other options include formal education, intercultural programs, group retraining, and positive mass media messages.[30] Education programs should particularly emphasize that race is not a biological reality. On the individual level, Allport provides the characteristics of a non-prejudiced personality, which can be used to develop goals for individual therapy plans for prejudiced people. A non-prejudiced personality deemphasizes individualism, develops self-insight, is intropunitive rather than extropunitive, has tolerance for ambiguity, and has a trusting approach.[31] Allport emphasizes that no one strategy is the answer and that a multimethod approach, on the structural and individual level, should be taken.

Evaluation

Methodological Benefits

This theoretical examination of prejudice relies on an exhaustive methodological review of earlier studies from a range of disciplines. Allport regularly pulls on interdisciplinary sources, such as *Journal of Personality, Fortune* (the magazine), *American Journal of Orthopsychiatry, Journal of Social Psychology, Journal of Educational Sociology,* and *Public Opinion Quarterly.* He moves through masses of research by providing specifics of studies, by using multiple examples to illuminate a particular facet of prejudice, and by summarizing the contributions of several researchers. For example, in Chapter 16 of *The Nature of Prejudice*, on the effect of contact among groups, he provides several tables from other studies, such as "Opinion of U.S. Soldiers Regarding Germans as Related to the Frequency of Their Contact with German Civilians," from the book *The American Soldier* (1949); "Percentage of Respondents Giving Indicated Reasons for Wanting to Exclude Negroes from Their

Neighborhood," from the unpublished work *Residential Contact as a Determinant of Attitudes Toward Negroes* (1950); and "Are They (the Negro People in the Project) Pretty Much the Same as the White People Who Live Here or Are They Different?" from *Interracial Housing: A Psychological Evaluation of a Social Experiment* (1951). Allport also relies on interviews or excerpts from first-person historical accounts. This use of supportive data from a range of studies and disciplines is typical of the methods employed by Allport throughout the book. Although Allport's theory does not rely on primary research, the range and rigor of sources used to illuminate the multiple facets of prejudice are impressive and invaluable for attaining a broad framework of prejudice.

Methodological Limitations

Limitations to Allport's methodology include the lack of research or testing of any specific approach to explaining prejudice. The methodology used is a collection of studies and commentary, rather than a scientific evaluation of any one proposed explanation, and the numerous sources cited in the book make it virtually impossible to evaluate the rigor of each study that Allport cites. Thus, the methodology is difficult to assess as a factor independent of the sources Allport uses. Allport's theory, then, relies on his synthesis of previous research rather than any type of primary data collection or analysis.

Theoretical Benefits

The interdisciplinary review of such a wide range of studies and theoretical approaches leads to a nuanced perspective on prejudice. As Allport notes in the beginning of his book, his aim is to provide a framework for future scholars—a theoretical foundation based on a holistic synthesis of the work on prejudice. The table of contents of the book provides a theoretical outline of how to approach the study of prejudice with 31 chapters, ranging from the introduction, "What Is the Problem?" to specific facets, such as "Stereotypes in Our Culture" and "Choice of Scapegoats," to a chapter toward the end on "Evaluation of Programs." Throughout the book, there is a carefully balanced view of explaining prejudice as a problem belonging to society and a problem belonging to individuals. Likely, the greatest theoretical benefit is that Allport successfully meets his goal of setting the stage for a theory of prejudice that successive scholars have relied on. As noted social psychologist Thomas Pettigrew remarks, "the book continues to be the definitive theoretical statement of the field."[32]

Theoretical Limitations

The limitation of a focus on prejudice is that the analysis does not clearly indicate why some groups are chosen as targets of prejudice and others are not. It also does not explain how some groups are able to progress through a period of targeted prejudice to eventually become accepted, while others are not. *The Nature of Prejudice* tends to focus on Black communities and Jewish communities (which makes sense, given that the book was published in the 1950s, when anti-Black and anti-Jewish sentiment was high), but there's no rigorous theoretical explanation as to why these two groups are persistently the targets of prejudice. Likewise, there's no reason given as to why Irish communities, who had previously been seen as different and had experienced severe discrimination, then came to be accepted by Whites. Prejudice, as a theoretical concept, tends to lack a sophisticated analysis of power that could help explain the structure of hierarchies. Overall, the strength of prejudice as an explanatory perspective is more on the individual, psychological level, while its theoretical limitation is in addressing power differentials, hierarchies, evolution in racial group dynamics, and similar processes.

Additional Contribution: Merton's Typology

Robert Merton's typology, which was published around the same time as Allport's book, is widely referenced for situating the complex relationship between prejudice and discrimination. Merton contends that there is not a direct causal relationship between prejudice and discrimination, in that prejudice always directly results in discrimination. Instead, he offers a typology to explain the multiple ways in which prejudice and discrimination can be related—and therefore the likelihood of when discrimination will occur. Merton proposes four types of prejudice–discrimination linkages: (1) unprejudiced nondiscriminators, (2) unprejudiced discriminators, (3) prejudiced nondiscriminators, and (4) prejudiced discriminators. Unprejudiced nondiscriminators, or all-weather liberals, believe in freedom and equality and seek out likeminded people; they are not ambivalent about social problems but often lack an awareness of them. Unprejudiced discriminators, or fair-weather liberals, tend to discriminate only if they feel it is necessary, particularly if it is in their self-interest. Fair-weather liberals often obey policies against discrimination because they prefer that their actions meet their unprejudiced views. Prejudiced nondiscriminators, or timid bigots, look upon many groups unfavorably and follow stereotypes, but they won't discriminate if there is law or social pressure against doing so. The fourth type is prejudiced discriminators, or active bigots, who believe in the inferiority of others and their right to act on that prejudice.[33] Because this is a typology, many people don't fall neatly into one of the four groups; nevertheless, the typology provides a useful guide to understand the varied relationship between prejudice and discrimination.

Conclusion

A theory of prejudice is useful for examining how individuals and societies develop and foster negative bias based on race and/or other identities, such as gender, religion, and class. Arguably, at the root of racism are an irrational perception of and a lack of empathy for people of color, both of which the theory of prejudice help explain. *The Nature of Prejudice* is still widely referenced and considered a foundation for the work on prejudice; in a 25th anniversary edition of the book, Kenneth Clark, the noted psychologist whose work was used in the 1954 *Brown v. Board of Education* Supreme Court case, noted that "its table of contents establishes the parameters for a scholarly social science approach to the discussion and understanding of this complex human problem."[34] Merton's typology, too, is still widely referenced and used in an array of sociology textbooks.

REFLECT AND DISCUSS

1. What is the difference between prejudgment and prejudice?

2. How are group differences, real or imagined, at the root of prejudice?

3. Describe the relationship between prejudice and discrimination.

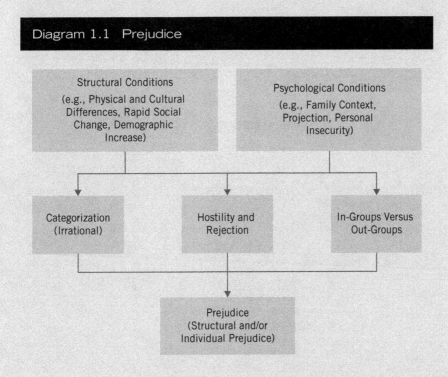

Diagram 1.1 Prejudice

Diagram 1.2   Merton's Typology

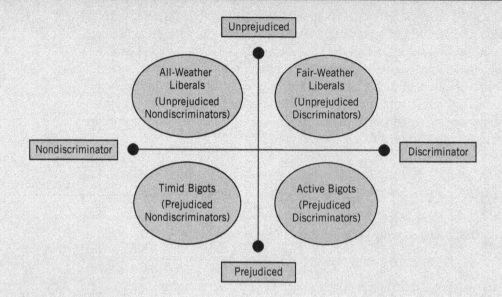

KEY TERMS

Category: "An accessible cluster of associated ideas which as a whole has the property of guiding daily adjustments."[35]

Ethnic prejudice: "An antipathy based upon a faulty and inflexible generalization. It may be felt or expressed. It may be directed toward a group or as a whole, or toward an individual because he is a member of that group."[36]

Group: "Any cluster of people who can use the term 'we' with the same significance."[37]

Prejudice: "Prejudgments become prejudices only if they are not reversible when exposed to new knowledge. A prejudice, unlike a simple misconception, is actively resistant to all

evidence that would unseat it. We tend to grow emotional when a prejudice is threatened with contradiction. Thus the difference between ordinary prejudgments and prejudice is that one can discuss and rectify a prejudgment without emotional resistance."[38]

Projection: "Whenever, and in whatever way, a correct-appraisal of one's own emotional life fails and gives way to an incorrect judgment of other people."[39]

Stereotype: "An exaggerated belief associated with a category. Its function is to justify (rationalize) our conduct in relation to that category."[40]

KEY PEOPLE

Gordon Allport (1897–1967): A psychologist who was known for pushing the boundaries

of the discipline, Allport developed the three-tiered hierarchy of personality traits and a theory of prejudice. Allport is ranked as number 11 of 100 of the most eminent psychologists of the 20th century by the American Psychological Association.

Robert Merton (1910–2003): Merton was a leading sociologist known for coining a series of foundational concepts, such as "roles," "status set," and "self-fulfilling prophecy." In 1994, he received the National Medal of Science for "founding the sociology of science," and he was the first sociologist to be awarded this honor.

WORKS CITED AND FURTHER READING

Allport, Gordon W. [1954] 1966. *The Nature of Prejudice.* Reading, MA: Addison-Wesley.

Clark, Kenneth. 1979. "Introduction." Pp. ix–xiii in *The Nature of Prejudice: 25th Anniversary Edition,* by G. W. Allport. New York: Basic Books.

Dovidio, John F., Peter Glick, and Laurie A. Rudman, eds. 2005. *On the Nature of Prejudice: Fifty Years after Allport.* Malden, MA: Blackwell.

Gilman, Sander L. and James M. Thomas. 2016. *Are Racists Crazy? How Prejudice, Racism, and Antisemitism Became Markers of Insanity.* New York: New York University Press.

Horowitz, Juliana Menasce, Anna Brown, and Kiana Cox. 2019. "Race in America 2019." Washington, DC: Pew Research Center.

Merton, Robert K. 1949. "Discrimination and the American Creed." Pp. 99–126 in *Discrimination and National Welfare,* edited by R. M. MacIver. New York: Harper and Row.

Parker, Kim, Juliana Menasce Horowitz, Rich Morin, and Mark Hugo Lopez. 2015. "Multiracial in America: Chapter 5." Washington, DC: Pew Research Center.

Pettigrew, Thomas. 1979. "The Ultimate Attribution Error: Extending Allport's Cognitive Analysis of Prejudice." *Personality and Social Psychology Bulletin* 5(4):461–76.

NOTES

1. Allport ([1954] 1966:xiii).
2. Ibid. (516).
3. Ibid. (27).
4. Ibid. (89).
5. Ibid. (13).
6. Ibid. (5).
7. Ibid. (9).
8. Ibid. (9, emphasis in original).
9. Ibid. (171).
10. Ibid. (173).
11. Ibid. (139).
12. Ibid. (138).
13. Ibid. (181).
14. Ibid. (179).
15. Ibid. (191, emphasis in original).
16. Ibid. (37).
17. Ibid. (125).
18. Ibid. (103).
19. Ibid. (7, emphasis in original).
20. Ibid. (221).
21. Ibid. (73, emphasis in original).
22. Ibid. (31–33).
23. Ibid. (289–324).
24. Ibid. (380, emphasis in original).
25. Ibid. (387–91).
26. Ibid. (396–407).
27. Ibid. (414–23).
28. Ibid. (57–58).

29. Ibid. (281).
30. Ibid. (512).
31. Ibid. (431).
32. Pettigrew (1979:462).
33. Merton (1949).
34. Clark (1979:xii).

35. Allport ([1954] 1966:171).
36. Ibid. (9).
37. Ibid. (37).
38. Ibid. (9).
39. Ibid. (380).
40. Ibid. (191).

2

White Privilege

Robert Amico | Peggy McIntosh |
Paula Rothenberg | Tim Wise

White privilege is now a regular part of the lexicon of racial and ethnic studies and is a popular concept in contemporary conversations on race and racism. Peggy McIntosh coined the term in 1988 when she wrote of 40 privileges that Whites receive but people of color do not. Since then, the concept of White privilege has been developed and used by many. In this chapter, the works of Robert Amico, Peggy McIntosh, Paula Rothenberg, and Tim Wise, all of whom undertake both a biographical and a scientific study of White privilege, are used.*

Photo 2.1 Robert Amico

Source: https://www.sbu.edu/academics/philosophy/faculty-and-staff/amico-robert-p-.

Photo 2.2 Peggy McIntosh

Source: https://commons.wikimedia.org/wiki/File:Peggy_McIntosh.jpg.

Photo 2.3 Tim Wise

Source: https://commons.wikimedia.org/wiki/File:Tim_Wise.jpg.

---

*Photo of Rothenberg unavailable.

Why This Theory

The study of racism often compares how people of color fare in relation to Whites on a host of indicators, such as education, employment, and pay. This comparative framework is common because inequalities become clear by comparing the group facing the problems—people of color—to the people who are deemed "normal"—Whites. This framework, however, often leads to a mistaken view of and/or singular focus on people of color "as the problem," rather than Whites' role in racism as the problem. Whites may be aware that racism, to some degree, exists but are unaware of how they benefit from that racism. The theory of White privilege, therefore, focuses on how Whites (1) participate in and perpetuate racism, intentionally or not, and (2) are oblivious to the benefits they receive because of racism. A greater goal of using this theory is helping Whites recognize their White privilege to help combat racism.[1]

Like other contemporary racial theories, the theory of White privilege emerged after the 1960s Civil Rights Movement to explain how racism persists despite existing laws against racial discrimination. Whites began looking inward to dissect how they experience privilege throughout their lives, both in daily interactions and at significant life moments, such as buying a house or getting a job. This chapter relies on the work of four White scholars: Robert Amico, Peggy McIntosh, Paula Rothenberg, and Tim Wise, all of whom have analyzed their own White privilege and who have systematically studied how White privilege sustains racism.

Description of the Theory

White privilege answers this question: If people of color are encountering racism, what are Whites experiencing? White privilege explains the "other side of racism," the benefits and resources given to Whites and that are denied to people of color. **White privilege** is a "*relational* concept. It positions one person or group over another person or group. It is a concept of racial domination that enables us to see this relationship from the perspective of those who benefit from such domination."[2] White privilege permits insight into who *benefits* from racism and how they do so; only by looking holistically at both the discriminatory and the beneficial nature of racism can the problem be fully addressed. Within this theory, **race** is defined as "a socially constructed category for the purpose of controlling, dominating, and exploiting some for the benefit of others,"[3] and **racism** is defined as "subordination of people of color by white people."[4]

Often, Whites think racism is defined by individual hateful actions that come from "bad people" and do not recognize racism's operation on the systemic and structural levels. White privilege theory, however, explains that racism against people of color and its corollary, White privilege, operate on a systemic and structural level as well as the individual level. Thus, White privilege is given to *all* Whites, not just White, wealthy, heterosexual men as the stereotypical image of White privilege recipients. Whites of all different classes, sexes, genders, sexual orientations, religions, and other intersecting identities receive White privilege, albeit how and to what degree White privilege is experienced vary across these intersecting identities. Whites receive White privilege whether they desire it or not, and they benefit from it whether they acknowledge those benefits or not, as, unlike people of color, all Whites are "born to belonging."[5] These benefits cannot be given away, and good intentions don't erase them, because White privilege is accorded not by an individual's behavior or beliefs but because of the status of "White" in society, or what is often referred to as "Whiteness."

Whiteness

To understand White privilege requires an explanation of the meaning behind "White" or what **Whiteness** represents. Whiteness is the power accorded to those deemed White. In the United States, Whiteness originated with plantation slavery, when "White" became synonymous with free and "Black" with slave. Policies in the United States then continued to place power, resources, opportunities, and achievements in the hands of Whites. Such practices and ideologies have given Whiteness special status, so that being "White" has been the way toward success. People from all racial and ethnic groups have fought to be identified as White, including Irish, Italians, Mexicans, Chinese, and Blacks who had a light enough skin tone that they could "pass" as White.[6] For those who were denied White racial status, many sought White approval. George Lipsitz explains this "possessive investment in whiteness" in how "the power of whiteness depended not only on White hegemony over separate racialized groups, but also on manipulating racial outsiders to fight against one another, to compete with each other for white approval, and to seek the rewards and privileges of whiteness for themselves at the expense of other racialized populations."[7]

Another defining aspect of Whiteness is the lack of awareness of race, of power, and of privilege; "to be an American and to be white is to be told a million different ways that the world is your oyster; it is to believe, because so many outward signs suggest it, that you can do anything and be anything your heart desires."[8] The constant and consistent valuing of Whiteness leads most Whites to understand this treatment as "normal," and they are therefore unaware that their racial status is according them benefits. Yet the relationship between Whiteness and privilege is of a constitutive nature; "without racial privilege there is no whiteness, and without whiteness, there is no racial privilege. Being white means to be advantaged relative to people of color, and pretty much *only* that."[9] Thus, there are direct reinforcing links between "White," "Whiteness," and "White privilege." *White* is the term used to identify a group of people who share phenotypical features understood as

"White," *Whiteness* refers to the power given to Whites, and *White privilege* denotes the benefits that Whites receive because they are White.

Facets of White Privilege

Given that much of White privilege scholarship relies on an autobiographical, self-reflective approach, the theory has not been neatly constructed into components. However, there are clear themes in how Amico, McIntosh, Rothenberg, and Wise systematically analyze White privilege, or, as Rothenberg says, there is "a kind of anatomy of privilege in all its complexity."[10] There are five main experiences that characterize White privilege: (1) opportunities received, (2) lack of authority enforcement, (3) a White ethnocentric curriculum, (4) racial segregation, and (5) a pattern of laws throughout time that benefit Whites. It should be noted, however, that though these five experiences help outline the theory of White privilege, they do not encapsulate all the varied and nuanced ways in which Whites experience their racial privilege.

Opportunities Received

A hallmark of White privilege is the "invisible" opportunities that Whites receive; these can be small, micro daily interactions or larger life-course markers that make it easier to move from one stage of life to another. For example, Wise reflects on how theater activities in school gave him a much-needed outlet in life, but his consistent assignment to key roles had more to do with the use of White roles rather than his acting ability.[11] Rothenberg describes how her family's White network got her into private school and away from more poorly performing public schools. Her father's network also aided her acceptance into the University of Chicago, and her parents helped buy her house by providing the down payment. Without the White networks, a perception of worthiness, and her family's wealth, Rothenberg would have gone without these educational and housing opportunities that affected her entire life course.[12] Whites receive privilege via the opportunities open to them through their networks, wealth, and other resources, as well as their perceived worth. This assignment of value and respect to Whiteness connects to the second main area of privilege: lack of authority enforcement.

Lack of Authority Enforcement

White privilege theory notes how Whites are presumed to be innocent, or if they are found to be deviant, the penalty is either insignificant or nonexistent. Wise recounts numerous times when he did not get into trouble, even though he was clearly violating the law: drinking and doing drugs as a teenager and, even more severe, his fake identification business that helped him and his underage friends drink at bars.[13] In another instance, a police officer chose to help Wise break into his car when he had locked himself out of it. Rather than the officer assuming Wise was illegally trying to break into a car, his Whiteness accorded him virtue; "for whites, innocence was presumed until proven otherwise, while for blacks, the presumption of guilt was the default position."[14] Lack of authority enforcement is also a common theme among a list of privileges that McIntosh delineates: She can shop without being followed around; she can be sure her children's teachers will tolerate them; she can be sure that if she is pulled over by a cop, it is not because of her race; and she can be late to a meeting without the tardiness reflecting on her race. McIntosh notes that several privileges allow her "to escape penalties or dangers that others suffer."[15]

White Ethnocentric Curriculum

White privilege also shapes what is considered knowledge or even epistemology. In an analysis of the major disciplines, such as history, philosophy, and science, the curriculum is Eurocentric, in that it focuses on the contributions and knowledge production of Whites. For example, Rothenberg had the following realization when she began teaching philosophy:

> Implicit in my syllabus was the notion that wisdom was the special attribute of one race, one sex, and one class, and thus one particular way of thinking about the world and framing questions was the only model for intelligence and rationality. That this way of defining knowledge and framing questions made the experience and wisdom of most of the world's people either invisible or irrelevant never occurred to me.[16]

She eventually came to realize that "we have privileged the distorted perspective of an infinitesimal fraction of the world's population."[17] Amico, too, as a professor of philosophy, came to realize that philosophy was primarily a White discipline that ignored the contributions of others and saw "the blind spots in [his] education that favor whiteness."[18] And McIntosh notes, "I can be sure that my children will be given curricular materials that testify to the existence of their race."[19] The White ethnocentric curriculum shows how Whites are taught from day one that White culture and knowledge are not only most significant but also correct.

Racial Segregation

White privilege is able to maintain itself through the residential and social isolation of Whites from people of color. Upon recognition of their White privilege, these scholars recognized that they had spent their lives largely in White spaces. It did not occur to them to question why people of color were absent in their neighborhoods, schools, clubs, jobs, and even the media. McIntosh notes such privilege in this way: "I can, if I wish, arrange to be in the company of people of my race most of the time" because Whites have created isolated spaces in any number of professional and social circles.[20] Wise notes how he had Black friends in middle school, but by high school, racial segregation had taken hold, and his friendship circle became largely composed of Whites. Rothenberg, in retrospect, realizes that there were no Blacks in her school or in her parents' segregated country club. As an adult, Rothenberg analyzes how "well-intentioned white liberals," knowingly or not, reinforce this segregated color line, for even when they desire to move into a diverse neighborhood, they often choose to send their children to private schools instead of the local public school.[21] By the time most White children get to college, they are not aware of how their racial segregation has become a norm, so, intentionally or not, they continue on with a life of White racial isolation.

Pattern of Laws

White privilege is not just a manifestation of contemporary culture; it is embedded in the structure and institutions of society. White privilege has been repeatedly enforced through policies and laws, beginning with plantation slavery and the genocide of the indigenous and continuing through today. Noting laws and policies such as the internment of Japanese people in the United States during World War II and the denial of citizenship to various communities of color throughout U.S. history, Rothenberg states that White skin privilege is part of the very fabric of the nation.[22] Wise refers to the highly restrictive immigration law of the Naturalization Act of 1790, discriminatory housing and mortgage polices, and the lack of enforcement of the Fair Housing Act.[23] Amico also addresses racist practices, such as restrictive immigration laws, the genocide of indigenous tribes, and the oppressive use of Chinese immigrant labor to build railroads.[24] And although not directly alluding to laws, McIntosh notes how the history of the United States speaks to the experiences of Whites in a positive manner: "When I am told about our national heritage or about 'civilization,' I am shown that people of my color [Whites] made it what it is." She points out that she "can remain oblivious to the language and customs of persons of color who constituted the world's majority without feeling in my culture any penalty for such oblivion."[25] White privilege has been enshrined not just in ideology but in the very laws that created and sustain the United States.

Confronting and Accepting White Privilege

When presented with White privilege, Whites often become hesitant to accept the information or develop White guilt. In the first regard, a primary reason Whites express hesitance is because they believe in the myth of meritocracy—that only those who work hard are appropriately rewarded—but White privilege exposes the falsity of this ideology. If Whites accept that they were given some systematic benefits in their life because of Whiteness, they must also believe that their life's accomplishments were aided by White privilege. Acceptance of this fact often leads to conflict with one's identity as White.

In addition to the myth of meritocracy, Amico outlines seven additional reasons why Whites generally have a hard time accepting the existence of White privilege: (1) the master narrative of U.S. history, (2) the myth of race,

(3) residential segregation, (4) individualism, (5) obliviousness, (6) racial identity development and cultural competencies, and (7) an individual's own racism. Amico says that these reasons can be compounded by four emotions: (1) a feeling of being threatened; (2) family loyalty; (3) fear, shame, and guilt; and (4) feelings of hopelessness and powerlessness.[26] There is a series of reasons and emotions, often overlapping and intersecting, that hinder Whites' recognition of their privilege, which is only evidence of the strength of privilege to obscure the truth.

When Whites do accept White privilege and realize that they are the recipients, a second outcome of confronting White privilege is White guilt. Whites feel guilt for the unfair advantages given to them and recognize that their opportunities and accomplishments are, at least in part, due to the unearned and unmerited bias afforded to those who are seen as White. A step further in the understanding of White privilege reveals that the unearned opportunities given to a White person also means that unmerited *disadvantages* were given to a person of color. When Whites come to grips with the years, decades, and centuries of benefits given to Whites and the corollary discrimination faced by people of color, guilt arises from being a member of the "White race," often because there is no clear way to rid oneself of these privileges.[27] However, as discussed later, the objective of White privilege theory is not to encourage Whites to feel guilty but to have this revelation lead to combating racism. Furthermore, White privilege theory posits that Whites can experience personal benefits from confronting their privilege. White privilege can keep Whites from having authentic relationships with people of color, can keep Whites ignorant about history, and can keep them from recognizing how they may be perpetuating a racist system. Therefore, confronting one's White privilege can lead to empowerment, confidence, healing, and community building.

How to Challenge Racism

To fix White privilege, Whites need to accept that it exists, that racism is structural and real, and that Whites have the agency to do something about it. Part of this effort can include a call for curricula to become much more diverse; knowledge and education in the United States are still largely Euro-centric, and a targeted effort to include the history, knowledge, and perspectives of people of color is needed. On the micro level, Amico suggests that Whites ask themselves a series of questions: What happens when they encounter people who are "different"? How has White privilege kept them isolated from others? When were they first aware that they were a member of an ethnic group?[28] Such questions can help White people interrogate how their race and privilege have played roles in their lives. Once individuals realize that they have White privilege, they can use that privilege to intervene. For example, they can use it to educate other Whites about their privilege or address a racist incident when it occurs. It can also be used to support organizations and policies that work for racial justice. As noted at the beginning of this chapter, part of the intent of this theory is to get Whites to become active antiracists. In fact, Amico argues that acknowledging White privilege means nothing without action:

> All my learning—about white privilege, systems of privilege, the history of white supremacy in American culture, the separate worlds of white people and people of color, the internalized white supremacy in myself, and so forth—is all for naught if it does not translate into action; action to change myself, my behavior, my worldview; action to dismantle systems of privilege, action to promote social justice and real community.[29]

The recognition of privilege can help challenge racism, but, as Wise suggests, there also can be dire consequences to Whites if they do not confront this privilege, because Whiteness presents unrealistic expectations of success:

> It strikes me that unless we get a hold of this, unless we begin to address the way that privilege can set up those who have it for a fall … we'll be creating more addicts, more people who turn to self-injury, suicide, eating disorders, or other forms of self-negation, all because they failed to live up to some idealized type that they'd been told was theirs to achieve.[30]

In this vein, White privilege is hurting Whites because they are given unreal and corrupted expectations of achievement and status. Thus,

---

By the Numbers

- Fifty-six percent of Whites—compared to 73% of Asians, 69% of Blacks, and 61% of Hispanics—say that being White helps a little to a lot in a person's ability to get ahead in the United States.

- White workers are more likely than Blacks and Latinos to have a good job, even when educational attainment is the same; 75% of Whites with a bachelor's degree or higher are likely to have a good job, compared to 68% of Blacks and 65% of Latinos with the same educational credentials.*

- Between 2009 and 2015, 27% of White students admitted to Harvard were legacies, the children of faculty or staff or children of parents who have donated or plan to donate money to Harvard. The acceptance rate for all legacies was 34%, compared to Harvard's acceptance rate of 4.89%.

Sources: Arcidiacono, Kinsler, and Ransom (2019); Carnevale et al. (2019); Horowitz, Brown, and Cox (2019).

---

challenging White privilege is good not only for addressing racism but also for cultivating healthier environments for Whites.

Evaluation

Methodological Benefits

White privilege is an analysis of racism that uses the perspective of Whites, which is a particularly powerful methodological approach. Whites have long been analyzing racism via studies on communities of color, so for Whites to look inward has provided novel insights. The overall method of these scholars is to be brutally honest about their personal lives and to invite people to see how transparency about White privilege can be liberating. This approach is engaging and can be particularly successful in getting Whites to think about White privilege in a manner that does not immediately put them on the defensive.

These scholars also tend to take a life-course perspective, thereby showing how White privilege operates from childhood through adulthood, from minor daily interactions to major life chances, and from personal family matters to professional lives. If the analysis had centered on only a certain part of life, there would have been many more opportunities to deny the all-encompassing nature of White privilege. Taking this holistic approach to analyzing White privilege from the perspective of a White person who has experienced it gives unique and powerful insights into the "other side of racism."

Methodological Limitations

Amico, McIntosh, Rothenberg, and Wise all note that it is time for White people to take a look at themselves and how their lives have benefited from racism. Rothenberg says that her book *Invisible Privilege* "grows out of a deeply felt need to reflect in a more personal way on what it means to be a privileged white woman coming to terms with that privilege."[31] Wise realizes that, on some level, he had not been honest with himself concerning his relationship to race/racism: "My racial identity had shaped me from the womb forward. I had not been in control of my own narrative. It wasn't just race that was a social construct. So was *I*."[32] McIntosh notes that her self-reflection came about after her frustration "with men who would not recognize male privilege." She continues, "I decided to try to work on myself at least by identifying some of the daily effects of white privilege in my life."[33] And throughout his book *Exploring White Privilege*, Amico uses personal vignettes that provide real-life examples that effectively expose White privilege in a personal manner. Although on some level this approach is effective by connecting with people through real-life personal examples, there's no systematic analysis of data or clear way to analyze whether these reflections are honest, reliable, or generalizable. This method of analysis makes it difficult to replicate to evaluate its applicability. In addition, because most of the information is personal, it is just that—information relative to the individual who experienced it; however, this can be mitigated by providing contextualizing information. For example, sometimes the reflections are complemented by information on racist laws, racial statistics, or information from other sources that confirms these personal reflections. Amico in particular offers important macro-level data on White privilege, which is complemented by personal anecdotes, rather than the other way around.

Theoretical Benefits

White privilege fills a significant gap in the analysis of racism. Prior to this concept, the majority of theories on racism focused on the discrimination people of color received. White privilege successfully moves the focus of the problem to the perpetuation of Whiteness and how Whites, knowingly or unknowingly, participate in and benefit from racism. Moreover, White privilege does not reduce racism to a problem of individuals or a "few bad apples" but pushes Whites to see that racism is a society-wide problem. This theoretical approach of White privilege puts the responsibility squarely on all Whites to recognize that meritocracy is a myth and that ending racism requires White participation. Amico calls upon Whites to confront their "internalized sense of racial superiority," because if Whites are not a part of the solution, they are a part of the problem.[34]

Another theoretical benefit is that these scholars analyze how White privilege varies in relation to other intersecting identities, such as class, gender, and religion, but is not negated by them. Wise comes from a relatively poor Jewish background but clearly argues that these other marginalized identities did not make him immune to receiving White privilege. For example, as a child, Wise angrily stood up to a teacher who told him to listen to a Christian group, and as he reflects on his audacity in confronting the teacher, he notes:

> It was white privilege that made the difference, far more so than some inherent courage on my part … it was predicated on the privilege that allowed even a lower-income white kid like myself to feel certain enough about my rights so as to challenge those who would abuse them … it was equally about the way that even Jews, with our historically inconsistent and situationally contingent whiteness, can still access the powers of our skin in ways that make a difference.[35]

Wise recognizes that he was oppressed in relation to his class and religious status, but his Whiteness still prevailed in providing the confidence of knowing he could stand up to a teacher without the threat of significant consequences. Rothenberg addresses how being a woman and an Orthodox Jew created barriers for her, while simultaneously White privilege mitigated some of those barriers and provided unique opportunities in other ways.[36] The intersectional approach that details oppression received in one area (class, gender, etc.) along with the simultaneous experience of White privilege counters the potential criticism that Whites who have other intersecting oppressed identities do not receive any White privilege.

Theoretical Limitations

The White privilege theory centers Whiteness in the discussions of how racism is perpetuated by Whites; this explanation is of theoretical import but can also run the risk of, ironically, putting Whites at the center of the conversation. Academia is largely a White enterprise, and knowledge that is validated historically has and continues to come largely through White producers. White privilege scholarship has been largely produced by White scholars, and therefore these White scholars become more validated to speak on racism because of the White privilege they have. Certainly, White privilege scholars recognize this conundrum; Tim Wise is known for addressing this issue during his talks when he notes that he gets large speaking engagements partially due to his White privilege. But White privilege theory needs to be careful not to reify the very problem that it aims to analyze and deconstruct.

Another drawback of White privilege theory is the conflation of macro-level systemic issues and micro-level individual experiences of privilege. For example, White privilege examples include the micro-level, individual experience of a White person who is not followed around in a store and the macro-level, systemic problem of the disproportionate incarceration of people of color. Of course, the macro level and micro level are interconnected, but White privilege attempts both to represent an individual experience that is a consequence of a system and to represent the system itself. White privilege can be used to articulate micro- and macro-level Whiteness, but White privilege does not theorize systemic racism well. strmic-pawl addresses this theoretical limitation of White privilege and argues that systemic racism is better conceptualized through the framework of White supremacy[37] (see Chapter 3 on White supremacy).

Conclusion

White privilege turned the focus of racism to bring attention to how Whites both actively and passively benefit from racism. Moreover, the importance of critically analyzing the pathologies of Whiteness as a negative consequence of racism pushes the conversation forward on how racism is detrimental to all. The theory of White privilege continues to be used, both in theoretical terms and in practice, in popular media, on educational campuses, and in racial training programs.

REFLECT AND DISCUSS

1. How is White privilege the "other side" of racism?

2. How are White privilege and Whiteness connected? How do White people, as individuals, fit into this equation?

3. How does White privilege vary in important manners—yet also remain prevalent—across class status and gender identity?

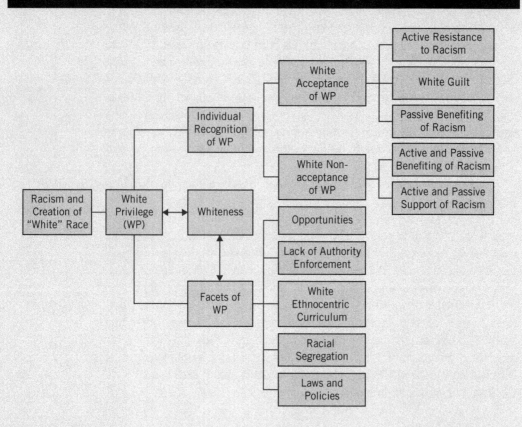

Diagram 2.1   White Privilege

KEY TERMS

Race: "A socially constructed category for the purpose of controlling, dominating, and exploiting some for the benefit of others."[38]

Racism: "Subordination of people of color by white people."[39]

White(ness): "Inequality and privilege are the only real components of whiteness. Without racial privilege there is no whiteness, and without whiteness, there is no racial privilege. Being white means being advantaged to people of color, and pretty much *only* that."[40]

White privilege: "A form of domination; hence it is a *relational* concept. It positions one person or group over another person or group. It is a concept of racial domination that enables us to see this relationship from the perspective of those who benefit from such domination."[41]

"I have come to see white privilege as an invisible package of unearned assets that I can count on cashing in each day, but about which I was 'meant' to remain oblivious. White privilege is like an invisible weightless knapsack of special provisions, assurances, tools, maps, guides, codebooks, passports, visas, clothes, compass, emergency gear, and blank checks."[42]

KEY PEOPLE

Robert Amico (1947–): Amico is Professor Emeritus of Philosophy at St. Bonaventure University in New York. His book *The Problem of Criterion* won the 1995 Choice Award for Outstanding Academic Book. His current research is on racism and social justice; in addition to writing *Exploring White Privilege* (2016), he also edited *Antiracist Teaching* (2015). Twitter @ rpamico

Peggy McIntosh (1934–): McIntosh was the former associate director of the Wellesley Centers for Women (of Wellesley College in Massachusetts) and was the founder of the National SEED (Seeking Educational Equity and Diversity) Project. She was also cofounder of the Rocky Mountain Women's Institute. McIntosh is widely recognized for coining the term *White privilege* in the 1988 paper "White Privilege and Male Privilege."

Paula Rothenberg (1943–2018): Rothenberg was a Senior Fellow at the Murphy Institute

at CUNY (City University of New York). She previously served for 7 years as the director of the New Jersey Project on Inclusive Scholarship, Curriculum, and Teaching at William Paterson University in New Jersey, where she was also Professor of Philosophy. Rothenberg published eight books that address social inequality and social justice. www.paularothenberg.com

Tim Wise (1968–): Wise is known for his public approach to his publications, having given talks in every state in the United States and at more than 1,000 college and high school campuses. Wise self-identities as an antiracist essayist, author, and educator and is the author of seven books. Wise is one of five people who were interviewed for a video exhibition on race relations in America. The video is featured at the National Museum of African American History and Culture in Washington, DC. www.timwise.org; Twitter @speakouttimwise

WORKS CITED AND FURTHER READING

Amico, Robert. 2016. *Exploring White Privilege.* New York: Routledge.

Arcidiacono, Peter, Josh Kinsler, and Tyler Ransom. 2019. "Legacy and Athlete Preferences at Harvard." *Working Paper 26316.* Cambridge, MA: National Bureau of Economic Research.

Carnevale, Anthony, Jeff Strohl, Artem Gulish, Martin Van Der Werf, and Kathryn Peltier Campbell. 2019. "The Unequal Race for Good Jobs." Washington, DC: Georgetown University.

Halley, Jean, Amy Eshleman, and Ramya Mahadevan Vijaya. 2011. *Seeing White: An*

Introduction to White Privilege and Race. Lanham, MD: Rowman and Littlefield.

Horowitz, Juliana Menasce, Anna Brown, and Kiana Cox. 2019. "Race in America 2019." Washington, DC: Pew Research Center.

Kendall, Frances E. 2013. *Understanding White Privilege: Creating Pathways to Authentic Relationships across Race.* 2nd ed. New York: Routledge.

Lipsitz, George. 2006. *The Possessive Investment in Whiteness: How White People Profit from Identity Politics.* Revised and expanded ed. Philadelphia, PA: Temple University Press.

McIntosh, Peggy. 1988. "White Privilege and Male Privilege." *Working Paper 189.* Wellesley, MA: Wellesley Centers for Women.

Rothenberg, Paula. 2000. *Invisible Privilege: A Memoir about Race, Class, and Gender.* Lawrence: University Press of Kansas.

Rothenberg, Paula. Ed. 2008. *White Privilege: Essential Readings on the Other Side of Racism.* 3rd ed. New York: Worth.

strmic-pawl, hephzibah. 2015. "More Than a Knapsack: The White Supremacy Flower as a New Model for Teaching Racism." *Sociology of Race and Ethnicity* 1(1):192–97.

Wise, Tim. 2011. *White Like Me: Reflections on Race from a Privileged Son: The Remix.* Revised and updated ed. Berkeley, CA: Soft Skull Press.

See also White Privilege Conference (www.whiteprivilegeconference.com) and the corollary journal, *Understanding and Dismantling Privilege* (http://www.wpcjournal.com).

NOTES

* A "good job" is defined by one that pays family-sustaining earnings.
1. Rothenberg (2008).
2. Amico (2016:2, emphasis in original).
3. Amico (2016:22).
4. Rothenberg (2000:172).
5. Wise (2011:3).
6. Lipsitz (2006).
7. Ibid. (3).
8. Wise (2011:85).
9. Ibid. (179, emphasis in original).
10. Rothenberg (2000:1).
11. Wise (2011).
12. Rothenberg (2000).
13. Wise (2011).
14. Ibid. (144).
15. McIntosh (1988:5).
16. Rothenberg (2000:111).
17. Ibid. (122).
18. Amico (2016:53).
19. McIntosh (1988:3).
20. Ibid. (3).
21. Rothenberg (2000:198).
22. Ibid.
23. Wise (2011).
24. Amico (2016).
25. McIntosh (1988:3–4).
26. Amico (2016:38–39).
27. Ibid.
28. Ibid. (69).
29. Ibid. (86).
30. Wise (2011:86).
31. Rothenberg (2000:2).
32. Wise (2011:viii, emphasis in original).
33. McIntosh (1988:3).
34. Amico (2016:30).
35. Wise (2011:62–63).
36. Rothenberg (2000).
37. strmic-pawl (2015).
38. Amico (2016:22).
39. Rothenberg (2000:172).
40. Wise (2011:179).
41. Amico (2016:2).
42. McIntosh (1988:2).

3

White Supremacy

Charles W. Mills | Andrea Smith | hephzibah v. strmic-pawl

White supremacy is a term most often associated with White superiority groups such as the Ku Klux Klan; however, in studies of race and ethnicity, White supremacy is a foundational concept for understanding how racism is embedded in the system. White supremacy is grounded in a historical analysis of race, with connections to how contemporary institutions operate to maintain power that benefits Whites. An in-depth theoretical description is best offered by philosopher Charles W. Mills, whose theory of the Racial Contract is the focus of this chapter. Two additional scholars' works are addressed in brief: Andrea Smith's "Heteropatriarchy and the Three Pillars of White Supremacy" and hephzibah v. strmic-pawl's "The White Supremacy Flower."*

Photo 3.1 Charles W. Mills

Source: https://www.gc.cuny.edu/ Faculty/Core-Bios/Charles-W-Mills.

Photo 3.2 hephzibah v. strmic-pawl

Source: http://www.hephzibahvsp. com/contact--booking.html.

---

*Photo of Smith unavailable.

Why This Theory

Charles W. Mills examines White supremacy by explaining how White normativity and superiority are embedded in the presumed egalitarian ideas of equality and justice. His theory of the Racial Contract is rooted in a foundational critique of the philosophical theory of the social contract. The *social contract* is a Western political theory that explains how human beings come to an agreement about the structure of civil society and government.[1] The primary dictate of the social contract is that all people are equal beneficiaries, and any presupposed or observed deviation from this practice is abnormal and a distortion of the social contract. In other words, the social contract states that all people are created equal and are treated as such. Mills, however, dispels the idea that the social contract is egalitarian, as it was implemented by White men and *intended* instead to have only White beneficiaries. Mills argues that society does not have a social contract but has a *Racial Contract,* as the oppression of people of color, rather than being an unintended perversion of the social contract, is actually a programmed result.

Mills' theory of the Racial Contract challenges the dominant assumption that the social contract works for the equality of all. Most of the world's population consists of people of color who have experienced racial oppression of some kind, but dominant philosophical analysis disregards this fact. For example, social contract theory ignores the concepts and history of race and racism, thus preventing a full knowledge and analysis of racial oppression. The Racial Contract, on the other hand, illuminates how White supremacy has been and is an integral and validated fact of the social system. Mills intends for the Racial Contract to bridge the stated ethics of Whites who are "preoccupied with discussions of justice and rights in the abstract" with the racial realities of people of color who are "focused on issues of conquest, imperialism, colonialism, white settlement, land rights, race and racism, slavery, Jim Crow, reparations, apartheid, cultural authenticity, national identity, *indigenismo,* Afrocentrism, etc."[2] In bringing these two discussions together, Mills reconciles the experiences of people of color with the color-blind logics of White philosophy. In addition, the Racial Contract provides both a descriptive account, how things are and how they got that way, as well as a prescriptive account, how society should be. The Racial Contract as a theory necessarily "puts race where it belongs—at center stage—and demonstrates how the polity was in fact a racial one, a white-supremacist state, for which differential white racial entitlement and nonwhite racial subordination were defining."[3]

Description of the Theory

Mills frames the Racial Contract within a broader conversation on the global nature of racism, which is in the form of White supremacy; he therefore defines **racism** as "*itself* a political system, a particular power structure of formal and informal rule, a socioeconomic privilege, and norms of the differential distribution of material wealth and opportunities, benefits and burdens, rights and duties."[4] The concept of the Racial Contract aims to explain the genesis of society and state, the way society is structured, the way government functions, and people's moral psychology.[5]

There are three crucial claims that underlie the theory: (1) an existential claim (one that purports the existence of an idea), (2) a conceptual claim (one that provides the framework for how to think about an idea), and (3) a methodological claim (one that describes the approach for how to analyze an idea). The existential claim is that White supremacy exists and has existed for years on local and global levels, the conceptual claim is that White supremacy is a political system, and the methodological claim is that White supremacy is a contract among Whites.[6]

The Racial Contract also has three subcontracts: (1) a political contract that arranges the people as a governed body and sets political guidelines, (2) a moral contract that determines ideas of right and wrong, and (3) an epistemological contract that "prescribes norms of cognition to which its signatories must adhere."[7] The epistemological subcontract is particularly important to understanding the Racial Contract because this subcontract describes how the "signatories"—that is, Whites who sign the contract—come to understand people of color as subhuman (this point will be described further shortly). Mills provides a specific definition of the **Racial Contract**:

> A set of formal or informal agreements or meta-agreements (higher-level contracts *about* contracts, which set the limits of the contracts' validity) between the members of one subset of humans, henceforth designated by (shifting) "racial" (phenotypical/genealogical/cultural) criteria C1, C2, C3 … as "white," and coextensive (making due allowance for gender differentiation) with the class of full persons, to categorize the remaining subset of humans as "nonwhite" and of a different and inferior moral status, subpersons, so that they have a subordinate civil standing in the white or white-ruled polities the whites either already inhabit or establish or in transactions as aliens with these polities, and the moral and juridical rules normally regulating the behavior of whites in their dealings with one another either do not apply at all in dealings with nonwhites or apply only in a qualified form (depending in part on changing historical circumstances and what particular variety of nonwhite is involved), but in any case the general purpose of the Contract is always the differential privileging of the whites as a group with respect to the nonwhites as a group, the exploitations of their bodies, land, and resources, and the denial of equal socioeconomic opportunities to them. All whites are *beneficiaries* of the Contract, though some whites are not *signatories* to it.[8]

In this definition, one can see that at the very essence of the racial contract is **White supremacy**. All Whites *benefit* from this Contract in that the arrangement systematically provides opportunities, resources, and benefits to Whites whether they desire them or not, though it is possible for Whites to acknowledge the oppressive nature of this Contract and not endorse or be "signatories" to the contract. This definition of the Racial Contract is further clarified through Mills' explanation of racing space, racing the individual, the evolution of the Racial Contract, and the enforcement of the Racial Contract.

Racing Space

The Racial Contract racializes the actual physical spaces of the land, thereby denoting a clear material aspect to the contract. As colonization and conquering of lands spread, and as the "frontier" moved and developed, the very lands became raced, wherein White spaces were known as "civilized" and spaces occupied by people of color were known as "savage." This racing of space operates on two levels. The first is the way in which Europe is constructed as the center of knowledge and how non-White spaces, where knowledge and production were created, were destroyed, explained away, and/or appropriated by Europeans as their own. The second is the way Whites describe spaces originally occupied by people of color as places that were "discovered" and "explored" as though the lands did not exist prior to White arrival; in this manner, cognition and knowledge also did not exist in these spaces until they were occupied by Whites. This racing of space persists in the contemporary description of spaces occupied by non-Whites as "urban" or "ghetto" and in blaming people of color for dysfunctional neighborhoods (with high levels of crime, violence, and welfare), instead of correctly identifying problems plaguing these neighborhoods as consequences of White supremacy.

Racing the Individual

The Racial Contract also operates through racing the body—some bodies are determined as "subpersons," and the status of subperson precludes full incorporation into the rights and protections of society. A **subperson** is defined in relation to Whiteness, in that subperson equals *not White*. Subpersons are identified as cognitively lacking, as those who are without the full capacities of rational thinking and therefore unable to contest any White knowledge or policy. For example, enslaved peoples, as subpersons, were prohibited from testifying against their owners. There is also an aesthetic racing of the body, so that the White body is the "somatic norm," wherein beauty is defined by light complexions and dark skin is equated with ugliness (see Chapter 12 on colorism). In this sense, Blacks are most alienated from their bodies because they are the least physically close to the complexion of Whites, and Black women in particular, given the sexist orientation toward women's beauty, uniquely feel the oppression of this White somatic norm. This racing of the body creates the division between person and subperson and is the foundational logic of White supremacy—it makes some bodies superior and eligible for participation in the "body politic" while deeming others as subpersons. This division then becomes the logic that is utilized to rationalize any detrimental treatment of non-Whites.

Evolution of the Racial Contract

The persistence of White supremacy can be observed through the ability of the Racial Contract to adjust and meet the context of the current time period. The social contract was written as a standing document, and then as time has progressed, people have continued to ratify and follow this contract. In contrast, the Racial Contract, as it constructs race and the relations among races, is constantly being rewritten. There are two primary time periods of the Racial Contract: (1) formal legal White supremacy and then (2) de facto White supremacy. During the first period, White supremacy was evident through the law of chattel slavery, the theft of Native lands and genocide, and racist labor laws. In the second period, White supremacy went into a de facto form, wherein laws protecting people of color were instituted, but the arrangement of social institutions (education, health, residence, law) persisted in benefiting Whites and denying opportunities and rights to people of color. The Racial Contract is harder to identify during this second time period because Whites deem non-Whites *legally as* persons, but the racial hierarchy is maintained so that "nonwhites find that race is, paradoxically, both everywhere and nowhere, structuring their lives but not formally recognized in political/moral theory."[9] For example, although discrimination is illegal, people of color consistently and systematically face racism in employment, politics, and the criminal justice system and are denied equal incorporation into society, as evidenced by substandard schooling, housing, healthcare, and other resources.

As time progresses, the Racial Contract can be modified to account for changing racial group eligibility; for example, some groups, such as German and Irish, who were previously discriminated against were then later welcomed into the White fold, while other groups have been pushed farther away from White eligibility. As Mills would say, some Whites are Whiter than others, and some non-Whites are Blacker than others. For example, during World War II, Japanese were put in internment camps, while today they have a much higher socioeconomic status compared to other people of color. In this vein, who counts as White is flexible; as Mills says, "the Racial Contract constructs its signatories as much as they construct it."[10] In other words, Whites sign the Contract, but the Contract also designates who counts as White.

Enforcement of the Racial Contract

As the Racial Contract evolves, the enforcement of the Contract is maintained through violence and ideological conditioning. In order for subpersons to exist, there needs to be a great deal of energy invested into creating, conditioning, and maintaining the idea of subpersons. During the first wave of overt White supremacy, this enforcement was maintained by extreme violence, such as "breaking" and "seasoning" enslaved Blacks. In the second wave of de facto White supremacy, the division has been maintained by teaching people of color that they are "less than," through honoring the contributions of Whites and dismissing knowledge production and cognition of non-Whites. Moreover, subpersons are taught to defer to Whites: "Racism as an ideology needs to be understood as aiming at the minds of nonwhites as well as whites, inculcating subjugation. If the social contract requires that all citizens and persons learn to respect themselves and each other, the Racial Contract prescribes nonwhite self-loathing and racial deference to white citizens."[11] The conditioning of Whites and non-Whites into the bind of the Racial Contract is an unrelenting force disseminated on both the macro and micro levels.

How to Challenge Racism

Mills makes the careful distinction between the individual and society, in that White supremacy and **Whiteness** are not about the faults of a few individuals but rather tied to a system. He writes that "the 'Racial Contract' decolorizes Whiteness by detaching it from whiteness.... *Whiteness is not really a color at all, but a set of power relations.*"[12] And in this distinction, Mills argues that no one race is inherently bad or inherently good; any group could potentially represent "Whiteness." The historical reality is that the European global conquest put Whites in power, but this reality can also be transformed. The Racial Contract is both a description of the problem and a prescription for fixing it; in other words, if one can see the system as racialized, the move to fix it becomes clear. Mills sees authentic confrontation with White supremacy as the first step: "Naming this reality brings it into the necessary theoretical focus for these issues to be honestly addressed. Those who pretend not to see them, who claim not to recognize the picture I have sketched, are only continuing the epistemology of ignorance required by the original Racial Contract."[13] Moreover, Mills situates his contribution within a set of scholarship that has long been ignored or disregarded: "The 'Racial Contract' locates itself proudly in the long, honorable tradition of oppositional black theory, the theory of those who were denied the capacity to theorize, the cognitions of persons rejecting their official subpersonhood."[14] The very writing and publication of *The Racial Contract* constitute a contestation of White supremacy.

By the Numbers

- In 2018, there were 1,020 hate groups identified in the United States; 148 were specifically White nationalist groups.

- In 1978, the Indian Claims Commission gave Native Americans less than $1,000 each in reparations for loss of land, and in 1988, $20,000 was paid to each Japanese American survivor of World War II internment. Descendants of enslaved Blacks have yet to receive any government reparations.

- In 2019, the White population in the United States was 61%, but Whites held 78% of congressional seats; nine people of color held seats as senators (out of 100).

Sources: Bialik (2019); Hassan and Healy (2019); Southern Poverty Law Center (2018).

Evaluation

Methodological Benefits

Mills critiques social contract theory to reveal how race(ism) is embedded into the seemingly race-neutral analyses of prominent philosophers. He dissects the foundational theories by Locke, Kant, and Hobbes to show where the articulation of the social contract falls short of recognizing the inherent Racial Contract. Indeed, Mills' book has so much strength because Mills moves through each one of his claims by rooting it in the historically oppressive acts that, he argues, Locke, Kant, and Hobbes all strategically ignore. He also references supportive historical and contemporary data to support his theoretical claims about the manifestation of White supremacy. For example, he cites the point that Europe held approximately 85% of the Earth as colonies,[15] the amount of income due to Blacks from unpaid slave labor,[16] evidence of job discrimination against non-Whites,[17] and descriptions of the violence undertaken across the globe during slavery and colonial times.[18] Such strong historical and contemporary data bolster his theoretical claims about the institutionalization and perpetuation of White supremacy. In fact, Mills outlines the historical facts of the Racial Contract as one of the benefits of the theory:

> [The Racial Contract] has the best claim to being an actual historical fact. Far from being lost in the mists of the ages, it is clearly historically locatable in the series of events marking the creation of the modern world by European colonialism and the voyages of "discovery" now increasingly and more appropriately called expeditions of conquest.[19]

Methodological Limitations

Mills provides historical and contemporary as well as local, national, and global evidence of White supremacy to support the existence of the Racial Contract. As noted previously, he moves systematically through these levels, which provide undisputed proof of the unfair rights, opportunities, and advantages given to Whites. Yet the way in which Mills attempts to cover so much can be a methodological limitation at times. The Racial Contract is an ambitious theory that explains White supremacy on a macro and dialogic level, yet this much material is difficult to cover. Mills moves from discussing the colonization of African lands to Japanese discrimination during World War II to the fight for Australian aboriginal rights in two pages.[20] He also cites a variety of scholars and disciplines in outlining his evidence: W. E. B. Du Bois (a sociologist), Richard Wright and James Baldwin (novelists), Sitting Bull (a Native American leader), Adolf Hitler (a German political dictator), and popular culture references such as the television show *Cheers*. This broad and encompassing group of sources and data could be perceived as a methodological limitation, as detail is lost in the breadth of coverage. And for readers who are unfamiliar with scholars/authors/activists from an array of disciplines, the references can be difficult to follow.

Theoretical Benefits

The term *White supremacy* is one of the most commonly used terms in theories of racism, particularly in critical race theory and related approaches, yet Mills' book provides a detailed examination of the processes of White supremacy. Of particular note is the description of racing of space and racing of individuals as tools to maintain the political, moral, and epistemological subcontracts of the Racial Contract. The theoretical originality of the Racial Contract is its revelation of White supremacy via the juxtaposition with the long-held, presupposed egalitarian social contract. Mills shows the hypocrisy and ignorance of the social contract by contrasting the moral egalitarianism of the social contract with the economic, political, and social reality of people of color. The clear theoretical import of the Racial Contract is outlined in Chapter 3 of Mills' book, "'Naturalized' Merits," wherein Mills moves through three major points that justify why the Racial Contract has explanatory and normative (prescriptive) power: (1) "The Racial Contract historically tracks the actual moral/political consciousness of (most) white moral agents," (2) "the Racial Contract has always been recognized by non-whites as the real determinant of (most) white moral/political practice and thus as the real moral/political agreement to be challenged," and (3) "the 'Racial Contract' as a theory is explanatorily superior to the raceless social contract in accounting for the political and moral realities of the world and in helping to guide normative theory."[21] In uncovering the hypocrisy of the social contract and the reality of the Racial Contract, the fixture of White supremacy in the social and political system is clear.

Theoretical Limitations

Mills writes that Whites are beneficiaries of the social contract and that most Whites are signatories of the contract, meaning that they have, in some sense, willingly signed on to the contract. As such, there are clear examples of Whites who have signed the contract—who actively produce or support laws, policies, or norms that support White superiority and opportunity— but what about Whites who are not actively creating laws and policies? How do most Whites sign the contract? The acts or beliefs Whites must uphold in order to be considered signatories of the Racial Contract are unclear. In addition, if Whites believe they are endorsing a social contract, even though in actuality they are supporting a Racial Contract, are they still active signatories or just beneficiaries? Is there a difference between active consent and coerced consent, or do all signatories equally support the regime of the Racial Contract? Mills also acknowledges that some Whites can refuse the Racial Contract, but here it is also unclear what acts or beliefs separate a signatory from a non-signatory.

In relation to this discussion, Whites are clearly the signatories of the Racial Contract, but the evolution of who counts as White is less clear. Mills defines *Whiteness* as a set of power relations, so that theoretically any group could end up at the top of the racial hierarchy; moreover, Mills acknowledges that racial groups have changed positions in the hierarchy throughout time. At one point, Japanese were disfavored by Whites, and at another time, they were favored. So how does one's relationship to the racial hierarchy, as part of a non-White racial group, affect the Racial Contract? Do some non-White groups suffer more or less from the consequences of the Racial Contract based on their positioning on the racial hierarchy? These unanswered questions do not undermine the power of this theory, but they can be limitations in the utility and application of the theory.

Additional Contributions to White Supremacy Theory: Smith and strmic-pawl

Smith: Heteropatriarchy and the Three Pillars of White Supremacy

In "Heteropatriarchy and the Three Pillars of White Supremacy," Andrea Smith addresses how White supremacy varies in relation to a goal: money, land, or imperial conquest.[22] Smith explains how there are **three pillars of White supremacy** that connect with three logics: (1) slavery and capitalism, (2) genocide and colonialism, and (3) Orientalism and war. One pillar of White supremacy is the logic of slavery, which is anchored in capitalism. In this system, Blacks are seen as enslavable, as property to be used to build wealth. Non-Blacks buy into this logic because then there is a permanently denigrated group from which they can strategically distance themselves. The second pillar is that of genocide, which is rooted in colonialism. People hold onto the value of colonialism, as it rationalizes the theft of land from indigenous people. The third pillar is Orientalism (speaking to a concept broader than the area known as the Orient or Asia), wherein certain peoples and nations are seen as perpetually foreign and threatening to the empire. The focus on "foreign threats" works as justification for war. Smith's identification of these three pillars allows insight into how White supremacy's manifestation varies in relation to different contexts and communities of color. This theory also reveals how communities of color may participate in one of the pillars in an effort to advance their social status and therefore be complicit with White supremacy. For example, non-Native peoples are complicit in order to get land, and non-immigrant communities are told they will be upwardly mobile if they support war efforts. This conceptualization of White supremacy, Smith suggests, can be used as a means to challenge racism:

> These approaches might help us to develop resistance strategies that do not inadvertently keep the system in place for all of us, and keep all of us accountable. In all of these cases, we would check our aspirations against the aspirations of other communities to ensure that our model of liberation does not become the model of oppression for others.[23]

strmic-pawl: The White Supremacy Flower

strmic-pawl's design uses a flower metaphor for describing the growth and manifestation of White supremacy.[24] This model does not purport to provide a new theory or description of White supremacy, but it is a theoretical mind map for understanding White supremacy, one that is intended to be accessible to students and newcomers. The proposed model, a White supremacy flower, also illuminates how White privilege is a manifestation of White supremacy rather than the other way around (see Chapter 2 on White privilege). In brief, the flower model consists of three main components: roots, stem, and bloom. The roots represent a historical grounding in White supremacy via theft of land, genocide of the indigenous, plantation slavery, and the writing of the Constitution for the benefit of White propertied men. The stem represents the growth of White supremacy over time, with laws and policies such as the Dawes Act, Jim Crow segregation, anti-immigration laws, and Japanese internment. The bloom of the flower signifies today's manifestation of White supremacy, with petals of the flower representing racialized inequalities, such as housing segregation, educational gaps, mass incarceration, and White privilege. In this sense, White privilege is just one manifestation of White supremacy—rather than the entire cause of racism. This model/metaphor of a flower clearly shows how the nation grew from its foundational roots in White supremacy and continues to manifest racialized social problems characterized by this foundation.

Conclusion

The theory of White supremacy is necessary for understanding the basis of racism and the underpinnings of other racial theories. While analyses of racism frequently reference White supremacy, Mills' Racial Contract provides a robust theoretical approach to examining the production, cause, and consequence of White supremacy. Smith's proposal encourages an analysis that shows how communities of color are differentially targeted and affected by three pillars and logics of White supremacy, and strmic-pawl's White supremacy flower provides an accessible model. An understanding of White supremacy is needed to illuminate the historical construction of the racial hierarchy and contemporary manifestations of the ongoing systemic and systematic valuing of those deemed as White.

REFLECT AND DISCUSS

1. How does the Racial Contract expose the falsity in the social contract?

2. How does the evolution of the Racial Contract explain the changing nature of racism?

3. How does the theory of White supremacy explain both the existence of White superiority groups and society's laws that purport to be race-neutral and egalitarian?

Diagram 3.1 Mills' Theory of the Racial Contract

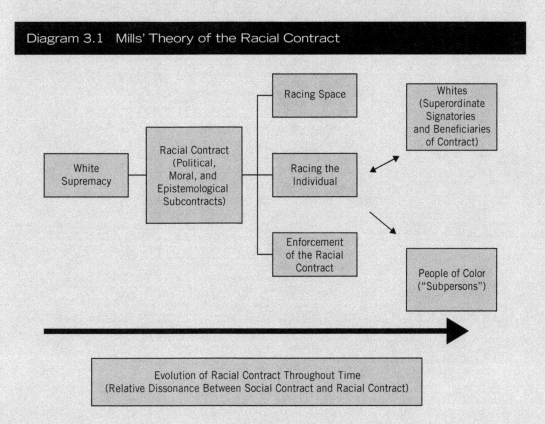

Diagram 3.2 Smith's Theory of the Three Pillars of White Supremacy

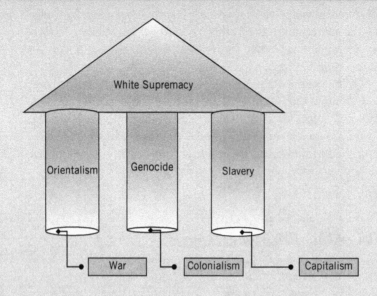

Diagram 3.3 strmic-pawl's White Supremacy Flower

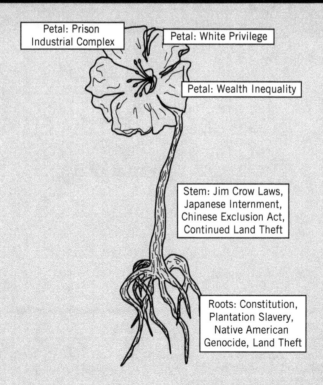

KEY TERMS

Racial Contract: "The differential privileging of the whites as a group with respect to the nonwhites as a group, the exploitations of their bodies, land, and resource, and the denial of equal socioeconomic opportunities to them. All whites are *beneficiaries* of the Contract, though some whites are not *signatories* to it."[25]

Racism: "A political system, a particular power structure of formal and informal rule, a socioeconomic privilege, and norms of the differential distribution of material wealth and opportunities, benefits and burdens, rights and duties."[26]

Subperson: "Humanoid entities who, because of racial phenotype/genealogy/culture, are not fully human and therefore have a different and inferior schedule of rights and liberties applying to them."[27]

Three pillars of White supremacy: Slavery/capitalism, genocide/colonialism, and Orientalism/war.[28]

Whiteness: "Whiteness is not really a color at all, but a set of power relations."[29]

White supremacy: "The systematic and systemic ways that the racial order benefits those deemed White and operates to oppress people of color."[30]

KEY PEOPLE

Charles W. Mills (1951–): Mills is Professor of Philosophy at the Graduate Center of City University of New York. Mills' *The Racial Contract* won the Gustavus Myers Outstanding Book Award for the study of bigotry and human rights in America and has been cited more than 2,500 times. He is known for his oppositional political theory centered on class, gender, and race and is the author of four additional books. In 2017, Mills was elected as a member of the American Academy of Arts and Sciences.

Andrea Smith (1966–): Smith is an Associate Professor of Media and Cultural Studies at the University of California Riverside. She is the author of two books, the editor of *The Revolution Will Not Be Funded*, and a cofounder of INCITE! Women of Color Against Violence. Smith has written extensively on Native Studies and claims Cherokee ancestry, but her Cherokee ancestry has come into question. There are two statements, "Open Letter from Indigenous Women Scholars Regarding Discussions of Andrea Smith" and "Cherokee Women Scholars' and Activists' Statement on Andrea Smith," that critically analyze and engage with the difficulties and harm incurred when scholars misrepresent their identity.

hephzibah v. strmic-pawl (1980–): strmic-pawl is Associate Professor of Sociology at Manhattanville College. Her research centers on multiracialism and the pedagogy of racism; she is the author of *Multiracialism and Its Discontents*, coeditor of the reader *Race and Ethnicity*, and founding Pedagogy Editor of the journal *Sociology of Race and Ethnicity*. In 2018, she received the Joseph B. Gittler Award from the Society for the Study of Social Problems. www.hephzibahvsp.com; Twitter @ hephzibahvsp

WORKS CITED AND FURTHER READING

Bialik, Kristen. 2019. "For the Fifth Time in a Row, the New Congress Is the Most Racially and Ethnically Diverse Ever." *Fact Tank*, February 8. Washington, DC: Pew Research Center.

Hassan, Adeel and Jack Healy. 2019. "America Has Tried Reparations Before. Here Is How It Went." *New York Times*, June 19.

Jung, Moon-Kie. 2015. *Beneath the Surface of White Supremacy: Denaturalizing U.S. Racisms Past and Present.* Stanford, CA: Stanford University Press.

Jung, Moon-Kie, João H. Costa Vargas, and Eduardo Bonilla-Silva, eds. 2011. *State of White Supremacy: Racism, Governance, and the United States.* Stanford, CA: Stanford University Press.

Mills, Charles W. 1997. *The Racial Contract.* Ithaca, NY: Cornell University Press.

Smith, Andrea. 2006. "Heteropatriarchy and the Three Pillars of White Supremacy: Rethinking Women of Color Organizing." Pp. 66–73 in *Color of Violence: The INCITE! Anthology*, edited by INCITE! Women of Color Against Violence. Boston: South End Press.*

Solomon, Akiba and Kenrya Rankin. 2019. *How We Fight White Supremacy: A Field Guide to Black Resistance.* New York: Bold Type Books.

Southern Poverty Law Center. 2018. "Hate Map." Montgomery, AL: Author.

strmic-pawl, hephzibah. 2015. "More Than a Knapsack: The White Supremacy Flower as a New Model for Teaching Racism." *Sociology of Race and Ethnicity* 1(1):192–97.

Yancy, George. 2017. *Black Bodies, White Gazes: The Continuing Significance of Race in America.* 2nd ed. Lanham, MD: Rowman and Littlefield.

NOTES

* Now published by Duke University Press (2016).
1. Mills (1997).
2. Ibid. (4).
3. Ibid. (57).
4. Ibid. (3).
5. Ibid. (5).
6. Ibid. (7).
7. Ibid. (11).
8. Ibid. (11, emphasis in original).
9. Ibid. (76).
10. Ibid. (78).
11. Ibid. (89).
12. Ibid. (127, emphasis in original).
13. Ibid. (133).
14. Ibid. (131).
15. Ibid. (29).
16. Ibid. (39).
17. Ibid. (75).
18. Ibid. (83–87).
19. Ibid. (20).
20. Ibid. (116–17).
21. Ibid. (120).
22. Smith (2006).
23. Ibid. (69).
24. strmic-pawl (2015).
25. Mills (1997:11).
26. Ibid. (3).
27. Ibid. (56).
28. Smith (2006).
29. Mills (1997:127).
30. strmic-pawl (2015:193).

Micro-Level Theories

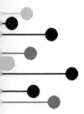

Implicit Bias

*Mahzarin Banaji, Anthony Greenwald,
and Brian Nosek*

The concept of implicit bias is based on the idea that individuals may hold biased thoughts of which they are unaware. Daily messages and experiences that shape cognition then lead to implicit racial biases, even when one may deliberately believe in and support racial equality. The Implicit Association Test (IAT), which evaluates automatic associations between racial groups and negative or positive attitudes and beliefs, reveals that most test-takers show an implicit preference for Whites. This chapter relies on the scholarship of the IAT's creators, Mahzarin Banaji, Anthony Greenwald, and Brian Nosek.

Photo 4.1 Mahzarin Banaji

Source: https://commons.wikimedia.org/
wiki/File:Implicit_Bias_Test_with_
Mahzarin_Banaji_and_Lloyd_Blankf
ein_(24898224967)_(cropped).jpg.

Photo 4.2 Anthony Greenwald

Source: https://faculty.washington.
edu/agg/.

Photo 4.3 Brian Nosek

Source: https://med.virginia.edu/
faculty/faculty-listing/ban2b/.

Why This Theory

The existence of racial bias is most easily recognized when individuals overtly embrace prejudiced attitudes and/or openly racially discriminate. This type of blatant racism, however, has been on the decline as egalitarian views, at least on a theoretical level, are becoming more widespread. Surveys on racial attitudes and beliefs show that most Whites now support racial equality. Sometimes, however, individuals have discriminatory or biased thinking of which they are not aware; these types of thoughts are captured by the concept of **implicit cognition**. Implicit thoughts are those that an individual has but are hidden from explicit (aware) cognition. Studies on implicit cognition have led to tests specifically crafted to reveal when people have implicit racial bias, even when that is contrary to their openly stated beliefs of racial equality. For example, one study used a virtual scenario where participants were told to shoot people whom they saw holding a gun. Tests revealed that participants were more likely to shoot Black people, regardless of whether they held a weapon or not. In this case, the participants reported no explicit racial animosity and believed themselves to be non-prejudiced, but the reflex shooting scenario showed that their racist implicit bias affected their actions.[1] This research pushes the conversation forward to consider the ways in which implicit bias may lead to unintentional racial discrimination.

The research on implicit bias has led to the development of the **Implicit Association Test**, or the **IAT** as it is commonly abbreviated. The purpose of the test is to tap into the "judgments that are under the control of automatically activated evaluation, without the performer's [test-taker's] awareness of that causation."[2] The IAT is a computer test that requires the participant to categorize images and words to evaluate automatic associations between a target concept and an associated attribute. The degree to which associations are made are then used to indicate any bias that a person may hold; for example, if a person associates Blacks with negative words more often than with positive words, the person likely has a negative implicit bias toward Blacks. Often when Whites are asked to self-report their values and beliefs about Blacks, the answers reflect non-prejudicial attitudes; however, the majority of Whites who take an IAT on race have results indicating a slight to a strong automatic preference for Whites over Blacks. The discrepancy in results between self-report measures versus IATs is at the crux of the contribution of this theory. The IAT taps into a set of data that are unavailable when relying on people to self-report.[3]

Description of the Theory

The fundamentals of implicit bias research consist of understanding the relationship between implicit and explicit cognition, the creation and design of the Implicit Association Test (IAT), the interpretation of IAT results, the use of the Project Implicit website, and changes and improvements to the IAT.

Implicit Versus Explicit

The theoretical approach of implicit bias is rooted in the differentiation between implicit and explicit cognition. Implicit cognition is shaped by previous experiences, which continue to inform an individual's thoughts, whether the individual is aware of that process occurring or not. Explicit cognition is the direct awareness of thoughts and recollection of previous experiences.[4]

A simple way to understand the difference between implicit and explicit cognition is through word retrieval tests. In such tests, individuals are shown a list of words to see if they can recall the words at a later time. An explicit test asks the person to simply recall the words, but an implicit test provides prompts. A prompt, such as providing the first letter or an affiliated concept, acts to stimulate the previous experience with the word and results in the participants more easily recalling the words because of the implicit association. Experiences in real life work in a similar manner. For example, if someone sees many commercials for cereal on television, that person may end up buying cereal at the grocery store due to implicit memory, even though the individual may not explicitly recall seeing cereal commercials. As Greenwald and Banaji explain, "the signature of implicit cognition is that traces of past experience affect some performance, even though the influential earlier experience is not remembered in the usual sense—that is, unavailable to self-report or introspection."[5] Thus, previous experience continues to shape current thought and action, even when that experience is not directly accessible by an individual's direct recollection.

Implicit bias has commonly come to be described as "unconscious" bias, but scientifically there is debate as to whether implicit cognition represents unconscious thought. Greenwald and Banaji argue that there is no clear, distinct connection between implicit as unconscious thought and explicit as conscious thought.[6] IAT scholars don't yet understand "what types of varied mental structures are produced by varied histories of experience with social stimuli or how those (still-to-be-identified) structures shape variations across persons in the conscious perception of a given stimulus situation."[7] In other words, at this point in the research, it is too early to state a definitive relationship among implicit, explicit, unconscious, and conscious. Instead, the key focus is understanding that the IAT captures cognition that explicit tests do not.

The Implicit Association Test

The IAT is a computer test that uses only two keys to respond to the prompts given. The test works by evaluating an individual's association between a target concept/category and an associated attribute:

When completing an IAT, participants rapidly classify individual stimuli that represent category and attribute (in the form of words, symbols, or pictures) into one of four distinct categories with only two responses. The underlying assumption is that responses will be facilitated—and thus will be faster and more accurate—when categories that are closely associated share a response, as compared to when they do not.[8]

In other words, an individual's quicker response in associating a target concept with one attribute (over another) indicates a bias toward that association.

The IAT can be made to test associations between any number of target concepts and attributes. Early design tests evaluated implicit associations based on the simple target concepts of insects and flowers, with the attribute concepts of good and bad. The IAT on the computer generally has seven stages through which the participant is guided. In the case of insects and flowers, Stage 1 instructions are to press the left computer key (usually the "E" key) when a flower word—such as *orchid*, *tulip*, or *rose*—appears and the right computer key (usually the "I" key) when an insect word—such as wasp, flea, or roach—appears. Stage 2 instructions are to press the left key when positive/good words—such as *cheer*, *happy*, or *love*—appear and the right key for negative/bad words—such as *evil*, *gloom*, or *damage*. Stage 3 uses the left key for flowers *or* for good words and the right key for bad words *or* insects. Stage 4 is a repeat of Stage 3. Stage 5 then switches the key relationship, so that the left key is now for bad/negative words and the right key is for good/positive words. Stage 6 inverses the relationship from Stage 3, so that the left key is for flower *or* bad words and the right key is for insects *or* good words. The final stage, Stage 7, is a repeat of the Stage 6 task. Individuals are asked to respond to the prompts as quickly as possible without producing multiple errors; the quick response style is used to avoid conscious overthinking. An IAT will also randomize the first few stages, so that the first association isn't always with flowers and good but could be flowers and bad; this randomness ensures that the test isn't inadvertently reinforcing flowers with good by presenting those stages first. The test can reveal an association between either good words and flowers or good words and insects, based on rapid, correct associations; the "burden is to retain the instructions to give the same response to two nonassociated categories (e.g., flower and unpleasant). There is no such apparent burden when the two categories that require the same response are strongly associated (e.g., flower and pleasant)."[9] An automatic association between good words and flowers would indicate a bias toward flowers over insects. The results of these early flower/insect IATs showed that any automatic association bias was also indicative of behavior; that is, people who showed a positive bias toward flowers cared more for flowers, while those who showed a positive bias toward insects had behavior that favored insects.[10] Given the reliable findings of such early IAT tests, the IAT was then extended to race.

The Race IAT operates on the same premise of the insect/flower IAT. The target concepts are Black and White, and the attribute concepts are positive or negative words. Participants follow the same stages of the test as outlined with flowers and insects but are instead shown faces of Blacks and Whites, along with positive or negative words. With a Race IAT, a faster response for White and positive words indicates an automatic preference for Whites.[11] Typically IATs measure attitudinal associations by using negative and positive words, but there is also a Race IAT that looks at associations between races and stereotypes. Greenwald and Banaji discuss the definition and importance of testing for **stereotypes**:

> A stereotype is a socially shared set of beliefs about traits that are characteristic of members of a social category. Whereas an attitude implies a consistent evaluative response to its object, a stereotype may encompass beliefs with widely diverging evaluative implications. For example, the stereotype of members of a certain group (e.g., cheerleaders) may simultaneously include the traits of being physically attractive (positive) and unintelligent (negative). Stereotypes guide judgment and action to the extent that a person acts toward another as if the other possesses traits included in the stereotype.[12]

In this manner, IATs that use stereotypes may capture more complex sentiments than attitudinal-only IATs. For example, stereotype IATs show that Whites are more often associated as Americans, and Blacks are more likely to be associated with weapons.[13] The IAT has been effectively designed to show such automatic associations, but another area of IAT research is interpreting the implications and significance of the test.

Interpreting the IAT

IATs on race show that a majority of people who take the test associate positive attributes and stereotypes with Whites, more so than they do with people of color. Yet there have been questions on how to interpret such results and what conclusions can be fairly deduced. There are three major considerations: (1) Are IAT results reflective of the culture, or are they specific to the individual who took the test? (2) What is the origin of implicit cognition? (3) Does implicit bias result in discriminatory action?

IAT Results: Your Culture or You?

One consideration is whether an individual's IAT result is an assessment of that person's culture or whether the result is specific to that person's cognition. IAT researchers argue that an IAT *is specific to the person* who took the test; if an IAT were reflective of the culture more so than the individual, self-report results would match those of an IAT. For example, if one's culture taught that Whites and Blacks are equal, one's self-report test would show no bias, and one's IAT would also show no bias. On the contrary, it is very often the case that a self-report survey shows attitudes supportive of racial equality, while that same person's IAT shows a preference for Whites. Moreover, if culture were the explanatory variable, all people who share the same culture would have similar IAT results, but IAT results vary among individuals, even though they belong to the same culture. Thus, IAT results are generally perceived as belonging to the person who took the test.[14]

The Origins of Implicit Cognition

An IAT reveals automatic associations of which an individual is unaware, but where does this implicit cognition come from? Greenwald and Banaji explain that "implicit attitudes and stereotypes may be acquired over many years from language and social experiences that cumulatively construct an overlearned repertoire of cultural expertise rooted in even more thousands of hours of experience than those invested by medical doctors, virtuoso musicians, or world-class athletes in their professional training."[15] Both minute and major interactions shape one's implicit cognition; it is a daily and ongoing process that is constantly at work. Thus, just as implicit cognition often goes unrecognized by the individual, so also does the process by which this implicit cognition is built: It is a result of the cumulation of the daily experiences that often pass as insignificant, and even unnoticed, but that shape an individual's thinking.

Implicit cognition, though it varies by individual, is also shaped by dominant macro ideologies. The effect of such social messages is evident by the fact that people of color who take IATs on race also show an automatic preference for Whites. IAT scholars explain this outcome with system justification theory. This theory posits that although people of color want to hold favorable views about themselves, they also want to hold favorable views about the system to which they belong. **Psychological system justification** is "the process by which existing social arrangements are legitimized, even at the expense of personal and group interest."[16] In other words, oppressed individuals will sometimes, unintentionally or without complete awareness, accept the dominant constructs and myths about themselves in order to avoid conflict with their society. For example, studies indicate that groups with low socioeconomic status show more belief in authoritarianism and political conservativism than groups with a high socioeconomic status; such contradictory beliefs likely exist as a motivation "to reduce ideological dissonance" but operate "in such a way that the status quo is preserved."[17] It should not be presumed, then, that an implicit bias toward Whiteness belongs only to Whites, as all people may develop implicit bias in an effort to live in accordance with their society's messaging.

Implicit Bias and Action

A third consideration in interpreting the IAT is the predictive value between one's IAT results and action: Does an IAT that shows bias predict discrimination? IATs, in fact, do have a stronger correlation with action than self-report measures. For instance, individuals can easily lie on a self-report survey and say that they support racial equality, while in practice they do not. Hiding such internal bias is more difficult on an IAT, due to the quick/auto response method of the test.[18] IAT measures do indicate favorable or unfavorable action toward the target group, and stereotype measures predict stereotype-consistent judgment toward target group members.[19] Another indication of the validity of the IAT is the evaluation of brain activation; IAT results predict greater activation of the amygdala, which is associated with emotion and fear response.[20] The predictive value of IATs is still under testing, but some data suggest the utility and validity of these tests for assessing racial bias that can result in discrimination.

The IAT Website

After evaluating and affirming the IAT through early tests, Anthony Greenwald, Mahzarin Banaji, and Brian Nosek in 1998 established **Project Implicit** as "a non-profit organization and international collaboration between researchers who are interested in implicit social cognition—thoughts and feelings outside of conscious awareness and control. The goal of the organization is to educate the public about hidden biases and to provide a 'virtual laboratory' for collecting data on the Internet."[21] This website is open and free to anyone who wishes to take an implicit bias test. There are currently 14 available tests, five of which are associated with race: (1) an Arab-Muslim IAT that consists of Arab-Muslim names and names that usually belong to other nationalities or religions, along with "good" or "bad" words; (2) an Asian IAT that consists of White faces and Asian American faces, along with places that are American or foreign; (3) a Native IAT that has Whites in modern dress and Native Americans in traditional clothing, along with pictures of locations that are in the United States or pictures of locations that are outside the United States; (4) a Race IAT that consists of faces of Whites and Blacks, along with "good" or "bad" words; and (5) a skin-tone IAT that consists of faces with light skin tone and dark skin tone, along with "good" or "bad" words.[22] After completing a test, participants are told whether they have "little to no," "slight," "moderate," or "strong" association for one of the target groups. For example, a Race IAT result that shows a slight bias toward Whites would state the result in this way: "Your data suggest slight automatic preference for European Americans over African Americans."[23] These descriptive results are based on an algorithm that evaluates the person's automatic association process during the IAT.

The Race IAT has been available on the website since 2002; between 2002 and 2017, approximately 4.6 million people completed this IAT. When taking an IAT on this website, individuals are also asked questions, which are optional, on basic demographics (race, gender, age, income, etc.), as well as a random set of 10 questions derived from a set of self-report questionnaires on racism, including a racial thermometer, a Bayesian Racism Scale, and Right-Wing Authoritarianism questions. These latter questions permit comparisons between implicit cognition and explicit, self-report answers. There are also a few debriefing questions that ask the participants their thoughts on test results. The answers from these questions and the IAT results are available as a data set for anyone to download and analyze.[24] Project Implicit became a non-profit in 2001 "to foster dissemination and application of implicit social cognition," and data sets are available, as "researchers may answer interesting and novel questions" with them.[25] The open-access nature of both the test and the data set results presents a unique opportunity to study this type of racism.

Changes and Improvements to the IAT

The first major article published on implicit bias and the IAT was "Measuring Individual Differences in Implicit Cognition: The Implicit Association Test," written in 1998 by Anthony Greenwald, Debbie McGhee, and Jordan Schwartz.[26] Since the publication of this article and the creation of the IAT website, both internal and external questions and criticisms have led to improvements in the validity, reliability, and value of the IAT. One central issue is choosing clear categories and attributes in test creation. The category concepts, such as choosing White or Black faces to reflect race, must be unambiguous to the participant, so that lack of clarity does not affect test results. The concepts also must be distinct and not easily conflated; for example, a skin-tone IAT with the target concepts of medium skin tone and dark skin tone would likely not work well because the concepts are not distinct enough. The configuration of categories and attributes also must be designed to ensure measurement of the intended bias. For example, tests have shown that individuals tend to prefer Black athletes to disliked White politicians when the IAT is on occupation, but individuals prefer White politicians to Black athletes when the IAT is on race. Thus, in this case, although the similar stimuli of Black athletes and White politicians were used in two tests, the results varied depending on whether the intended bias to be measured was occupation or race.[27] The test process has also been improved by making clear all the images and words that will be used in a test before taking it. For example, prior to taking the Race IAT, the Project Implicit website provides the images that represent Black and White faces and the words used to represent positive and negative.

The algorithm for measuring implicit bias has also been a point of conversation in improving the IAT. Greenwald, Nosek, and Banaji have addressed this point by looking at a series of factors that can affect an IAT score, such as participant error, length of time to respond and choose a key, and previous experience taking IATs.[28] They suggest an improved algorithm for assessing one's implicit bias with three major alterations: (1) use of practice-block data, (2) use of error penalties, and (3) use of individual-respondent standard deviations to provide the measure's scale unit.[29] These changes address previous concerns of IAT measurement and overall

> (a) better reflect underlying association strengths, (b) more powerfully assess relations between association strengths and other variables of interest, (c) provide increased power to observe the effect of experimental manipulations on association strengths, and (d) better reveal individual differences that are due to association strengths rather than other variables.[30]

Improving the measurement algorithm is intended not to change the IAT itself but to measure the association more accurately, with as few offsetting or extraneous factors as possible.

How to Challenge Racism

The IAT appeals to a wide audience, as indicated by the number of people who have voluntarily participated in taking an IAT on the Project Implicit website. Test-takers are often surprised at their results and interested in ameliorating their personal bias, as they are concerned it could manifest in biased action. As mentioned earlier, there is a predictive value of the IAT, in that some research shows that implicit bias correlates with behavior. Thus, it is possible that individuals who become aware of their implicit beliefs may be able to take steps to counter consequential action. In this manner, the online IAT provides a free and easily accessible service to individuals who are interested in their implicit cognition and in modifying personal behavior.

There has also been increasing interest in using the IAT in education, law, policy, and business to help people become aware of their unknown biases.[31] For example, the Kirwan Institute for the Study of Race and Ethnicity has an "Implicit Bias Module Series" that teaches about "how our minds operate" and helps people "understand the origins of implicit associations." The institute aims for people to uncover their "biases and learn strategies for addressing them."[32] The Berkeley Lab, associated with the University of California system, has "The UC Managing Implicit Bias Series," which is "designed to increase awareness of implicit bias and reduce its impact at the University. The series reinforces the UC diversity, equity, and inclusion values that enable the University to attract and retain a top talent workforce."[33] Large corporations, such as Google and Starbucks, have also utilized implicit bias trainings in an effort to curb employee bias and cultivate more inclusive environments.[34] Cities including Cincinnati, Chicago, and New York also offer voluntary or mandatory implicit bias training to various government employees. Although the leading researchers on implicit bias have not published research specifically on using the IAT to challenge racism, there clearly has been an increase on the part of both individuals and institutions to use implicit bias training to address racism.

By the Numbers

- In studies of facial expressions, Whites with stronger implicit racial bias are more likely to see an expression on a Black face as angry but perceive it as happy or neutral when it appears on a White face.

- Implicit negative associations toward Asian Americans are linked to a resistance to hiring Asian Americans for national security jobs.

- When given a fake memorandum with grammar errors, law partners identified an average of 2.9 grammar errors when they believed the memo was written by a White associate, compared to 5.8 errors when they believed the memo was written by a Black associate.

Sources: Godsil et al. (2014); Hugenberg and Bodenhausen (2003); Yogeeswaran and Dasgupta (2010).

Evaluation

Methodological Benefits

Previous to the IAT, a measure of individual prejudice or bias largely relied on self-report surveys. Although self-report surveys have evolved to use sophisticated questions, such tests still rely on individuals honestly answering questions. The IAT avoids this self-report problem by having the participant provide rapid answers to simple categorization tasks, thereby making it difficult to misguide the results of the test. Moreover, the IAT has been rigorously tested and retested by multiple leading researchers, who have made modifications to make the test more valid and reliable. Greenwald, Nosek, and Banaji recognize that the utility of "the IAT may be due to its combination of apparent resistance to self-presentation artifact, its lack of dependence on introspective access to the association strengths being measured, and its ease of adaptation to assess a broad variety of socially significant associations."[35]

Methodological Limitations

There are several factors that can affect the outcomes of an IAT and therefore provide inaccurate measurements of implicit associations. One such factor is the use of the concepts and attributes included in the test. As noted earlier, one test tends to show positive association for Black athletes over White politicians when evaluating occupation but positive association for White politicians when evaluating race. Another study showed that people responded to gay women more positively than they did to gay men, so that an IAT on sexual orientation could differ depending on an individual's personal acceptance of gay women or men.[36] These examples indicate that it is possible that an IAT may not always be measuring what is intended, and it can be difficult to predict how individuals may personally connect to particular target concepts or associated attributes.

Another primary factor is the reliability of the test. Any number of variables, such as level of alertness, daily emotions, and contemporary social context, can affect test results. All test-taking is affected by a number of issues, and an IAT is no different. Furthermore, if one takes the same IAT repeatedly, results can vary, which indicates to critics that the results are unreliable. IAT lead researchers, however, argue that although no one IAT is completely reflective of an individual's implicit cognition, a series of IAT tests taken by an individual can be informative on an aggregate level.

Theoretical Benefits

The research on implicit bias has successfully built on previous studies on semantic priming and unconscious thinking to identify a layer of cognition that had not been previously systematically tested. Evaluation of implicit cognition can lend great insight into personal biases and the effects of racial messaging. The fact that individuals who take an IAT feel surprise at their results is revealing of the ways in which society's messages affect cognition, whether one is a willing participant in those messages or not. Even people who do not subscribe to sentiments of White superiority are exposed to daily messages that promote it: for example, advertisements that predominantly use White models and show light skin tone as beautiful or school curricula that tell history via a White ethnocentric perspective. It is important to remember that every person's cognition is shaped by an array of ideologies and values of the society in which they live; awareness of implicit bias reminds people of this fact.

Another theoretical benefit of the IAT is its adaptability for testing multiple types of bias. The theoretical basis for the IAT measure is "the difference in average latency between two combined tasks," which provides an individual's automatic association.[37] Thus, any number of IATs could be built using different target groups and attribute associations to test different types of racial biases. Project Implicit currently has five tests related to race, but more could be added to reflect other racial groups. The stereotype-based IATs also provide an additional way to test for more complex racialized associations. The proposal of implicit bias is a rich theoretical addition to understanding racism, and the adaptability of the IAT allows for a wide range of tests.

Theoretical Limitations

The utility, arguably, of measuring and acknowledging implicit bias is the opportunity to use that knowledge in addressing racism. However, there are concerns as to whether the IAT can predict behavior or whether implicit cognition can be modified. There are several scientists who, through their own evaluation of the IAT, find little to no correlation between IAT outcomes and discriminatory behavior.[38] The IAT is not designed to predict behavior, so this criticism is not so much a methodological limitation as it is a limitation on making a robust theoretical connection between implicit cognition and action. The theoretical import of implicit bias is somewhat weakened if there is not a direct connection to behavior, as behavior then can be neither predicted nor potentially changed in relation to implicit bias.

A secondary theoretical limitation of implicit bias is related to the nature of implicit cognition. Blaming discriminatory action on implicit bias can become an escape route for those who are racially biased by claiming that they were unaware of their bias and therefore not responsible for it. Implicit cognition can easily become entangled in a conversation on intention, which may be important on an individual level, but such conversations on intention do little to challenge or change racism on the macro level.

Conclusion

The theoretical approach of implicit cognition lends novel insight into how individuals can have racially biased attitudes without being aware of them. Research on how implicit cognition operates led to the development of the IAT, which provides a clear and accessible way to measure for implicit cognition. The design of the IAT based on associations between target concepts and associated attributes provides flexibility for evaluating bias related to a wide range of racial dynamics.

REFLECT AND DISCUSS

1. How do past experiences shape implicit cognition?

2. How can one have explicit nondiscriminatory views and implicit discriminatory attitudes concurrently?

3. Explain why people of color who take an IAT test may show a preference for Whites.

Diagram 4.1   Implicit Bias

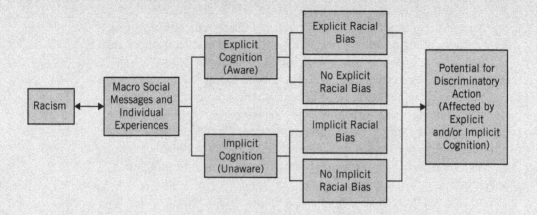

KEY TERMS

Implicit Association Test (IAT): "When completing an IAT, participants rapidly classify individual stimuli that represent category and attribute (in the form of words, symbols, or pictures) into one of four distinct categories with only two responses. The underlying assumption is that responses will be facilitated—and thus will be faster and more accurate—when categories that are closely associated share a response, as compared to when they do not."[39]

Implicit cognition: "The signature of implicit cognition is that traces of past experience affect some performance, even though the influential earlier experience is not remembered in the usual sense—that is, unavailable to self-report or introspection."[40]

Project Implicit: "A non-profit organization and international collaboration between researchers who are interested in implicit social cognition—thoughts and feelings outside of conscious awareness and control. The goal of the organization is to educate the public about hidden biases and to provide a 'virtual laboratory' for collecting data on the Internet."[41]

Psychological system justification: "The process by which existing social arrangements are legitimized, even at the expense of personal and group interest."[42]

Stereotype: "A socially shared set of beliefs about traits that are characteristic of members of a social category. Whereas an attitude implies a consistent evaluative response to its object, a stereotype may encompass beliefs with widely diverging evaluative implications."[43]

KEY PEOPLE

Mahzarin Banaji (1956–): Banaji is the Richard Clarke Cabot Professor of Social Ethics at Harvard University. Banaji is cofounder, along with Greenwald and Nosek, of Project Implicit. In 2017, along with Greenwald, she received the Distinguished Scientific Contributions Award from the American Psychological Association. In 2016, she received the William James Fellow Award for a "lifetime of significant intellectual contributions to the basic science of psychology" from the Association for Psychological Science; she was president of the organization from 2010 to 2011. Twitter @banaji

Anthony Greenwald (1939–): Greenwald is Professor of Psychology at the University of Washington. Greenwald is cofounder, along with Banaji and Nosek, of Project Implicit. In 2013, he received the William James Lifetime Achievement Award from the Association for Psychological Science. In 2017, along with

Banaji, he received the Distinguished Scientific Contributions Award from the American Psychological Association.

Brian Nosek (1950–): Nosek is Professor of Psychology at the University of Virginia. Nosek is cofounder, along with Banaji and Greenwald, of Project Implicit. Nosek is also cofounder and the executive director of the Center for Open Science, which operates the Open Science Network. In 2015, *Nature*, the international weekly journal of science, listed Nosek on "*Nature's* 10" as part of its "10 people who mattered this year." Twitter @briannosek

WORKS CITED AND FURTHER READING ———————————

Banaji, Mahzarin R. and Anthony G. Greenwald. 2016. *Blindspot: Hidden Biases of Good People.* New York: Bantam Books.

Berkeley Lab. 2019. "Implicit Bias Awareness." Berkeley, CA: Author. Retrieved September 23, 2019 (https://diversity.lbl.gov/implicit-bias-awareness).

Feloni, Richard. 2016. "Here's the Presentation Google Gives Employees on How to Spot Unconscious Bias at Work." *Business Insider.* Retrieved September 23, 2019 (https://www.businessinsider.com/google-unconscious-bias-training-presentation-2015-12).

Godsil, Rachel, Linda Tropp, Phillip Atiba Goff, and john powell. 2014. "Addressing Implicit Bias, Racial Anxiety, and Stereotype Threat in Education and Health Care." Perception Institute. Retrieved March 5, 2020 (https://perception.org/publications/science-of-equality-vol-1).

Greenwald, Anthony G. and Mahzarin R. Banaji. 1995. "Implicit Social Cognition: Attitudes, Self-Esteem, and Stereotypes." *Psychological Review* 102(1):4–27.

Greenwald, Anthony G. and Mahzarin R. Banaji. 2017. "The Implicit Revolution: Reconceiving the Relation between Conscious and Unconscious." *American Psychologist* 72(9):861–71.

Greenwald, Anthony G., Mahzarin R. Banaji, and Brian A. Nosek. 2015. "Statistically Small Effects of the Implicit Association Test Can Have Societally Large Effects." *Journal of Personality and Social Psychology* 108(4):553–61.

Greenwald, Anthony G., Debbie E. McGhee, and Jordan L. Schwartz. 1998. "Measuring Individual Differences in Implicit Cognition: The Implicit Association Test." *Journal of Personality and Social Psychology* 74(6):1464–80.

Greenwald, Anthony G., Brian A. Nosek, and Mahzarin R. Banaji. 2003. "Understanding and Using the Implicit Association Test: I. An Improved Scoring Algorithm." *Journal of Personality and Social Psychology* 85(2):197–216.

Greenwald, Anthony G., Mark A. Oakes, and Hunter G. Hoffman. 2003. "Targets of Discrimination: Effects of Race on Responses to Weapons Holders." *Journal of Experimental Social Psychology* 39(4):399–405.

Greenwald, Anthony G., T. Andrew Poehlman, Eric Luis Uhlmann, and Mahzarin R. Banaji. 2009. "Understanding and Using the Implicit Association Test: III. Meta-Analysis of Predictive Validity." *Journal of Personality and Social Psychology* 97(1):17–41.

Hugenberg, Kurt and Galen V. Bodenhausen. 2003. "Facing Prejudice: Implicit Prejudice and the Perception of Facial Threat." *Psychological Science* 14(6):640–43.

Jost, John T., Mahzarin R. Banaji, and Brian A. Nosek. 2004. "A Decade of System Justification Theory: Accumulated Evidence of Conscious and Unconscious Bolstering of the Status Quo." *Political Psychology* 25(6):881–919.

Kirwan Institute. 2018. "Implicit Bias Module Series." Columbus: Ohio State University. Retrieved September 24, 2019 (http://kirwan institute.osu.edu/implicit-bias-training).

Lane, Kristin, Mahzarin R. Banaji, Brian A. Nosek, and Anthony G. Greenwald. 2007. "Understanding and Using the Implicit Association Test: IV: What We Know (So Far) About the Method." Pp. 59–102 in *Implicit Measures of Attitudes*, edited by B. Wittenbrink and N. Schwarz. New York: Guilford Press.

Oswald, Frederick L., Gregory Mitchell, Hart Blanton, James Jaccard, and Philip E. Tetlock. 2013. "Predicting Ethnic and Racial Discrimination: A Meta-Analysis of IAT Criterion Studies." *Journal of Personality and Social Psychology* 105(2):171–92.

Project Implicit. 2011. "Project Implicit." Retrieved September 24, 2019 (https://implicit. harvard.edu/implicit).

Project Implicit Wiki. 2019. "Project Implicit Demo Website Datasets." Charlottesville, VA: Center for Open Science. Retrieved September 24, 2019 (https://osf.io/y9hiq/wiki/home).

Starbucks. 2018. "Starbucks to Close All U.S. Stores for Racial-Bias Education." *Starbucks Stories and News,* April 17. Retrieved September 24, 2019 (https://stories.starbucks.com/press/ 2018/starbucks-to-close-stores-nationwide-for-racial-bias-education-may-29).

Yogeeswaran, Kumar and Nilanjana Dasgupta. 2010. "Will The 'Real' American Please Stand Up? The Effect of Implicit Stereotypes about Nationality on Discriminatory Behavior." *Personality and Social Psychology Bulletin* 36(10):1332–45.

NOTES

1. Greenwald, Oakes, and Hoffman (2003).
2. Greenwald, McGhee, and Schwartz (1998:1464).
3. Ibid.
4. Greenwald and Banaji (2017:861).
5. Greenwald and Banaji (1995:4–5).
6. Greenwald and Banaji (2017).
7. Ibid. (869).
8. Lane et al. (2007:62).
9. Greenwald and Banaji (2017:866).
10. Lane et al. (2007).
11. Greenwald et al. (2009).
12. Greenwald and Banaji (1995:14).
13. Lane et al. (2007).
14. Ibid.
15. Greenwald and Banaji (2017:866–67).
16. Jost, Banaji, and Nosek (2004:883).
17. Ibid. (910).
18. Greenwald et al. (2009).
19. Greenwald, Banaji, and Nosek (2015).
20. Lane et al. (2007).
21. Project Implicit (2011).
22. Ibid.
23. Ibid.

24. Project Implicit Wiki (2019).
25. Ibid.
26. Greenwald et al. (1998).
27. Lane et al. (2007).
28. Greenwald, Nosek, and Banaji (2003).
29. Ibid. (213).
30. Ibid. (215).
31. Greenwald et al. (2009).
32. Kirwan Institute (2018).
33. Berkeley Lab (2019).
34. Feloni (2016); Starbucks (2018).
35. Greenwald, Nosek, and Banaji (2003:97).
36. Lane et al. (2007).
37. Greenwald et al. (2009:18).
38. Oswald et al. (2013).
39. Lane et al. (2007:62).
40. Greenwald and Banaji (1995:4–5).
41. Project Implicit (2011).
42. Jost et al. (2004:883).
43. Greenwald and Banaji (1995:14).

Microaggressions

Derald Wing Sue

Microaggressions are the small interpersonal hostile or derogatory comments that assault an individual's marginalized identity. The term *microaggression* was introduced in the 1970s, but the theoretical development of the concept and popular awareness of microaggressions are more recent. Attention to how the small comments that characterize microaggressions can have detrimental consequences, particularly in schools and in the workplace, has grown. The theoretical explanation of microaggressions in this chapter is based on the work by Derald Wing Sue, a psychologist who is recognized for his expansive development of microaggression theory.

Photo 5.1 Derald Wing Sue

Source: https://www.tc.columbia.edu/faculty/dw2020/.

Why This Theory

The theory of microaggressions is an example of the shifting nature of contemporary racism, which is characterized by a covert racism that is often difficult to detect. The term *microaggression* was first coined in the 1970s by Chester M. Pierce in his work on how Blacks experience subtle verbal and nonverbal discrimination.[1] Derald Wing Sue, whose work this chapter is based on, has built on Pierce's concept of microaggression and the theories of aversive racism and implicit bias to construct a compelling theory of microaggressions.

Microaggression theory is akin to the theories of aversive racism and implicit bias in the recognition of how subconscious discriminatory thoughts and values can shape action. The theory of aversive racism analyzes how Whites see themselves as moral and decent citizens who would not intentionally discriminate, but they have unconscious biased attitudes that result in discrimination.[2] The theory of implicit bias (see Chapter 4) also looks at how people hold beliefs and values that can unknowingly affect their decision-making processes and result in discrimination against people of color. **Microaggression theory**, however, focuses "primarily on describing the dynamic interplay between perpetrator and recipient, classifying everyday manifestations, deconstructing hidden messages, and exploring internal (psychological) and external (disparities in education, employment, and health care) consequences."[3]

Microaggressions may seem to have minimal effects because they are small exchanges, but Sue endeavors to show how lifelong exposure to microaggressions has psychological and biological health consequences and how microaggressions result in unequal outcomes observable on the macro level. Sue writes that

> microaggressions are constant and continuing experiences of marginalized groups in our society; they assail the self-esteem of recipients, produce anger and frustration, deplete psychic energy, lower feelings of subjective well-being and worthiness, produce physical health problems, shorten life expectancy, and deny minority populations equal access and opportunity in education, employment, and health care.[4]

Microaggression theory addresses three key aspects of racism: (1) unconscious or unintentional discrimination often exhibited by well-intentioned people; (2) analysis of micro-level, minute, daily-level exchanges; and (3) the connection between these micro-level exchanges and macro-level and/or long-term consequences.

Description of the Theory

Sue situates his conversation on microaggressions within a broader conversation on **racism**, which he defines as "any attitude, action, institutional structure, or social policy that subordinates persons or groups because of their color."[5] Racism can be at the individual (one-on-one), institutional (policy, practice, procedure, or structure in institution), or cultural level (expressions of superiority and imposition of standards of one group over another).[6] Sue notes that most people can be educated to see conscious racism on the individual, institutional, and cultural levels, but microaggressions can be harder to recognize, as they tend to operate on a covert level and through normalized daily use that is overlooked. **Microaggressions** are defined as "the brief and commonplace daily verbal, behavioral, and environmental indignities, whether intentional or unintentional, that communicate hostile, derogatory, or negative racial, gender, sexual-orientation, and religious slights and insults to the target person or group."[7] Recipients of microaggressions are at the "edge of a system" in some manner—cultural, social, political, and/or economic—and "when microaggressions make their appearance in interpersonal encounters or environmental symbols, they are reflections of marginality and/or a worldview of inclusion/exclusion, superiority/inferiority, desirability/undesirability, or normality/abnormality."[8] Perpetrators of microaggressions are often, though not always, well-intentioned people who subconsciously or unintentionally discriminate. Because perpetrators are often unaware that they have participated in microaggressive behavior, microaggressions are particularly difficult to assess and contest.

As microaggressions are interpersonal exchanges, the analysis and consequences of microaggressions are also usually in relation to the individual. Microaggressions, however, also have macro-level, system-wide consequences via the cumulative effect of denying equal access and opportunities to people of color. In his book *Microaggressions in Everyday Life: Race, Gender, and Sexual Orientation,* Sue outlines types and themes of microaggressions, a response model for processing microaggressions, and both the micro- and macro-level consequences of microaggressions.[9] He also addresses how Whites both perpetuate and are affected by microaggressions.

Types of Microaggressions

There are three main types of microaggressions: (1) microassaults, (2) microinsults, and (3) microinvalidations. The three types of microaggressions are useful in understanding how racialized comments are delivered differently and can communicate different racist themes. **Microassaults** are the "conscious, deliberate, and either subtle or explicit racial, gender, or sexual-orientation biased attitudes, beliefs, or behaviors that are communicated to marginalized groups through environmental cues, verbalizations, or behaviors."[10] These microaggressions are most akin to "old-fashioned," overt racism, as they are intended to threaten and harm the recipient. Microassaults more often occur if the perpetrator can assume some level of anonymity, if the perpetrator is in a group of like-minded people, or if the perpetrator loses control. Examples include telling racial jokes, forbidding an interracial relationship, or ignoring the presence or importance of a group. It may seem counterintuitive, but microassaults can be easier to deal with because they are obvious, so less energy is spent trying to interpret them.

The second type, **microinsults**, represents "subtle snubs, frequently outside the conscious awareness of the perpetrator, but they convey an oftentimes hidden insulting message to the recipient."[11] Examples of microinsults are statements such as "You're pretty for a dark-skinned girl" or "You are so articulate" or actions such as crossing the street when one sees a man of color nearby. As seen with these examples, microinsults can be subtle discriminatory statements or actions that perpetrators might even believe to be complimentary but reveal an unconscious disdain or bias toward people of color.

The third type, **microinvalidations**, is seen by Sue as potentially the most damaging, as they deny the experiential reality of people of color. Microinvalidations are

> characterized by communications or environmental cues that exclude, negate, or nullify the psychological thoughts, feelings, or experiential reality of certain groups such as people of color, women, and LGBTs. In many ways, microinvalidations may potentially represent the most damaging form of the three microaggressions because they directly and insidiously deny the racial, gender, or sexual-orientation reality of these groups.[12]

Examples of microinvalidations include assuming that someone of Asian descent was not born in the United States and asking, "Where are you from?"; believing that one is color-blind and saying, "I don't see race"; and universally using the pronoun "he" to refer to all people. Like microinsults, microinvalidations tend to be subtle comments, but the difference between the two is in the underlying meaning of the microaggression: Microinsults are about an offensive comment to the person, while microinvalidations challenge or deny the feelings or experiential reality of people of color.

Along with the three main types of microaggressions, there are also three ways in which these microaggressions can be delivered: (1) verbal, (2) nonverbal, and (3) environmental. The verbal mechanism of delivery is usually the most obvious, that is, when a person verbally provides a statement or question either directly or indirectly to a person of color. Nonverbal delivery, such as through facial expressions and body language, is the second method. The third type of delivery, environmental, can be more difficult to detect, especially for White communities that are not attuned to the ways in which environmental cues such as location, decoration, and spatial arrangement/ organization can reflect investment in Whiteness. Sue defines *environmental microaggressions* as "demeaning and threatening social, educational, political or economic cues that are communicated individually, institutionally, or societally to marginalized groups" and that "may be delivered visually or from a stated philosophy such as 'color-blindness.'"[13] Environmental examples include art that reflects only White communities, an organization that has all or predominantly White employees, or the use of indigenous mascots. Environmental microaggressions do not have to include interpersonal communication; the space alone can communicate the superiority of Whites and/or the inferiority of people of color.

Although microaggressions can come in any number of statements and cues, there are some predominant recurring themes of microaggressions.[14] A few of these dominant themes, as described by Sue, are being alien in one's own land, the assumption of criminal status, the myth of meritocracy, and being a second-class citizen. Being alien in one's own land entails the assumption that someone is foreign-born and is often accompanied by the question "Where are you from?"; criminal status assumes that someone is a criminal or potential criminal and can be demonstrated, for example, when a woman clutches her purse as a man of color walks near; the myth of meritocracy suggests that employment and education opportunities are fair and open to everyone and is seen in statements such as "I believe the most qualified person should get the job"; and being a second-class citizen is illustrated when the presence of people of color is negated or ignored, such as when taxi drivers pass by a person of color to pick up a White person. In each instance, the presence of a microaggression may not be clear due to the subconscious meaning or unintentional delivery of a microaggression, but in each instance, there is an underlying meaning that insults or invalidates the lives of people of color.

Processing Microaggressions

Because microaggressions can be particularly difficult to detect and assess, Sue outlines how people go through stages of processing after experiencing a microaggression. Each time a microaggression occurs, a recipient must take the time to interpret the microaggression and then decide how to react. Yet the most common response to microaggressions is for the recipient to do nothing. A lack of response occurs for six main reasons: (1) "attributional ambiguity," or the inability to ascertain whether a microaggression has actually occurred; (2) "response indecision," or not knowing the best way to respond; (3) "time limited," which points to the quick period of time in which a microaggression is delivered and therefore the short window of time for a response; (4) "denying experiential reality," which is the lack of desire to believe that the microaggression occurred, particularly if the perpetrator is someone in a close relationship with the recipient; (5) "impotency of actions," or the belief that a response would be both futile and energy depleting; and (6) "fearing the consequences," or weighing the costs of taking action.[15]

The **Microaggression Process Model** frames the steps that a recipient goes through when experiencing a microaggression.[16] This model consists of five phases: (1) incident, (2) perception, (3) reaction, (4) interpretation, and (5) consequences. The first phase is the actual incident; an event or situation occurs. The second phase is perception, which requires the recipient to analyze the event or situation as a possible microaggression. At this phase, there can be an internal struggle to identify the incident as a microaggression, and this struggle can often result in energy depletion. The perception and labeling of an incident can be affected by the relationship between the perpetrator and the recipient, the racial identity development of the recipient, the content of the incident, and the prior personal experiences of the recipient. The third phase, reaction, can be an immediate cognitive or behavioral response that includes an internal processing of the event and/or a behavioral action in response to the event. Four common reactions are "healthy paranoia," when a recipient ends constant internal questioning of an incident and validates the experience; "sanity check," when a recipient shares the experience in order to have it validated by others; "validating self," when a recipient puts the blame on Whites' unconscious, biased beliefs and values instead of internalizing the negative microaggression; and "rescuing offenders," when a recipient inquires into the state and care of the perpetrator so that the *offender* feels better about delivering a microaggression. The fourth phase of the process model, interpretation, is trying to discern the meaning behind the microaggression and what the perpetrator might be thinking about the victim. Commonly assigned perpetrators' beliefs about victims are that victims are abnormal, are intellectually inferior, are not trustworthy, or are all the same. The last phase of the Microaggression Process Model is the consequence and impact for the recipient, which can be short-term and/or long-term, and can include behavioral, emotive, or cognitive consequences. Common consequences are a feeling of powerlessness or invisibility, forced compliance, and pressure to feel that one is always representing the group of one's identity. As seen with this description of the process model, a victim of a microaggression potentially expends much energy in responding to a microaggression every time one occurs.

The Microaggression Process Model provides an outline of five distinct phases, but in reality Sue notes that the phases may occur in a different order, overlap, be cyclical, or interact. A factor that complicates this process is Whites' lack of seeing and understanding microaggressions as real and detrimental: "As long as microaggressions remain invisible to the aggressor, reactions to them by marginalized groups place them in an unenviable position: they are damned if they don't (not take action) and damned if they do (take action)! This is the catch-22 posed by microaggressions."[17]

Consequences of Microaggressions

One of the popular criticisms of the theory of microaggressions is that the seriousness assigned to them is out of proportion to the incident: If microaggressions are small, limited moments of exchange, how consequential can they be? Given this criticism, Sue is careful to provide a lengthy discussion of the long-term biological, emotional, cognitive, and behavioral consequences. Sue states that microaggressions have been shown to have more effects on an individual than other stressful life events, as microaggressions are symbols of racism, they are continuous, and they affect all aspects of life; in comparison, other stressful events often have a clear, recognizable cause and are rarely persistent.

Biological consequences include hypertension, diabetes, asthma, and other cardiovascular complications. The continuous assault of microaggressions across the course of life induces and amplifies stress, which lowers immunity and leads to these health conditions. Emotional consequences such as lower self-esteem, depression, and other mental health conditions are also connected to the persistent onslaught of microaggressions. Among the cognitive costs are "cognitive disruption," which includes difficulty solving problems and/or feeling distracted from tasks at hand, and "stereotype threat," which is when people of color meet low expectations due to the apprehension of constant judgment or the desire to reject a task at hand in order to protect oneself from White judgment.

Behavioral consequences include five common outcomes: (1) hypervigilance and skepticism, which result in a lack of close relationships and externalization of all personal failings onto other people and situations; (2) forced compliance, which manifests in internalized racism and a desire to meet and please the oppressor's expectations; (3) rage and anger, which result in a constant state of agitation and pushing people away; (4) fatigue and helplessness, when recipients have little energy to deal with life stressors, which can sometimes manifest in depression; and (5) strength through adversity, when recipients become adept at reading nonverbal and contextual cues, develop bicultural flexibility, and have a strong sense of group identity.[18] The biological, emotional, cognitive, and behavioral consequences of microaggressions show the severe detrimental effects long after the immediate processing of the incident.

Microaggressions and the Perpetrator

After explaining microaggressions, the ways in which they're communicated, and their consequences, Sue then examines the reasons why Whites participate in this form of oppression and the effects on Whites of their participation. The first part of understanding why Whites deliver microaggressions is making the connection between Whites, as a racial group, and White racism. This connection is explained by Sue in a four-step process model that he calls the **Whiteness-to-Racism Conversion**, which consists of Whiteness + White Supremacy + Power Imposition + Tools of Imposition = White Racism.[19] **Whiteness**, the concept used to refer to people who are seen and labeled as White, is not bad in and of itself: Whiteness refers to the phenotypical features that are recognized as White. However, Whiteness becomes perverted when the next step in the process is added: **White supremacy**, the doctrine of White racial superiority combined with non-White inferiority. The third step in the process is adding power imposition, which is how Whites define reality using a White supremacist ideology. The fourth step is the addition of tools of imposition, wherein Whites use institutions such as education, mass media, and organizations to communicate and enforce their power. Whiteness, plus White supremacy, plus power imposition, plus tools of imposition equal the last step in the process: **White racism** is "the individual, institutional, and cultural expression of the superiority of one group's cultural heritage over another and the power to impose and enforce that worldview upon the general populace"[20]. White racism includes **White privilege** or "unearned advantages and benefits that accrue to Whites by virtue of a system normed on the experiences, values, and perceptions of the group"[21] and the justification of unequal treatment of people of color. A significant part of White racism is White privilege, and Sue explains that "Whites are socialized into Eurocentric values, beliefs, standards and norms" so that they fail to see how Whites become a "default standard by which all other group norms and behaviors are consciously and unconsciously compared."[22] Thus, microaggressions are supported by White racism, and "the deleterious effects of racial microaggressions are cloaked within an invisible White veil," so that Whites "resist the realization that Whiteness, White supremacy and White privilege are three interlocking forces that disguise covert forms of racism."[23]

Whites tend to resist recognizing their White privilege and the existence of White racism, thereby obstructing the existence and consequences of microaggressions. Whites contest the reality of microaggressions because they fear appearing racist, they fear acknowledging that they have been racist, they fear recognizing their own White privilege, and they fear taking the personal responsibility necessary to end racism. Getting Whites to confront these fears and move past them is necessary to have Whites see their participation in perpetuating microaggressions.

There are also costs to Whites themselves for not ending their role in racism. Whites can experience affective costs, such as fear, anxiety, guilt, and low empathy; they can have behavioral costs, such as impaired interpersonal relationships and callousness toward others; and they can feel a spiritual or moral cost by losing a connection to one's humanity in exchange for maintaining power. Therefore, it is important not only to understand why microaggressions exist but also to see and understand that microaggressions are harmful to the perpetrator as well.

How to Challenge Racism

Sue explicitly addresses how to challenge racism by focusing on three main areas where microaggressions exist and what can be done to change these environments; he looks at microaggressions (1) in the workplace, (2) in schools, and (3) in mental health treatment. In the workplace, microaggressions often exist due to a hostile or unwelcoming environment and a nonexistent or underdeveloped vision of multiculturalism. To address this problem, Sue suggests listening to the voices of people of color in the organization, developing strong leadership that follows a meaningful mission statement of diversity, building a system for developing the organization's progress, creating a division of individuals who are held accountable for progress, and creating a long-term program that educates the entire workforce on diversity issues and barriers that block authentic multiculturalism.[24]

The second area is education and teaching, where microaggressions can often originate with the teachers themselves; they can also occur through a biased curriculum and/or a predominantly White staff. Sue suggests creating a working definition and understanding of microaggressions to help maneuver difficult dialogues, analyzing oneself as a racial being so that the invisible becomes visible, confronting one's own cultural conditioning and biases, and cultivating an emotional comfort in discussing race and racism. Sue also suggests that teachers learn how to control the process and not the content, so that students can communicate their thoughts and feelings in a manner that can be critically engaged, instead of halting conversation. During this process, it's important not to allow passivity or silence to win, so teachers should communicate appreciation to students when they participate in this dialogue.[25]

The third area is mental health; Sue's field is psychology, so his engagement in this area likely comes from his own experience in the field. Microaggressions coming from a therapist can be particularly problematic, as they can hurt a patient's healing or lead to a patient ending therapy. Some of the strategies for mental health practitioners are similar to those suggested for the workforce and education. Suggestions include having therapists invest in healing themselves and becoming aware of their own values, biases, and assumptions; crafting a vision to frame values, goals, and objectives of a practice that are affirmative of multiculturalism; developing culturally appropriate strategies for patients; and acting against racism in one's own practice and life. Therapists can also make a point to develop relationships with people of color to learn from their experiential

By the Numbers

- Forty percent of Black women, 32% of Latina women, and 29% of Asian women report that they have their judgment questioned in their area of expertise at work.

- Forty-two percent of Black women, 30% of Latina women, and 36% of Asian women report that at work they need to provide more evidence of their competence in comparison to others.

- Black students report 70% more general ethnic discrimination and almost twice as many racial microaggressions as White students.

Sources: Lean In and McKinsey & Company (2018); Ibid.; Williams, Kanter, and Ching (2018).

reality. Sue's recommendations show how distinct steps can be taken to address microaggressions and create environments where they are less likely to occur.[26]

Evaluation

Methodological Benefits

Sue has numerous other publications based on his own research and collaboration with coauthors; this body of work is the foundation of the book *Microaggressions in Everyday Life*. The book's chapters take the reader from definitions and effects to themes and methods of intervention. Sue relies on both quantitative and qualitative research, often with an interdisciplinary approach. The book also strategically uses first-person narratives of microaggressions via quotes, dialogues, and mini–case studies. In addition, Sue's method of citing numerous other previous studies to support his analyses, the thematic points, and the tables and diagrams provide a methodologically rich way to present the data.

Another methodological benefit is found in Sue's personal reflections and anecdotes, which add accessibility to an otherwise dense theory. For example, Chapter 3 opens with a detailed story of how Sue was asked to move seats on an airplane, while three White men were told they could sit anywhere. In this account, Sue provides his feelings about the incident, details the energy he needed to use to interpret the incident, and reflects on how he chose to react. By providing this personal account, Sue follows his own research and advice by validating his own experience and then using it as an example to show how people of color experience and feel about such incidents.

Methodological Limitations

The data in *Microaggressions in Everyday Life* are an amalgamation of first-person narratives, current events, results from previous studies, and personal accounts. While the mixed-methods approach provides a rich breadth of data, it is also unclear what methods can or should be used to study microaggressions. The common insertions of Sue's personal experience or narratives of pop culture events following results from a psychology research study can come across as cushioning the data or, at the very least, an unscientific method of analysis.

Another methodological limitation is drawing on focus groups and interviews with subjects who may be predisposed to agree that microaggressions exist and are harmful. Moreover, subjects are often aware that they are part of a study on microaggressions and could therefore potentially bias the results of the study. A common criticism of microaggression research is the reliance on self-reporting to determine whether an action/statement is a microaggression and the contention that a perpetrator does not get a say in the intention behind an action/statement.[27]

Theoretical Benefits

Sue is not the first or only scholar to research microaggressions, but *Microaggressions in Everyday Life* is arguably the most thorough analysis and theoretical development of microaggressions. The book provides theoretical models and conceptual classifications, not just of microaggressions themselves but also of their interpretation, response, and consequences. A criticism of microaggression theory is that people are reading too much into comments and/or are being too sensitive and that microaggressions, even for those who understand them, can still be difficult to decipher. A table of sample racial, gender, and sexual-orientation microaggressions addresses this issue by providing themes, giving an example of the corresponding microaggression, and stating the underlying message of the microaggression. The theme of "alien in one's own land," for example, is the assumption that Asian Americans and Latinx Americans are foreign-born. The underlying message of the questions/statements "Where are you from?" or "You speak English very well" is that "You are not American" or "You are a foreigner." Providing thematic examples such as this one brings the theory into focus. In addition, within each chapter, Sue often identifies and enumerates subthemes so that each major area of microaggressions is more clearly detailed and understood. For example, the reasons why people often do nothing after experiencing a microaggression is identified and enumerated with six clear points,[28] and the psychological health consequences experienced by African Americans are labeled and defined in five bullet points.[29] There is clear theoretical development of the types of microaggressions and explication of how they work.

Two additional theoretical strengths are Sue's attention to how microaggressions vary among communities of color and the attention to Whites as perpetrators. To the first point, the chapter on microaggressions and racism provides unique themes of microaggressions for African Americans, Asian Americans, Latinx Americans, and Native Americans. For example, Asian American microaggressions are how they are perpetually seen as foreign and ascribed intelligence, while African American microaggressions are the assumptions of criminality and intellectual inferiority. It is valuable to recognize the different sociohistorical experience of these racial groups and contemporary political, economic, and social conditions that connect to particular racial microaggressions. To the second point, Sue also expands the theoretical boundaries of microaggressions by focusing on Whites—why they deliver microaggressions and the harm they experience from doing so. By detailing Whites' roles, Sue makes the oft-invisible privilege of Whites visible; it's critically important to see how Whites are responsible for perpetuating this racism. It's also significant that Sue details the consequences that Whites experience for participating in microaggressions, as there is a cost experienced by oppressors for oppressing.

Theoretical Limitations

A limitation to microaggression theory is the reliance on the subjective interpretation of statements by the receiver. Other theoretical models of racism point to empirically measured outcomes of racism, such as inequality in pay, health, and transportation, but the meaning or consequence of microaggressions is interpreted by the individual who receives it. Sometimes a statement may or may not be interpreted and received as a microaggression; for example, "Where are you from?" may be understood as a friendly inquiry, or it may be felt as a microinsult. Because the labeling and consequence of a microaggression are in relation to the recipient, it is difficult to say when a microaggression has or has not occurred and therefore makes a definitive push for intervention unclear. Lilienfeld, noted for his criticisms of microaggression theory, states:

> The "eye of the beholder" assumption implicit in the MRP [Microaggression Research Program] generates other logical quandaries. In particular, it is unclear whether any verbal or nonverbal action that a certain proportion of minority individuals perceive as upsetting or offensive would constitute a microaggression. Nor is it apparent what level of agreement among minority group members would be needed to regard a given act as a microaggression. As a consequence, one is left to wonder which actions might fall under the capacious microaggression umbrella.[30]

In this criticism of microaggression, Lilienfeld summarily states the prevailing criticism of the theory of microaggressions: who determines a microaggression and how many people have to agree that it is a microaggression in order for that determination to be valid. The very theoretical nature of a microaggression, its subtlety and often unconscious delivery, presents difficulties for some to see the theory of microaggressions as valid.

Conclusion
· ·

There are ensuing debates on defining microaggressions, estimating their consequences, and proposing policies and solutions to address them. However, Sue's research has done much to frame the intricate dynamics of microaggressions and establish a conceptual framework. Sue's theoretical development of microaggressions makes this contemporary theory of racism useful and relevant across a range of academic fields and to private companies addressing diversity.

REFLECT AND DISCUSS

1. How can statements be received as harmful microaggressions even when the perpetrator did not intend any harm?

2. How do microaggressions vary by type, delivery, and context?

3. How are microaggressions damaging in both the short term and the long term?

Diagram 5.1   Microaggressions

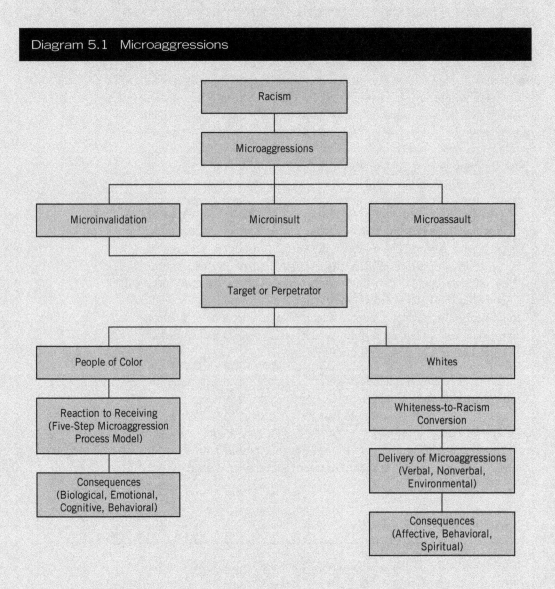

KEY TERMS

Microaggression Process Model: The five phases that a recipient goes through when experiencing a microaggression: incident, perception, reaction, interpretation, and consequences.[31]

Microaggressions: "The brief and commonplace daily verbal, behavioral, and environmental indignities, whether intentional or unintentional, that communicate hostile, derogatory, or negative racial, gender, sexual-orientation, and religious slights and insults to the target person or group."[32]

Microaggression theory: "Describing the dynamic interplay between perpetrator and recipient, classifying everyday manifestations, deconstructing hidden messages, and exploring internal (psychological) and external (disparities in education, employment, and health care) consequences."[33]

Microassaults: "Conscious, deliberate, and either subtle or explicit racial, gender, or sexual-orientation biased attitudes, beliefs, or behaviors that are communicated to marginalized groups through environmental cues, verbalizations, or behaviors."[34]

Microinsults: "Represent subtle snubs, frequently outside the conscious awareness of the perpetrator, but they convey an oftentimes hidden insulting message to the recipient."[35]

Microinvalidations: "Characterized by communications or environmental cues that exclude, negate, or nullify the psychological thoughts, feelings, or experiential reality of certain groups such as people of color, women, and LGBTs. In many ways, microinvalidations may potentially represent the most damaging form of the three microaggressions because they directly and insidiously deny the racial, gender, or sexual-orientation reality of these groups."[36]

Racism: "Any attitude, action, institutional structure, or social policy that subordinates persons or groups because of their color."[37]

Whiteness: "The constellation of physical features most characterized by fair or light skin color/tone. Other physical features may be considered ideal (associated with Western traits) such as blond hair, blue eyes, or elongated face. Whiteness alone conveys neither positive nor negative valence."[38]

Whiteness-to-Racism Conversion: "Whiteness + White Supremacy + Power Imposition + Tools of Imposition = White Racism."[39]

White privilege: "Unearned advantages and benefits that accrue to Whites by virtue of a system normed on the experiences, values, and perceptions of the group."[40]

White racism: "The individual, institutional, and cultural expression of the superiority of one group's cultural heritage over another and the power to impose and enforce that worldview upon the general populace."[41]

White supremacy: "A doctrine of White racial superiority and non-White inferiority that justifies domination and prejudicial treatment of minority groups. It strongly attributes positive qualities to Whiteness and negative qualities to non-White groups"[42]

KEY PEOPLE

Derald Wing Sue (1942–): Sue is Professor of Psychology and Education in the Department of Counseling and Clinical Psychology at Teachers College and the School of Social Work of Columbia University in New York. Sue is the cofounder and first president of the Asian American Psychological Association and is also past president of the Society of Counseling Psychology and the Society for the Psychological Study of Ethnic Minorities. Sue has been working on antiracism research since the 1970s; his coauthored piece "Racial Microaggressions in Everyday Life" has been cited more than 3,000 times and is considered a foundational piece in the study of microaggressions. Twitter @deraldwingsue

WORKS CITED AND FURTHER READING

Dovidio, John F. and Gaertner, Samuel L. 1996. "Affirmative Action, Unintentional Racial Biases, and Intergroup Relations." *Journal of Social Issues* 52(4):51–75.

Lean In and McKinsey & Company. 2018. "Women in the Workplace." Retrieved March 5, 2020 (https://wiw-report.s3.amazonaws.com/ Women_in_the_Workplace_2018.pdf).

Lilienfeld, Scott O. 2017. "Microaggressions: Strong Claims, Inadequate Evidence." *Perspectives on Psychological Science* 12(1): 138–69.

Nadal, Kevin L. 2011. "The Racial and Ethnic Microaggressions Scale (REMS): Construction, Reliability, and Validity." *Journal of Counseling Psychology* 58(4):470–80.

Sue, Derald Wing, ed. 2010a. *Microaggressions and Marginality: Manifestation, Dynamics, and Impact.* Hoboken, NJ: Wiley.

Sue, Derald Wing. 2010b. *Microaggressions in Everyday Life: Race, Gender, and Sexual Orientation.* Hoboken, NJ: Wiley.

Sue, Derald Wing, Christina M. Capodilupo, Gina C. Torino, Jennifer M. Bucceri, Aisha M. B. Holder, Kevin L. Nadal, and Marta Esquilin. 2007. "Racial Microaggressions in Everyday Life: Implications for Clinical Practice." *American Psychologist* 62(4): 271–86.

Williams, Monica T., Jonathan W. Kanter, and Terence H. W. Ching. 2018. "Anxiety, Stress, and Trauma Symptoms in African Americans: Negative Affectivity Does Not Explain the Relationship between Microaggressions and Psychopathology." *Journal of Racial and Ethnic Health Disparities* 5(5):919–27.

See also Microaggressions Project blog (www. microaggressions.com).

NOTES

1. Sue (2010b:24).
2. Dovidio and Gaertner (1996).
3. Sue (2010b:9).
4. Ibid. (6).
5. Ibid. (7).
6. Ibid. (8).
7. Ibid. (5).
8. Ibid. (14).
9. Ibid.
10. Ibid. (28).
11. Ibid. (31).
12. Ibid. (37).
13. Ibid. (25).
14. Ibid. (see tables on pp. 32–34).
15. Ibid. (55–57).
16. Ibid. (67–69).
17. Ibid. (58).
18. Ibid. (105).
19. Ibid. (115–20).
20. Ibid. (117).
21. Ibid.
22. Ibid. (114).
23. Ibid. (115).
24. Ibid. (209–29).
25. Ibid. (231–53).
26. Ibid. (255–79).
27. Lilienfeld (2017).
28. Sue (2010b:55–57).
29. Ibid. (149–51).
30. Lilienfeld (2017:143).
31. Sue (2010b:69).
32. Ibid. (5).
33. Ibid. (9).
34. Ibid. (28).
35. Ibid. (31).
36. Ibid. (37).
37. Ibid. (7).
38. Ibid. (117).
39. Ibid.
40. Ibid.
41. Ibid.
42. Ibid.

Macro-Level Theories

Racial Formation

Michael Omi and Howard Winant

The theory of racial formation identifies race as a critical organizing principle of society, sheds light on how the state directs racial processes, and analyzes how racial projects shape the ongoing nature of race and racism. Although this theory is more focused on the dynamics of race, not racism, the theoretical explanation of race leads to an account of how racism operates. This chapter is based on *Racial Formation in the United States* by Michael Omi and Howard Winant, originally published in 1986 and now in its third edition. This book is commonly known as a foundational text for scholars who study race.

Photo 6.1 Michael Omi

Source: http://ethnicstudies.berkeley.edu/people/faculty-profile/michael-omi-1.

Photo 6.2 Howard Winant

Source: https://www.soc.ucsb.edu/faculty/howard-winant.

Why This Theory

Racial Formation in the United States outlines Michael Omi and Howard Winant's theory of racial formation. This theory is a direct response to the gaps that were present in the then-dominant theories of racial inequality: the three paradigms of ethnicity, class, and nation.[1] The first part of the book reviews these three paradigms to reveal how each approach is insufficient in its explanation of race. All the paradigms, Omi and Winant argue, have three common weaknesses: (1) They do not grasp the shifting nature of racial dynamics in the postwar United States; (2) they reduce race to a manifestation of some other larger social force; and (3) they do not recognize the uniqueness, flexibility, immediacy, and centrality of race in society. To understand Omi and Winant's theory of racial formation, it is necessary to review each of the three paradigms that they critique.

Ethnicity-Based Theory

The ethnicity paradigm rose in the early 1900s as a challenge to biologistic notions of race, which saw race as an immutable trait that determined people's capabilities. Ethnicity theory, however, recognized ethnicity as mutable and nondeterministic, and racial identities such as Black were made analogous to other ethnicities, such as Irish or German. Later, from 1930 to 1965, a revised ethnicity paradigm focused on the model of assimilation, wherein new migrants to the United States could gradually shed cultural values and identity from their home country in order to move up the social ladder and become American. This story of assimilation is typified with Irish and Germans, who started as poor immigrants but became middle-class Americans. The third phase of the ethnicity paradigm rose after 1965 as a conservative/neoconservative backlash to the Civil Rights Movement; this phase suggested that Blacks were the cause of their own failures because other ethnic groups, such as the Irish, Germans, and Polish, had started at the bottom but worked to achieve upward mobility. In this vein, the ethnicity paradigm presumed that Blacks had the same opportunities and treatment as White immigrants and ignored the structural barriers unique to people of color. Omi and Winant criticize the ethnicity paradigm for blaming the victim, for making race synonymous with ethnicity, and for failing to recognize diverse intraracial identities within communities of color. Ethnicity theory acknowledges different White ethnic identities, such as Irish and German, but not different Black ethnic identities, such as African American, West Indian, and various African nationalities. The ethnicity paradigm subsumes race under ethnicity, thereby ignoring structural barriers unique to race.

Class-Based Theory

In their critique of the class paradigm, Omi and Winant point out that it has three main approaches: (1) market, (2) stratification, and

(3) class conflict. The market system looks at supply and demand as driving market equilibrium; thus, in this model, racial discrimination is identified as an anomaly in the system. The stratification approach recognizes how economic resources are distributed unevenly among classes; in this case, racial inequality may overlap with class inequality, but class is the primary driver of stratification. The third approach, class conflict, explains that economic exploitation is common to all workers in a capitalist system, but any focus on race is seen as a hindrance to developing a working-class consciousness. Although recognizing that class stratification is a social problem, Omi and Winant see race as the driver of social inequality, not class conflict: "Racial dynamics must be understood as determinants of class relationships and indeed class identities, not as mere consequences of these relationships."[2]

Nation-Based Theory

For Omi and Winant, the nation-based paradigm represents the most promise because it clearly recognizes race and racial oppression. The nation paradigm analyzes how subjects of colonialism experience political disenfranchisement, territorial and institutional segregation, and cultural domination. This paradigm sees racial inequality as continuing from origins in nation-based/colonial oppression. Omi and Winant summarize the nation paradigm as having three primary demands: (1) Movements need to be composed of the colonized, (2) the colonized need cultural autonomy, and (3) national liberation is needed to create a new society without colonial heritage. The nation-based paradigm accounts for race, but like the class and ethnicity paradigms, race is still constructed as a consequence of another, more central driving force. Furthermore, the nation paradigm doesn't adequately explain Black racism in the United States, as Blacks were not a colonized population but a group forcefully brought to a new land. Omi and Winant write that the nation-based theory "fails to demonstrate the existence of racial minority or colonized 'nations' internal to the US and structurally separated from the majority society."[3]

A Theory of Racial Formation

Omi and Winant acknowledge some merit and utility in the three approaches: The ethnicity paradigm shows the mutability of identity, the class paradigm reveals patterns of exploitation and mobility, and the nation paradigm connects the United States to global patterns of oppression and the legacy of colonialism. Yet for them, each paradigm "neglects the specificity of race as an autonomous field of social conflict, political organization, and cultural/ideological meaning."[4] Thus, Omi and Winant propose their theory of "racial formation" to explain how "race has been a fundamental axis of social organization in the United States."[5]

Description of the Theory

Omi and Winant propose the theory of racial formation in order to analyze the social meaning assigned to race and how it changes at both the macro and micro levels. At the micro level, race is related to the individual and is usually connected to a racial identity. At the macro level, race is a collectivity and is embedded in the economic, political, and cultural institutions of society. Central to the concept of racial formation is that race is not biological but is a social construction. There are no inherent physical or cultural characteristics of any racial group, and the meanings assigned to racial groups are provided by society and are historically specific.[6] Omi and Winant define **race** as *"an unstable and 'decentered' complex of social meanings constantly being transformed by political struggle."*[7] In the third edition of their book, Omi and Winant add that race is *"a master category*—a fundamental concept that has profoundly shaped and continues to shape the history, polity, economic structure, and culture of the United States."*[8] Race, then, is a stable, dominant category in that it has and continues to be a strong force that shapes society, *and* race is a set of meanings that is constantly shifting in relation to social forces. It appears contrary that race can be stable and unstable simultaneously, but a look at the use of racial categories in the U.S. Census proves this point to be correct. The U.S. Census has always used racial categories to classify people; from the first Census in 1790 until today, every Census has had a race question, which shows the stability of the race concept. Yet the racial categories used have been constantly changed and modified, such as "free white" and "slave" in 1790; "Black," "Mulatto," "Quadroon," and "Octoroon" in 1890; "Hindu" in 1920; and "Mexican" in 1930.[9] The addition, removal, and modification of racial categories show how racial categories and racial meanings are unstable. Thus, race is both stable as a "master category" and unstable as a "complex of social meanings."

To explain how racial categories and the meanings attached to racial categories change throughout time, Omi and Winant use the concept of "racialization." **Racialization** is "the extension of racial meaning to a previously racially unclassified relationship, social practice or group. Racialization is an ideological process, an historically specific one."[10] Racialization explains how racial groups are created, destroyed, and transformed; for example, on the U.S. Census, there were two categories for Blacks from 1870 to 1880, four categories for Blacks in 1890, one category for Blacks from 1900 to 1990, and then the option to choose Black and another race starting in 2000. In this example, the racialization of Blacks/Blackness changes throughout time, and it is clear how racialization is an ideological process contextualized within a specific historical time period.

Racial meanings emerge through interactions at the micro and macro levels, a process described as **racial etiquette**:

> The set of interpretive codes and racial meanings which operate in the interactions of daily life ... "etiquette" is not mere universal

adherence to the dominant group's rules, but a more dynamic combination of these rules with the values and beliefs of subordinating groupings … everybody learns some combination, some version, of the rules of racial classification, and of their own racial identity, often without obvious teaching or conscious inculcation.[11]

Racial etiquette exists in everyday interactions, so that the meanings attached to racial groups emerge "naturally" and are often absorbed without one's conscious recognition of this process occurring. For example, recognition of different groups and their relative status is observed through minor interactions, such as opening the door for someone, stepping aside to let someone pass on a busy sidewalk, or using a type of greeting. Such racial etiquette teaches one how to understand one's own race and status in relation to other races in society.

Through these conceptual understandings of race, racialization, and racial etiquette, Omi and Winant come to define their theoretical approach of racial formation. They define **racial formation** as

the process by which social, economic, and political forces determine the content and importance of racial categories, and by which they are in turn shaped by racial meanings. Crucial to this formulation is the treatment of race as a *central axis* of social relations which cannot be subsumed under or reduced to some broader category or conception.[12]

In 1994, they updated and shortened the definition of *racial formation* to "the sociohistorical process by which racial categories are created, inhabited, transformed, and destroyed."[13] In other words, race is a primary component of society, and its meanings are shaped by society, *but* race also then shapes society itself—it's a two-way street. Through this process, race becomes so engrained into society that it is understood in an almost taken-for-granted, commonsense manner.

Racial formation is the theoretical concept that illustrates how race operates, and Omi and Winant build on this foundation to explain how racism persists. Their analysis of the state and the concept of "racial projects" is central to this explanation.

The State

Omi and Winant center their theory of racial formation on the relationship between the state and race. Rather than seeing the state as impartial or objective in the process of racial meaning, the state is "itself increasingly the pre-eminent site of racial conflict."[14] In this sense, the state actively shapes the meanings of race; race is shaped by society, *and* race also then shapes society itself, thereby creating a cycle of the state shaping race, race shaping the state, and so on. The relationship between the state and race is outlined by understanding (1) the components of the state, (2) how change occurs, and (3) how the centrality of race is maintained.

The Components of the State

Omi and Winant define *the state* as "composed of institutions, the policies they carry out, the conditions and rules which support and justify them, and the social relations in which they are embedded. Every state institution is a racial institution, but not every institution operates in the same way."[15] It is important to understand that each institution has its own procedures and policies, so their engagement with race will look different, but their enforcement of racial politics is still present. Moreover, the state has key policy makers and judicial rules that help maintain consistency across the state. The state takes shape under "conditions and rules." These conditions and rules integrate racial polices of different state agencies, they define the scope of state activity, they set procedures of shaping policy, and they set the limits of what counts as legitimate political activity. An example of a state institution and policy is the U.S. Department of Health and Human Services (the institution), which regulates welfare (the policy) and who is eligible for it (social relations). In this example, the relationship between state and race can be seen in the idea that Black communities use welfare, which results in the myth that Blacks are lazy and abuse the welfare system, which then results in more restrictive policies. The restrictive polices then result in a low success rate of economic mobility, resulting in the perpetuation of Black poverty. In this manner, there is a dynamic relationship between the state and race.

How Change Occurs

State institutions and policies are under constant modification, and each new racial order is a result of a process of conflict and compromise between racial movements and the state. Omi and Winant explain a **racial trajectory** of change: "The pattern of conflict and accommodation which takes shape over time between racially based social movements and the policies and programs of the state ... the central elements of this trajectory are the state and social movements, linked in a single historical framework of racial formation."[16] This trajectory of change is evident in the Civil Rights Movement (CRM), where Black and allied organizations fought against racist policies. The state eventually responded with some changes, and then a new racial order emerged.

Within this process of change, Omi and Winant outline specific stages. The "first stage" is unstable equilibrium, a state of tenuous acceptance of the current racial order in society ("first stage" is in quotation marks to denote that because it is a cycle, there is really no beginning or ending stage). In the example of the CRM, this period is the acceptance of legal segregation, which existed between the end of Reconstruction and the "beginning" of the CRM in the 1950s.

The second stage is crisis, a state of conflict between racial movements and the state. Racial movements then demand change via different strategies of dissent. Omi and Winant argue that movements changed from a Gramscian understanding of a war of maneuver to a war of position. In a war of maneuver, the state has strong dictatorship, leaving little room for opposition, so resistance occurs *outside the political arena*. In a war of position, more characteristic of contemporary times, the rule is hegemonic, and resistance is more likely to occur *inside the political arena*. In the CRM, numerous organizations operated to put pressure on the state to change laws, including the Black Panther Party for Self Defense, the Southern Christian Leadership Conference (SCLC), and the Student Nonviolent Coordinating Committee (SNCC).

In reaction to the pressure for change, the state then engages in the third stage of absorption and insulation. Absorption reflects the state's realization that the presence of racial movements' demands are greater threats to the society's racial order than acceptance on some moderate level. In other words, a racial movement maintaining a vocal presence in society can be more threatening than subduing the movement by accepting some of the demands. There is also insulation, which is how the state confines the demands to symbolic or non-crucial areas of society. In the example of the CRM, activists addressed a range of problems, such as segregation, voting restrictions, poverty, and police brutality. In order to subdue the mounting pressure from organizations, some of these demands were absorbed, including the end of legal segregation and the adoption of the Voting Rights Act. However, some of these demands were made only on an insulation level; for example, schools were instructed to desegregate, but there was no national timeline or enforced method for achieving this integration.

After absorption and insulation, a new unstable equilibrium is attained. When this new equilibrium is put into effect, the racial movement breaks into factions, wherein the passive movement makers help integrate and articulate the new racial ideology, while the other movement makers become radicalized. In the case of the CRM, by the end of the 1960s, most of the organizations had fallen apart or at least had lost clear coherence, and many of the movement leaders went into politics or higher education, as seen with Julian Bond and John Lewis. In this cycle of change, there is a dual process of the deterioration of the old dominant racial ideology, followed by the creation of a new alternative one.

How the Centrality of Race Is Maintained

In evaluating change or lack thereof in race and racism, Omi and Winant center the role of the **racial state**: "The racial state does not have precise boundaries. Although based in formally constituted institutions and grounded in a contentious historical process, the state extends beyond administrative, legislative, or judicial forms of activity. It inhabits and indeed organizes large segments of social and indeed psychological identity, as well as everyday life."[17] In this manner, the racial state is virtually all-encompassing. Thus, there is an ongoing process between racial movements that aim to rearticulate the racial ideology and the persistence of race and racism in society. For example, after the legal successes of the CRM, many wondered if there would be a postracial society, one where race was no longer a central factor in inequality. The CRM did accomplish a major racial rearticulation of race relations, but race remains a central organizing principle. Omi and Winant explain that because of the process of absorption and insulation, racial movements do not get their demands fully implemented, and racism remains. Moreover, it is important to remember that social movements for equality are often met with backlash, and social movements that instigate change can be from a liberal or conservative standpoint. For example, the CRM initiated by Blacks is identified as a classic example of a race-based social movement for equality, but the conservative backlash in the 1980s against racial progress was led by Whites and is also a racialized social movement. Thus, in this process: "State racial policy ultimately defines the extent and limits of racial democracy, of racial despotism and inequality, of racial inclusion or exclusion."[18]

Racial Projects

In addition to understanding the role of the state, Omi and Winant propose the concept of racial projects to explain how racism operates. **Racial projects** are

> *simultaneously an interpretation, representation, or explanation of racial identities and meanings, and an effort to organize and distribute resources (economic, political, cultural) along particular racial lines.* Racial projects connect what race *means* in a particular discursive or ideological practice and the ways in which both social structures and everyday experiences are *organized,* based upon that meaning.[19]

Racial projects give races meaning and assign resources (power) to races; this process occurs through micro-level racial interactions and through macro-level policies and practices. For example, a racial project can be a police officer conducting "stop and frisk" on Latinx assumed to be undocumented (micro level) or national deportation policies (macro level). Racial projects, however, are not necessarily racist and can instead challenge racism, such as replacing the term *illegal* with *undocumented* (micro level) or supporting national policies to allow undocumented students to attend college (macro level).

Racial projects are embedded in society, so that the presence and meaning of race appear as common sense. A racial project is apparent every time race is invoked. To speak of race is to locate it within a racial hierarchy where meaning and power are assigned, and "every racial project attempts to reproduce, extend, subvert, or directly challenge that system."[20]

How to Challenge Racism

Omi and Winant show that racism can be challenged through social movements and antiracist racial projects. Conflict is always present at the macro and micro levels; the level of conflict varies, and the origin of the conflict also varies, but conflict is persistent, thereby always presenting the option for a racial movement to occur, so that "both racial movements and the racial state experience such transformations, passing through periods of rapid change and virtual stasis, through moments of massive mobilization and others of relative passivity."[21] An example of this conflict and change is clear in Omi and Winant's analysis of how the CRM brought forth a new racial era through organizations that challenged the racist policies of the state. They also point out that all racial projects are not racist in nature; while **racist racial projects** "create or reproduce structures of domination based on racial significations and identities,"[22] there are also **antiracist racial projects** that *"undo or resist structures of domination based on racial significations and identities."*[23] In other words, antiracist racial projects can be used to challenge racism and the unequal distribution of power. Within this analysis of change, Omi and Winant are careful to note that as powerful as racism is, it does not discount the potentially "emancipatory dimensions of racial identity, racial solidarity, or racially conscious agency, both individual and collective."[24] This point means that race is not always negative, and movements based on a racial identity can be a foundation for freedom.

By the Numbers

- In 1954, the U.S. Supreme Court determined segregated schools to be illegal, but currently 27% of students are enrolled in predominantly non-White districts, and 26% of students are enrolled in predominantly White districts.

- The U.S. Census determines the categories for races in the United States; the 2020 Census has five racial groups, the option to choose more than one racial group, and the choice for people of any race to identify their ethnicity as Hispanic.

- Fifty-five percent of Latinx reported that regardless of their legal status, they worry a lot or some that they, a family member, or a close friend could be deported, an 8% increase since the election of Donald Trump.

Sources: EdBuild (2019); U.S. Census Bureau (2019); Lopez, Gonzalez-Barrera, and Krogstad (2018).

Evaluation

Methodological Benefits

The methodological benefits of racial formation include the systematic manner in which the theory is explained. First, Omi and Winant carefully review the tenets and application of the ethnicity, class, and nation paradigms—in turn showing how each paradigm falls short by not centering race. The second part of the book details the components of racial formation theory, and the third section applies the theory to the movements of the 1950s and 1960s. Specifically, Omi and Winant's methodological strength shows through in the application of the trajectory of change. In their original edition, they analyze how the theory of racial formation applies to the CRM and why racism persists post-1960s; the four states of change are clearly applied: unstable equilibrium, crisis, absorption and insulation, and finally a new unstable equilibrium. The direct application of racial formation theory to the 1950s and 1960s shows the utility of this theory. This application is extended in the third edition, where there are two additional chapters that look at "Racial Reaction" and "Colorblindness, Neoliberalism, and Obama." These chapters help bring racial formation theory to contemporary discussions, thereby also exhibiting the theory's continuing applicability.

Methodological Limitations

Omi and Winant apply racial formation to the movements of the 1950s and 1960s by largely focusing on African American and Black movements. They focus on these movements because they were the largest racial movements pre-1980s, but there were other racial movements that are not included in their analysis. The American Indian Movement and the Chicano Movement receive no attention in the book, despite the magnitude of these racial movements. Another methodological limitation is in the sweeping overview of the ethnicity, class, and nation paradigms. Although authors can address only so much, a fair criticism of a paradigm is difficult when events and groups are so summarily made. For example, in the first edition, the explanation of cultural nationalism lacks a thorough connection to global colonization.

Both methodological limitations, however, are given some attention in the third edition. The explanations of each paradigm have been expanded, and more attention has been given to individuals, groups, and events. For example, in the nation-based chapter, there are now several pages dedicated to Pan-Africanism, cultural nationalism, and internal colonialism. The third edition is also improved by being inclusive of more voices of color. For example, the ethnicity chapter addresses Asian and Latinx immigration, and the nation chapter expands on the historical origin of the "white nation" and the cultural nationalism of "black, brown, red, and yellow power."[25]

Theoretical Benefits

The theory of racial formation has had a significant influence on studies of race across a range of disciplines. This theory is cited in at least 6% of sociology publications on race and has set a foundation for examining the social construction of race.[26] Omi and Winant provide a clear definition of race, which is rooted in conflict and power, and they give a theoretical understanding of how racial meanings change. Racial formation shows *how race is formed* through a *process* of constant creating and re-creating. Because the meanings attached to racial groups are always in flux, racial formation theory explains how race cannot be biological—an important theoretical point, as biological notions of race are consistently revived. Furthermore, Omi and Winant center the state as the active agent in this process. If political institutions are active creators of race, it is impossible that those institutions are neutral; therefore, claims that we are in a color-blind society are negated. Racial projects help explain how racism manifests on the micro and macro levels and how racial meaning is constantly in *process*. The terminology that Omi and Winant use also serves as an engaging, theoretical tool; in order to discuss race, one has to use words that emphasize process, such as *formation* and *projects*. Thus, Omi and Winant provide a foundation that subsequent research and theory production can and has relied on.

Theoretical Limitations

Omi and Winant's book on racial formation is now in its third edition, with each edition addressing some criticisms of the earlier editions and addressing new trends in race and the racial hierarchy. Some terms, such as *race*, *racial projects*, and *racial formations*, have been updated and clarified in each edition. For example, in the first edition, Omi and Winant gloss over the physical and bodily dimensions of race and racism. In the third edition, there is much greater attention to the corporeal aspect of race: They expand on their definition of *race* to include "a representation or signification of identity that refers to different types of human bodies, to the perceived corporeal and phenotypic markers of difference and the meanings and social practices that are ascribed to these differences."[27] They also clarify how and when a racial project is racist or antiracist, and they account for intersectional analysis, which is factored in at points throughout the book (how race shapes and is shaped by other lines of stratification, such as gender and class).

However, a remaining limitation of the theory is the inadequate explanation of how the racial hierarchy operates and shifts. Omi and Winant say that the United States has a White supremacist hierarchy,[28] but a thorough theoretical discussion of the racial hierarchy is lacking (see Chapter 3 in this book on White supremacy). They do not discuss how the racial hierarchy changes, how groups are formed in relation to each other, or how those groups might change position in the hierarchy throughout time. And, specifically, they do not discuss the role of Whites in creating or perpetuating the racial hierarchy. Joe Feagin and Sean Elias wage this criticism; they write that "no critical and explicit discussion of whites as a racial group shaping and maintaining the racial oppression and dynamics central to US society appears in [Omi and Winant's] book."[29] By omitting a discussion of Whites' active role in the creation and maintenance of the hierarchy, the position of other racial groups in relation to one another also becomes ambiguous (see Chapter 7 in this book on systemic racism). For example, at one point, Omi and Winant do state that in certain neighborhoods, communities of color could potentially racially subordinate other communities of color. However, an explanation of how a community of color could hold racialized power is relatively absent. For a theory on race that proposes how races form, there is a theoretical gap in explaining the racial hierarchy, how racial groups place on this hierarchy, and the active role of Whites in perpetuating the hierarchy.

Conclusion

Racial formation theory indisputably outlines the state as an active agent in the construction of race and racism in society, and it describes how racial identities and racism change. Racial projects are invoked on the micro and macro level every day, and such projects are constantly shaping the racial formation process. Race is never fixed but is always present. The theory of racial formation makes it clear that race is not reducible to some other manifestation and is a central principle organizing power and resources in society.

REFLECT AND DISCUSS ————————————————

1. Explain the central problem that Omi and Winant find in the ethnicity, class, and nation-based paradigms.

2. How is race constantly transformed by political struggle yet also a constant across time?

3. Describe the dynamics of racist racial projects and antiracist racial projects.

Diagram 6.1   Racial Formation

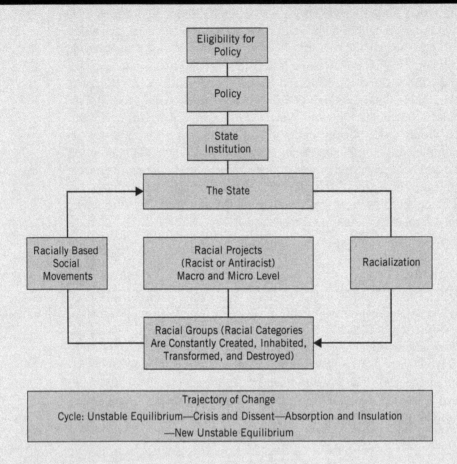

KEY TERMS

Antiracist racial project: A project to "undo or resist structures of domination based on racial significations and identities."[30]

Race: "A concept that signifies and symbolizes social conflicts and interests by referring to different types of human bodies."[31]

"Race is a master category—a fundamental concept that has profoundly shaped, and continues to shape, the history, polity, economic structure, and culture of the United States."[32]

Racial etiquette: "A set of interpretive codes and racial meanings which operate in the interactions of daily life ... 'etiquette' is not mere universal adherence to the dominant group's rules, but a more dynamic combination of these rules with the values and beliefs of subordinating groupings ... everybody learns some combination, some version, of the rules of racial classification, and of their own racial identity, often without obvious teaching or conscious inculcation."[33]

Racial formation: "The sociohistorical process by which racial identities are created, lived out, transformed, and destroyed."[34] Racial formation is a "synthesis, a constantly reiterated outcome, of the interaction of racial projects on a society-wide level."[35]

Racialization: "The extension of racial meaning to a previously racially unclassified relationship, social practice, or group. Racialization is an ideological process, an historically specific one."[36]

Racial project: "Simultaneously an interpretation, representation, or explanation of racial identities and meanings, and an effort to organize and distribute resources (economic, political, cultural) along particular racial lines. Racial projects connect what race means in a particular discursive or ideological practice and the ways in which both social structures and everyday experiences are racially organized, based upon that meaning."[37]

Racial state: "The racial state does not have precise boundaries. Although based in formally constituted institutions and grounded in a contentious historical process, the state extends beyond administrative, legislative, or judicial forms of activity. It inhabits and indeed organizes large segments of social and indeed psychological identity, as well as everyday life."[38]

"State racial policy ultimately defines the extent and limits of racial democracy, of racial despotism and inequality, of racial inclusion or exclusion."[39]

Racial trajectory: "Racial movements and the racial state experience such transformations, passing through periods of rapid change and virtual stasis, through moments of massive mobilization and others of relative passivity."[40]

Racist racial project: A project that "create[s] or reproduce[s] structures of domination based on racial significations and identities."[41]

KEY PEOPLE

Michael Omi (1951–): Omi is Associate Professor of Asian American and Asian Diaspora Studies in the Department of Ethnic Studies at University of California, Berkeley. He has served as chair of the Daniel E. Koshland Committee for Civic Unity at the San Francisco Foundation, he has served on the Project Advisory Board for the American Anthropological Association on "Race and Human Variation," and he currently serves as the associate director of the Haas Institute for a Fair and Inclusive Society.

Howard Winant (1946–): Winant is Distinguished Professor of Sociology at the University of California, Santa Barbara. He founded and directed the University of California Center for New Racial Studies. He has published five other books in addition to *Racial Formation in the United States*. Winant's *The World Is a Ghetto* received the Oliver Cromwell Cox Book Award from the American Sociological Association Section on Racial and Ethnic Minorities.

WORKS CITED AND FURTHER READING

EdBuild. 2019. "$23 Billion." Retrieved March 5, 2020 (https://edbuild.org/content/23-billion).

Feagin, Joe and Sean Elias. 2013. "Rethinking Racial Formation Theory: A Systemic Racism Critique." *Ethnic and Racial Studies* 36(6): 931–60.

HoSang, Daniel Martinez, Oneka LaBennett, and Laura Pulido, eds. 2012. *Racial Formation in the Twenty-First Century.* Berkeley: University of California Press.

Lopez, Mark Hugo, Ana Gonzalez-Barrera, and Jens Manuel Krogstad. 2018. "More Latinos

Have Serious Concerns about Their Place in America under Trump." Washington, DC: Pew Research Center.

Omi, Michael and Howard Winant. 1986. *Racial Formation in the United States: From the 1960s to the 1980s.* New York: Routledge.

Omi, Michael and Howard Winant. 1994. *Racial Formation in the United States: From the 1960s to the 1990s.* 2nd ed. New York: Routledge.

Omi, Michael and Howard Winant. 2015. *Racial Formation in the United States.* 3rd ed. New York: Routledge.

Pew Research Center. 2015. "What Census Calls Us: A Historical Timeline." Washington, DC: Author, June 10.

Saperstein, Aliya, Andrew M. Penner, and Ryan Light. 2013. "Racial Formation in Perspective: Connecting Individuals, Institutions, and Power Relations." *Annual Review of Sociology* 39:359–78.

U.S. Census Bureau. 2019. "Quick Facts: Race." Washington, DC: Author.

See also "Symposium—Rethinking Racial Formation Theory." 2013. *Ethnic and Racial Studies* 36(6): 931–99.

NOTES

1. Omi and Winant (1986).
2. Ibid. (37).
3. Ibid. (51).
4. Ibid. (52).
5. Ibid. (13).
6. Ibid. (60).
7. Ibid. (68, emphasis in original).
8. Ibid. (106, emphasis in original).
9. Pew Research Center (2015).
10. Omi and Winant (1986:65).
11. Ibid. (62).
12. Ibid. (61–62).
13. Omi and Winant (1994:55).
14. Omi and Winant (1986:76).
15. Ibid. (76–77).
16. Omi and Winant (1994:78).
17. Omi and Winant (2015:138).
18. Ibid. (2015:172).
19. Ibid. (125, emphasis in original).
20. Ibid. (125).
21. Omi and Winant (1986:80).
22. Ibid. (128).
23. Omi and Winant (2015:129, emphasis in original).
24. Ibid. (128).
25. Ibid. (88).
26. Saperstein, Penner, and Light. (2013:361).
27. Omi and Winant (2015:111).
28. Ibid. (130).
29. Feagin and Elias (2013:939).
30. Omi and Winant (2015:129).
31. Ibid. (110).
32. Ibid. (106).
33. Omi and Winant (1986:62).
34. Omi and Winant (1994:109).
35. Omi and Winant (2015:127).
36. Ibid. (111).
37. Ibid. (125).
38. Ibid. (138).
39. Ibid. (172).
40. Ibid. (148).
41. Ibid. (128).

CHAPTER

7

Systemic Racism

Joe Feagin

The theory of systemic racism suggests that racism is built into the very founda-tion of the United States and is intergenerationally transmitted. Rather than see-ing race and racism as an illness in an otherwise healthy society, Joe Feagin, in his book *Systemic Racism: A Theory of Oppression,* explains how racism is *of* society. This theory also centers Whites' participation in the creation and maintenance of racism. Through a dissection of the dimensions of systemic racism and an analy-sis of three historical eras, Feagin explores the foundation and perpetuation of racism on the macro and micro levels.

Photo 7.1 Joe Feagin

Source: https://liberalarts.tamu.edu/
sociology/profile/joe-feagin/.

Why This Theory

· ·

The theory of systemic racism, as developed by Joe Feagin, explains how racism is central to the United States. He investigates why racial oppression has been a persistent feature of the nation by interpreting "the racialized character, structure, and development of this society."[1] Central to Feagin's theory of systemic racism is a response to scholars for either ignoring or not providing a robust analysis on three interrelated issues: (1) intergenerational reproduction of resources, (2) Whites' central role in racism, and (3) the persistence of racism. To the first point, wealth, power, and privilege were instituted at the founding of the nation and reproduced with every generation, so that each generation of Whites accumulated more wealth as a group than the one previous. Feagin takes scholars to task for their focus on how White immigrants adapted and assimilated, rather than on how the institutional arrangements have benefited Whites for generations. This intergenerational (re)production of White wealth is evident in policies that permitted only Whites to vote, own property, attend higher education, and more. The second point, Whites' role in racism, logically follows from the first. Feagin exposes how other race scholars often compare the lack of social mobility for communities of color to that of Whites, but rarely is there an interrogation of how Whites, as active agents, make decisions that reproduce their status within a racially discriminatory system. Whites have repeatedly chosen to sustain racist policies and practices, such as voting restrictions, residential segregation, and private healthcare systems. Third, Feagin argues that scholars view contemporary race relations as though there is a collection of racial groups, rather than a distinct hierarchy of races whose access to power is connected to racism. Races cannot be studied without also studying racism; the existence of race necessarily implies the existence of a racial hierarchy. He explains that "all racial-ethnic relationships and events, past and present" reflect a system of racial oppression.[2]

Feagin also specifically addresses Omi and Winant's theory of racial formation (see Chapter 6). He supports the theory's use of "racial projects" and focus on how races are created and destroyed but suggests they do not give enough emphasis to the ways that contemporary racism, just as in the past, manifests in a severe racial hierarchy and racial ideologies. Feagin's theory of systemic racism correctly sees "the grounding of U.S. society today, as in the past, in the provision of large-scale wealth-generating resources for white Americans" and "the intergenerational transmission of these critical material and related social assets."[3]

Feagin suggests three components for an improved theory of racial oppression: (1) The theory should indicate major features, structures, and counterforces; (2) the theory should show relationships between structures and forces; and (3) the theory should assist in understanding patterns of social change and the lack thereof.[4] Thus, Feagin's theory is a large-scale holistic theory that explains the "big picture," and the ways in which society was founded on the oppression of people of color, specifically, African Americans.

Description of the Theory

Feagin defines **U.S. racism** as "both complex and highly relational, a true system in which major racial groups and their networks stand in asymmetrical and oppositional relations. The social institutions and processes that reproduce racial inequality imbed a fundamental inegalitarian relationship—on the one hand, the racially oppressed, and on the other, the racial oppressors."[5] He further specifies this definition with the theoretical approach of systemic racism; Feagin notes the etymology of the word *systemic*, which is to place or stand together, so that **systemic racism** is about "an organized societal whole with many interconnected elements."[6] He diagrams the theory to show the interconnected parts and the chronological nature of systemic racism (see Diagram 7.1 toward the end of the chapter).[7] Though each of the seven dimensions he proposes are diagrammed in separate boxes, he notes that each dimension is "*integrally connected* to one another" and "none stands alone, and each is but an aspect of a much larger whole."[8] The **seven dimensions of systemic racism** are (1) White economic domination (at the center of the diagram), (2) the White racial frame, (3) alienated social relations, (4) the racial hierarchy, (5) related racial domination, (6) Whites' unjust enrichment, and (7) constant struggle and resistance.[9] The intergenerational nature of this process is addressed at the bottom of the diagram by a timeline noting three major eras: (1) slavery, (2) legal segregation, and (3) contemporary racial oppression.

White Economic Domination

At the center of the diagram of systemic racism and at the core founding of the United States is the economic enrichment of Whites and the consequential economic oppression and suffering of Blacks and Native Americans via enslavement and theft of land. Early colonists massacred Native Americans and increasingly stole land as they moved westward. As the colonies expanded, so did the demand for labor, a demand that resulted in the growth of the African slave trade. The United States would not have become the "economic superpower" it is today without the constitutional support of the economic exploitation of these groups. The constitutional convention was composed of 55 White men, 40% of whom had once owned or were current slave owners; a critical point because the Constitution is often taken as a document that promised equality in the United States. In actuality, this document was written by slave owners with policies to protect slavery.[10] Feagin notes that by 1860, nearly one-fifth of U.S. national wealth was in the value of enslaved Blacks, which means that Whites accumulated wealth from stolen Black labor and Blacks received little to nothing in return.[11] This White economic domination over Blacks and other laborers of color has not ended; today, the disparate economic status is evident through the racial income gap and wealth gap. Feagin puts White economic domination at the center of the theory's diagram because systemic racism "is at bottom a highly unjust system for creating and extending the impoverishment of large groups of people, such as African Americans, to the profit of other large groups of people, principally White Americans."[12]

The White Racial Frame

Racism is perpetuated through institutional and individual practices in concert with a racial ideology; a **racial ideology** is "an interrelated set of cognitive notions, understandings, and metaphors that whites have used to rationalize and legitimate systemic racism."[13] Feagin conceptualizes the racial ideology that guided the founding of the United States as the White racial frame. The **White racial frame** is an "organized set of racialized ideas, stereotypes, emotions and inclinations to discriminate"; this frame leads to conscious and unconscious discriminatory actions by Whites.[14] The White racial frame is cognitive in that it affects thinking and interpretation, but it also includes racialized emotions, metaphors and concepts, and images. The frame works on the daily minute-by-minute interactions at the micro level and at the macro institutional level. The White racial frame is embedded in Whites' psyches, so that learning or understanding information outside this frame is difficult. For example, Whites often come to believe that they deserve everything they have, so much so that they deny that racism played any role in their success. This denial of racism leads Whites to believe in a meritocratic society and reject policies intended to ameliorate racial discrimination. A potential consequence of this frame is what Feagin and Hernán Vera call "social alexithymia," or the inability to understand the pain and experience of oppressed communities. The widespread and persistent oppression of people of color implies that social alexithymia is common among oppressors.[15]

Alienated Social Relations and the Racial Hierarchy

The creation and maintenance of a racial hierarchy is characterized by separation of and distance between groups. The **U.S. racial hierarchy** "runs from the privileged white position and status at the top to an oppressed black position and status at the bottom, with different groups of color variously positioned *by whites* between the two ends of this central racial-status continuum."[16] As holders of the top of the hierarchy, Whites force or coerce people of color to act for the benefits of Whites, so that often communities of color are working against their own self-interests. For example, Whites may only hire people of color who accept White cultural ideals and values, such as "proper" residence, language, fashion, hair styling, and modes of interaction. Thus, in this racist system, oppressed communities are "alienated from control over their own bodies as well as from an ability to make decisions about many aspects of their lives."[17] Systemic racism is perpetuated via hierarchical racial division and control.

Related Racial Domination

Other types of discrimination also intersect with racism. For example, sexism maintains discrimination against women, and class divisions oppress the poor (see Chapter 13 on intersectionality). However, the relative subordination of groups is in relation to their racial positioning on the hierarchy; for example, during plantation slavery, while White landowners (Whiteness and wealth) were more privileged and held a powerful position over working-class White men (Whiteness and poor), Whites of all classes were always privileged over Blacks. Today, Whites, regardless of their class status, maintain a psychological sense of racial superiority over communities of color. This point is not to suggest that an intersectional analysis is not important, but, at the same time, other intersecting oppressions do not erase the power of race(ism).

Whites' Unjust Enrichment

The unjust enrichment of Whites, over generations, is often overlooked. Whites have systematically been given privileges and opportunities that have led to their sustained position of power. For example, the institution of education is often seen as a major route toward mobility, yet it has been constantly denied to people of color. Blacks were excluded from schools during plantation slavery; they were forced into segregated schools during Jim Crow; and today Blacks, particularly from low-income backgrounds, attend schools that are underfunded, are poorly staffed, and have low graduation rates. Whites also receive unequal privileges in major institutions, including housing, politics, and healthcare. Whites have greater access and opportunities in society and impose a Eurocentric culture that pressures everyone to conform to White norms.[18] This arrangement of institutions and culture leads to the sustained unjust enrichment of Whites.

Constant Struggle and Resistance

Although racial oppression is persistent and constant, it is important to remember that in all time periods, people of color have resisted White domination and racism; "oppression in each historical epoch has dialectically triggered distinctive anti-oppression efforts."[19] For example, during plantation slavery, the enslaved resisted with a variety of efforts, including violence and running away; during the Civil Rights Movement, there were major policy and legal changes that resulted in desegregation; and currently union movements and policy changes have led to increased opportunities for people of color. Systemic racism theory includes the dimension of resistance because dissent is as much of the story of the United States as is oppression.

Systemic Racism Across Time

The maintenance of racism across time is accounted for by the inclusion of a timeline that moves from slavery to legal segregation to the contemporary era (generally identified as post–Civil Rights Movement). This timeline allows insight into how racism operated at a particular historical moment, as well as how racism persists over time. Despite resistance and change at the micro and macro level, systemic racism remains because the "deep structure" of society has not been fundamentally altered. This "social inertia" is a result of Whites' conscious and unconscious efforts to maintain the system in both overt and covert manners. On the macro level, there are large-scale racist institutions, such as the economy and the government, both of which maintain White norms and White-controlled social networks. On the micro level, racism is reproduced through socializing Whites into the White racial frame, so that they learn how to be a part of the dominant group in a racist society. Thus, from individuals to family, communities, and institutions, systemic racism is reproduced at every level and across time.[20] Feagin takes the reader through an application of the theory through three time periods: (1) slavery, (2) segregation, and (3) the contemporary era. In each era, he shows the realities of systemic racism from the perspective of both the oppressed and the oppressor.

Era 1: Systemic Racism During Slavery

Feagin looks at accounts of both Blacks and Whites during the era of plantation slavery (1600s–1865). He understands slavery not as a unique racist creation of the United States or an aberration in an otherwise equal society but as the foundation of the country that set the stage for the future. To show the perspective of enslaved Blacks, Feagin largely relies on the narratives of Frederick Douglass, William Wells Brown, and Harriet Jacobs; the narratives show how they understood their material oppression, their exclusion, and their perspectives on Whites. Analysis of these narratives provides insight into plantation slavery, including the brutal violence, the separation of families, and gendered racial oppression via sexual violence. Because resistance is a fundamental dimension of systemic racism, the strategies of enslaved Blacks are also accounted for; these strategies included playing dumb, playing lazy, physical violence, and escaping to the North for freedom. Feagin concludes that "from the black perspective, economic exploitation is central to slavery, as are recurring barbarity and violence in its major forms—physical, sexual, and psychological. The social relations of exploitation are central to this experience and have created much income and wealth, much racial capital, for many generations of whites."[21]

The analysis of slavery is also given from the perspective of Whites. Feagin uses the writings of Thomas Jefferson, James Madison, and George

Washington as the "highest ranking icons in U.S. civil religion," who have "had a profound impact on their time and continue to have an impact on our time."[22] All three men owned enslaved Blacks, interacted with them on a daily basis, and had sexual relationships with them. Jefferson rationalized slavery by saying that Blacks were more tolerant of heat and needed less sleep; Madison made sure that the Constitution had provisions to protect slavery, such as the three-fifths clause; and Washington made sure that his slaves were sent back to Virginia every 6 months, as Pennsylvania (Philadelphia was the nation's capital at the time) was a free state, so any enslaved resident there for more than 6 months was eligible for freedom. These men took action to defend their slavery interests and wrote stereotypically about Blacks; their narratives show that they had only a White, landowning perspective of the slavery system and did not identify the fundamental violence of the institution. Feagin thus argues that "we gain a much more insightful analysis of slavery's impact on whites in enslaved blacks' accounts than in those of these white founders. The dimension of systemic racism most demonstrated in their account seems to be the white racial frame, which is used to interpret and defend whites' interests."[23]

Era 2: Systemic Racism During Segregation

The second era of analysis is that of legal segregation. The vivid stories that Blacks recounted of this time are used to "see not only the thick texture of their lives at the microlevel, but also the ways in which the macrolevel of institutional oppression constantly intrudes on their daily experience."[24] During this time, Blacks were segregated by residence and in social encounters and were systematically denied equal opportunities in schooling, employment, politics, and more. Those who were viewed as resisting White domination had their homes and businesses burned and regularly faced physical violence. This violence was often condoned, if not actually endorsed or carried out by police officers. Resistance strategies by Blacks included ignoring or confronting segregation rules, moving to another region/state, socializing their children to resist the White racial frame, and avoiding Whites.

To see Whites' accounts of life during Jim Crow, Feagin looks at both Whites of a high status and those of the White working class. Their actions and rationalization of those actions reveal a continued use of the racial ideology created during slavery. High-status Whites, including senators, representatives, and President Eisenhower, attacked the 1954 *Brown v. Board of Education* desegregation case as threatening of their traditions and ways of life. Working-class Whites enforced segregation by calling the police or taking matters into their own hands.[25] These thoughts and actions were reinforced on the emotive level with fears of interracial relationships, Black sexuality, and Black criminality. Whites may not have been cognizant of their White racial frame because racial oppression remained so foundational and fundamental to society, but there was "active agency of whites in maintaining the racial hierarchy and its associated set of economic, social, and political burdens."[26]

Era 3: Contemporary Racial Realities

The maintenance of systemic racism is revealed through the continuing racial realities for Blacks and Whites in the contemporary period. After the Civil Rights Movement, a dominant narrative was that the United States had finally moved past race and into an era where equal opportunities were available to everyone. Although the Civil Rights Movement accomplished important changes, it was unsuccessful in fundamentally altering the system, and there was a White backlash against the gains that people of color were making. In this section of the book, Feagin relies on nearly 1,000 interviews with Blacks and Whites.

Black communities continue to be aware of and sensitive to racism while also cognizant of the racialized history of the United States. Economic domination persists via employment discrimination practices, such as stereotyping Black employees, favoring Whites in promotions, and cultivating hostile work climates. Racism is also present in other major institutions, such as in housing, where Blacks are regularly denied mortgages; education, where Blacks are more likely to attend segregated, poor schools; and health, where Blacks experience less reliable healthcare and attention. Blacks resist this oppression through challenging White managers and supervisors, by relying on strong family networks, and by reporting racism. The use of interviews and supportive statistics demonstrates that "racial oppression remains *systemic*" so that "it is not something superficial that is appended to an otherwise healthy U.S. society."[27]

In the contemporary era, the majority of Whites know that overt racism is not generally accepted, so they have modified their language and actions and sometimes rely on a "backstage" and a "frontstage." In frontstage spaces (mixed racial company), Whites maintain a sense of racial respect, while in backstage spaces (segregated all-White spaces), Whites allow each other to express more blatant racism. Whites also largely continue to live in predominantly White spaces, which supports the preservation of racist thought and reinforces alienated relationships between Blacks and Whites. Whites not only hold racist thoughts about Blacks and other communities of color but also hold "sincere fictions" about the superiority of Whites; "whiteness is centrally about prizing white beauty, values, opinions, stereotypes, and culture."[28] When confronted with Black resistance and moves for racial equality, Whites have acted to oppose policies (such as Affirmative Action) and create political parties and movements that work for the benefit of Whites. Feagin writes that "whites today remain firmly in control."[29]

How to Challenge Racism
••

One of the dimensions of systemic racism is constant struggle and resistance. Feagin is diligent about noting the resistance efforts of the oppressed in all time periods. Thus, it is not surprising that in the epilogue of *Systemic*

Racism, Feagin suggests several possible actions, on both the macro and micro levels, to challenge racism. On the micro level, people should be vigilant about calling out racism when they see it and push themselves to speak out against racism. Families, communities, and schools can also teach children the full history of the United States and work to replace the White racial frame with a social justice frame that emphasizes racial justice and equality. On the macro level, Feagin suggests major overhauls, such as a writing a new constitution that would be framed by an equal representation of all stakeholders, a democratic Supreme Court (not one primarily dominated by White men, as it has been), and writing an economic bill of rights that would seek to change people's current material reality.

Evaluation

Methodological Benefits

One of the primary strengths of this book is the varied data sources and organization used to support how systemic racism operates. The choice to organize the theoretical assessment by three general eras is more convincing than if Feagin had given only a general historical overview and then moved on to discuss contemporary racism. The examination of each era is made stronger by devoting a chapter to Blacks and then a chapter to Whites; this comparative framing makes it easy to see how the same events and actions are assessed and understood differently, depending on one's placement on the racial hierarchy. Moreover, the focus on White narratives also brings the White racial frame to the fore.

The comparative framing and chronological organization are sustained by the multiple data sources that are used. In the chapters on slavery, Feagin draws on the personal writings of three enslaved people and three U.S. presidents. In the case of the slave narratives, he chooses to use the primary accounts of Douglass, Wells Brown, and Jacobs, rather than second-hand accounts of slavery. Likewise, it is methodologically strong to use the writings of Jefferson, Madison, and Washington, as they reveal the White racial frame and strong racist ideology of the country's founding fathers, who are normally understood as model citizens and leaders. In the chapters on segregation and contemporary racial realities, Feagin continues to rely on first-person accounts from both Blacks and Whites. In addition to the use of these narratives and interview data, Feagin supplements his analysis with information on historical laws, policies, and documents; statistics on primary indicators of social well-being, such as income, housing, education, and health; and surveys or data from other research. In other words, Feagin makes it difficult to contest his findings.

Methodological Limitations

The methodological limitations lie in the choice of data in some of the chapters. In the chapters on slavery, the analysis is based on three accounts from the perspective of Blacks and three from Whites; the in-depth account provides richness of detail but has the drawback of providing data from limited sources. Certainly, three accounts of slavery are not an adequate summary for a system of oppression that lasted more than 200 years. In the following chapters on segregation, Feagin notes that he is drawing on personal perspectives from Blacks "on interviews done in various settings" and who are "from rank-and-file citizens, while a few are drawn from black leaders,"[30] and from Whites, both "those with substantial power and those in the rank and file."[31] The details on any of these interviews are unclear: how many, what age, what region, how long, who interviewed them, and the substance of the questions. When one refers to the notes in the back of the book, quotes come from a range of sources, such as data from other papers, books, NPR interviews, and a Jim Crow website. It is therefore difficult for one to determine specific details about the original data. For example, Feagin says, "In interview studies of nearly one thousand black and white Americans,"[32] but the notes do not reference any specific study of 1,000 interviews, so it seems that these data are culled from multiple sources, including several different research projects by Feagin and associates. This lack of details does not invalidate the data, but the relative inaccessibility to the information on the origins of the data makes it hard for the reader to evaluate sources and have a clear grasp of the methods.

Theoretical Benefits

Systemic racism is a macro-level, holistic, theoretical explanation of racism. The multiple, interconnected dimensions of the theory show how racism is at the foundation of the United States. The explicit connection between the contemporary era and the racialized history of the nation make it clear that racism has not faded. In contemporary times, when many conversations suggest that racism is on the decline or a result of a just "a few bad apples," systemic racism shows that racism is not only still pervasive but embedded in our institutions and framework of society.

This theory also effectively shows the connections between the macro and micro level. Although the theory is rooted in a historical system analysis, the connections to the micro level and daily lived experience come through the narratives of Blacks and Whites. In particular, the White racial frame shows the micro-level socialization process at work, and the concept of social alexithymia exemplifies how Whites' emotions and empathy become perverted in conjunction with Whites' oppressor status on the racial hierarchy. A key theoretical contribution of systemic racism is the focus on and examination of Whites' role in creating and sustaining racism, which puts the responsibility and the agency of Whites at the center of the conversation; this point counters a tradition of focusing on people of color when addressing the problem of racism. At the same time, this theory also gives critical attention to the resistance efforts of people of color, a facet that is often overshadowed in other theories of racism.

Theoretical Limitations

The theory of systemic racism is set in the context of the White–Black binary and points to the ways in which oppression of Black communities is at the foundation of the U.S. racial hierarchy. There is certainly support for this theoretical approach, but consequentially systemic racism ends up largely leaving out the stories of other communities of color. For example, Feagin mentions the genocide of the indigenous tribes but without any detail or focus; had it not been for expanding territory via the theft of land through the mass killing of tribes, slavery would not have been nearly as successful an economic enterprise. The relative absence of attention to the experiences of other communities of color serves to obfuscate this important history and therefore also ignores how the racial hierarchy and racism operate outside the White–Black binary.

Another limitation is a lack of clarity concerning how the nation moves from one time period to the next and how racism evolves throughout these time periods. The evolution of racism is somewhat addressed through accounts of resistance in the chapters, but there's no extensive explanation as to how the country moved from slavery to Jim Crow to Civil Rights to today. In other words, how does racism morph and adapt, while systemic racism persists? Related to this point, in a review of *Systemic Racism*, Omi and Winant argue that Feagin needs to pay more attention to how racial categories change and how political processes play into the changing dynamics of race and racism; they write that this theory needs to address "struggles over the meaning of race, both in large-scale political structures and in everyday experience and identity" as they "remain inseparable from struggles against racism."[33]

Conclusion

Systemic racism is a theory that accounts for the historical foundation of racism and how racism is embedded into the fabric of the nation. It also speaks to complex processes that result from White supremacy, such as unjust enrichment of Whites across generations, the teaching and learning of the White racial frame, and the development of social alexithymia. Systemic racism is a particularly useful theory for understanding Whites' active role in the production and persistence of racism across time while accounting for the resistance efforts of people of color.

REFLECT AND DISCUSS

1. How does racism from colonial times continue to shape and affect racism in current times?

2. How does the White racial frame help explain Whites' participation in sustaining racism?

3. Why are perspectives on racism from people of color more reliable than those of Whites?

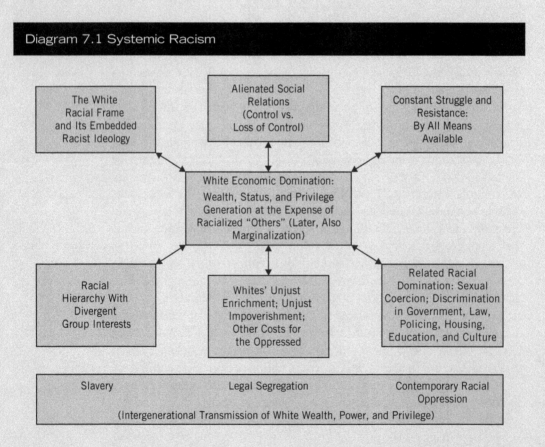

Diagram 7.1 Systemic Racism

Source: Feagin, Joe. *Systemic Racism: A Theory of Oppression*. Routledge, 2006. Reprinted with permission.

KEY TERMS

Racial ideology: "An interrelated set of cognitive notions, understandings, and metaphors that whites have used to rationalize and legitimate systemic racism."[34]

Seven dimensions of systemic racism: (1) White economic domination, (2) the White racial frame, (3) alienated social relations, (4) the racial hierarchy, (5) related racial domination, (6) Whites' unjust enrichment, and (7) constant struggle and resistance.[35]

Systemic racism: "Encompasses a broad range of white-racist dimensions: the racist ideology, attitudes, emotions, habits, actions, and institutions of whites in this society. Thus, systemic racism is far more than a matter of racial prejudice and individual bigotry. It is a material, social, and ideological reality that is well-imbedded in major U.S. institutions."[36]

U.S. racial hierarchy: "Runs from the privileged white position and status at the top to an oppressed black position and status at the bottom, with different groups of color variously positioned *by whites* between the two ends of this central racial-status continuum."[37]

U.S. racism: "Both complex and highly relational, a true system in which major racial groups and their networks stand in asymmetrical and oppositional relations. The social institutions and processes that reproduce racial inequality imbed a fundamental inegalitarian relationship—on the one hand, the racially oppressed, and on the other, the racial oppressors."[38]

White racial frame: "An organized set of racialized ideas, stereotypes, emotions, and inclinations to discriminate. This white racial frame generates closely associated, recurring, and habitual discriminatory actions."[39]

KEY PEOPLE

Joe Feagin (1938–): Feagin is the Ella C. McFadden Professor of Sociology at Texas A&M University in College Station, Texas. He is a prolific author on race and racism, with more than 50 authored or coauthored books. His 1973 book with Harlan Hahn, *Ghetto Revolts,* was nominated for a Pulitzer Prize, and his 1994 book with Melvin Sikes, *Living With Racism,* won the Gustavus Myers Center's Outstanding Human Rights Book Award, as did his 1995 book with Hernan Vera, *White Racism.* Feagin was the 91st president of the American Sociological Association (2000), and in 2013, he received the W. E. B. Du Bois Career of Distinguished Scholarship Award. Twitter @ JoeFeagin

WORKS CITED AND FURTHER READING

Collins, Chuck, Dedrick Asante-Muhammed, Josh Hoxie, and Sabrina Terry. 2019. "Dreams Deferred: How Enriching the 1% Widens the Racial Wealth Divide." Washington, DC: Institute for Policy Studies.

Elias, Sean and Joe Feagin. 2016. *Racial Theories in Social Science: A Systemic Racism Critique.* New York: Routledge.

Feagin, Joe. 2006. *Systemic Racism: A Theory of Oppression.* New York: Routledge.

Feagin, Joe. 2013. *The White Racial Frame: Centuries of Racial Framing and Counter-Framing.* 2nd ed. New York: Routledge.

Feagin, Joe. 2014. *Racist America: Roots, Current Realities, and Future Reparations.* 3rd ed. New York: Routledge.

Feagin, Joe and Zinobia Bennefeld. 2014. "Systemic Racism and U.S. Health Care." *Social Science & Medicine* 103:7–14.

Horowitz, Juliana Menasce, Anna Brown, and Kiana Cox. 2019. "Race in America 2019." Washington, DC: Pew Research Center.

McGirt, Ellen. 2018. "raceAhead: Only Three Black CEOs in the Fortune 500." *Fortune*, March 1.

Omi, Michael and Howard Winant. 2009. "Review: Thinking through Race and Racism." *Contemporary Sociology* 38(2):121–25.

Zillman, Claire. 2019. "The Fortune 500 Has More Female CEOs Than Ever Before." *Fortune*, May 16.

NOTES

1. Feagin (2006:2).
2. Ibid. (7).
3. Ibid. (6–7).
4. Ibid. (7).
5. Omi and Winant (2009:23).
6. Feagin (2006:8).
7. Ibid. (17).
8. Ibid. (16, emphasis in original).
9. The diagram in this chapter is a replication of the diagram Feagin uses in his book.
10. Feagin (2006:12).
11. Ibid. (19).
12. Ibid. (20).
13. Omi and Winant (2009:28).
14. Feagin (2006:25).
15. Ibid. (28).
16. Omi and Winant (2009:21, emphasis in original).
17. Feagin (2006:21).
18. Ibid. (24–25).
19. Ibid. (32).
20. Ibid. (37).
21. Ibid. (79).
22. Ibid. (86).
23. Ibid. (87).
24. Ibid. (127).
25. Ibid. (156–68).
26. Ibid. (186).
27. Ibid. (194, emphasis in original).
28. Ibid. (237).
29. Ibid. (258).
30. Ibid. (127).
31. Ibid. (155).
32. Ibid. (194).
33. Omi and Winant (2009:124).
34. Ibid. (28).
35. Ibid. (17).
36. Ibid. (2).
37. Ibid. (21, emphasis in original).
38. Ibid. (23).
39. Ibid. (25).

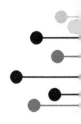

Critical Race Theory

Derrick Bell

Critical race theory was advanced in the 1980s by several scholar activists who concluded that racism was a permanent fixture of society and that law was not a neutral tool that could be effectively used to end racism. The theory has influenced a range of disciplines, including politics, education, sociology, Latinx critical studies, Asian critical studies, indigenous critical studies, and queer critical studies. The first part of this chapter is a summary of critical race theory tenets as identified by Richard Delgado and Jean Stefancic. The remainder of the chapter is based on *Faces at the Bottom of the Well: The Permanence of Racism* by Derrick Bell, who is widely considered the founder of critical race theory.

Photo 8.1 Derrick Bell

Source: https://upload.wikimedia.org/
wikipedia/commons/0/03/Derrick_
Bell_by_David_Shankbone.jpg.

Why This Theory

∙∙

The U.S. Civil Rights Movement, which took place from approximately the 1950s to the 1970s, resulted in legal gains for people of color in a range of areas, including education, voting, housing, and social life. Of utmost significance was the end of the extreme racist practices of Jim Crow. The toppling of Jim Crow and other specific wins, such as *Brown v. Board of Education* in 1954, the Civil Rights Act of 1964, and the Voting Rights Act of 1965, appeared to mark the ability of civil rights law to gain equality. Yet these gains were met with legal and social backlash, such as Whites cultivating segregated neighborhoods and schools, the use of redlining to make homeownership more difficult for people of color, and court cases that limited the use of Affirmative Action. Such backlash led to racial inequality in income, educational attainment, voting, and a host of other areas. While the wins of the Civil Rights Movement were important, overall the failure of law, precedent, and the legal process to sustain racial progress and equality spurred thinkers to revisit civil rights law as a tool of liberation. Critical race theorists are a group of scholars who came together around their shared realization that law could not be neutral or objective.[1] They identified the concept of **empathic fallacy**, which is the "belief that one can change a narrative simply by offering another, better one,"[2] so that people come to the mistaken idea "that sweeping social reform can be accomplished through speech and incremental victories within the system."[3]

Critical race theory emerged in the 1980s with the presumption that racism is a permanent feature of U.S. society. This idea, however, was understood not as a loss but instead as an integral insight into how racism honestly operates and therefore an insight into more realistic opportunities to address it. Critical race theory's theoretical approach to racism merges aspects of the Civil Rights Movement, the critical legal studies movement, radical feminism, and ethnic studies.[4] From the Civil Rights Movement, it takes the imperative to address wrongs and the need to develop legal theory to do so. From critical legal studies, there is a focus on legal indeterminacy, the idea that cases do not have one "correct" outcome but are settled in relation to who is in power at that time. This point is important, as it clarifies that court cases and laws are not objective or neutral but instead reflect the "morality" of the people who made them; for example, the U.S. Constitution was founded on equality but excluded the rights of African Americans. Critical legal studies also contribute the idea that favorable precedent tends to lose its power over time, so that legal wins are not sustainable. From radical feminism, critical race theory uses the understanding that identities such as gender and race are social constructions. Ethnic studies provide an emphasis on the particular histories and perspectives of oppressed communities of color.[5] Critical race theory builds on these ideas and adds attention to the futility of legal challenges, the historical relationship between the law and those in power, and the centrality and permanence of racism in society. This chapter first outlines the main tenets of critical race theory as put forth by Richard

Delgado and Jean Stefancic and then describes the book *Faces at the Bottom of the Well* by critical race theorist Derrick Bell.

Description of the Theory

Critical race theory (CRT) questions the very foundation of liberalism: for example, what other theories of law and society often take for granted, such as egalitarianism, legal reasoning, rationalism, and the neutrality of the Constitution, CRT asserts as false.[6] There is no neutral decision or legal rationalism because all decisions are infused with the ideals and ideologies of the people who made them, thereby inherently reflecting their views and the views of that time period. In an introductory book on CRT, Richard Delgado and Jean Stefancic outline six general interconnected tenets of the theory that most CRT theorists subscribe to: (1) race as a social construction, (2) racism as a regular and permanent part of society, (3) Whiteness and racism providing direct rewards to Whites, (4) the relationship between CRT and the related theories of intersectionality and anti-essentialism, (5) the unique and valuable perspective that belongs to people of color, and (6) the use of counter-narrative and legal storytelling as important tools. General agreement with these six tenets is at the basis of the work of critical race theorists.

Race Is a Social Construction

Beginning with "slave" and "free" in 1790 and into current times, with more than 60 possible racial identifications on the U.S. Census, U.S. society has long been organized by racial categories. Despite this long-standing reliance on racial categorization, **race** is not a biological phenomenon, and races do not have any inherent cultural or physical characteristics. CRT objects to any classification of race based on biological traits such as skin tone, hair texture, or facial features; instead, it is understood that race represents a perceived set of shared phenotypical characteristics that are assigned meaning and value by society. It is also recognized that racialization of communities (identity and value assigned to that identity) can shift throughout time, so that racial groups will move positions in the racial hierarchy in response to social, economic, and political needs.

Racism Is a Regular Part of Society

The United States is governed by a constitution that proclaims equality and liberty for all, yet racism is central to the United States, as slavery and its corollary, racial hierarchy, were a foundation of the nation and codified into the Constitution. CRT requires that people be honest about the racist foundation of the United States and maintenance of racism throughout the country's history. Taking a long view reveals that racism is not an aberration to society but a regular part of it. In this vein, the proposition that law is objective and neutral is also inconceivable; if racism is *of* our society, it is impossible that the laws created in this society are neutral.

Whiteness and Racism Provide Direct Rewards to Whites

The racial hierarchy consists of Whites at the top and Blacks at the bottom; other people of color are situated between Whites and Blacks as society's needs and conditions change. This racial hierarchy provides both psychological and material benefits to Whites. Higher-socioeconomic-status Whites in particular receive both significant material and psychological benefits via their social positioning. Lower-socioeconomic-status Whites may not have many material rewards but still receive psychosocial benefits in knowing that they are above people of color, no matter their economic status (see Chapter 2 on White privilege). Whites, therefore, have little to no incentive to change the racial hierarchy or to eradicate racism.

The Importance of Intersectionality and Anti-Essentialism

CRT, akin to anti-essentialism, emphasizes that racial experiences and racial groups cannot and should not be overly simplified and condensed into essentialist notions. Intersectionality (see Chapter 13) explains how people do not unilaterally occupy a race, class, or gender but rather simultaneously hold a matrix of multiple identities. For example, one cannot refer to "*the* Black experience" because there are multitudes of Black experiences. CRT adopts an intersectional and anti-essentialist perspective to understand that individuals' experiences and identities vary from group to group, within groups, and across time.

People of Color Have a Unique, Valuable Perspective

History books recounting the events of plantation slavery, the Civil War, colonization of indigenous lands, and more have largely been written by Whites and with a White, Eurocentric perspective. CRT explains that people of color, as the oppressed who experience racism, have a uniquely valuable insight into how race and racism operate—an insight that White people cannot have. Race is not a biological fact, but racism is a social fact that people of color experience every day; therefore, the objective experiences, feelings and emotions of facing racism can be told only by people of color. Thus, CRT holds that the perspectives of people of color should be an integral and valued part of the conversation and scholarship on racism.

Narrative and Legal Storytelling Are Important Tools

CRT understands that law is not objective; it is inherently racialized. Thus, CRT moves to use personal narrative and/or storytelling as a response to the presumed "objectivity" of law and as an important tool to help people understand and accept the existence of racism. Critical race scholars use personal stories, allegories, metaphors, analogies, and other related methods of storytelling. Stories are particularly useful because they can appeal to those who otherwise might not listen, they can be more successful in cultivating empathy, and they can be particularly counter-hegemonic through the telling of the same events but from a different, non-dominant perspective. "The 'legal storytelling' movement urges black and brown writers to recount their experiences with racism and the legal system to apply their own unique perspectives to assess law's master narratives."[7] The use of storytelling is particularly clear in Bell's book *Faces at the Bottom of the Well*.

Critical Race Theory: *Faces at the Bottom of the Well* by Derrick Bell

Faces at the Bottom of the Well by Derrick Bell (1992) is widely considered a foundational book of CRT.[8] Bell writes each of nine chapters as a story that communicates a different lesson about race and racism. Each chapter uses the CRT strategy of storytelling to engage with difficult issues of race and racism. The stories do not necessarily provide answers to the problems posed or even a definitive account of how a problem should be viewed, but they are successful in encouraging the reader to critically think about, interrogate, and reflect on racialized problems in new ways. Bell intentionally does not follow the academic traditions of legal scholarship, so a systematic overview of concepts and components of CRT via using *Faces at the Bottom of the Well* isn't provided. Instead, a brief synopsis of each chapter's story provides a way to see the strengths of Bell's use of CRT.

Chapter 1: Racial Symbols: A Limited Legacy

In this story, a law professor and a cab driver debate the merits of a Martin Luther King Jr. holiday and related symbols of racial progress. The cab driver argues that generally too much emphasis is put on holidays as indicators of progress and suggests that they are merely tokens offered by White society to keep Blacks pacified; he says, "Tell me how a holiday for Dr. King helps the poor, the ignorant, the out-of-work, and hungry blacks all over this racist land?"[9]

The law professor in the cab is on his way to give a speech for MLK Day; he recognizes the symbolic importance of an MLK Day while also noting the continued significant barriers to equality. This story relates questions on what constitutes progress, how much progress has been made, and how to maintain a spirit of resistance in spite of ongoing oppression.

Chapter 2: The Afrolantica Awakening

In the Afrolantica Awakening, a beautiful, rich island emerges from the ocean, an island on which it is discovered that only Blacks can breathe;

Whites try to descend on the island but find it uninhabitable. Blacks debate the merits of immigration to the island; some believe that departing the United States means leaving behind progress, while others seek the island as a place of liberation and a homeland. Whites begin a campaign to stop Black emigration, as their departure might threaten the social and economic superiority of Whites if there are no Blacks to oppress. A community of Blacks decides to emigrate, only then to see the island disappear, but they realize that by creating an organized movement to depart, they had "an Afrolantica Awakening, a liberation—not of place, but of mind."[10] This story connects to a desire for material and psychological liberation from White control. Since plantation slavery, Black communities have debated the merits of staying in the United States or leaving the place where they were born to return to their ancestors' homeland of Africa.

Chapter 3: The Racial Preference Licensing Act

In this story, a new law permits businesses to discriminate, but only if the business owners purchase a "racial preference license." If the license is purchased, the business must display it prominently and is required to discriminate against all members of the group, without exception. The income derived from the cost of the license is used to support home mortgages, loans, and scholarships for Blacks. This point is taken within the context that traditional civil rights law has failed and resulted in racism becoming more covert, not less powerful. The idea of a discrimination license also speaks to the difficulties in legally regulating individual morality. This story may indicate a need to evaluate all suggestions for combating racism, even those considered overtly offensive, such as racial preference license.

Chapter 4: The Last Black Hero

The Black leader of Quad A, a Black liberation organization, falls in love with a White woman. A Black woman who is loyal to Quad A and its leader, Jason, is also in love with Jason and feels betrayed by his love for a White woman. She questions how Jason, a militant Black organization leader, could marry a White woman. His rationale is that "the sum of my existence is not confined to a knowledge of black history and a love of black culture. My identity cannot be so readily appropriated by *any* white woman."[11] This story addresses long-held concerns on whether Black resistance requires endogamy and racial segregation.

Chapter 5: Divining a Racial Realism Theory

An all-White pro-gun organization is created to protect Blacks in the case of an upcoming war against them. The organization believes (1) in **racial realism**, that the United States showed its true colors during slavery and no Black person should feel safe in society, and (2) that Whites should build a network of shelters for Blacks, as "America's race problem is a white problem."[12] A White leader of this organization had previously attended law school but realized the futility of the law to sustain change and racial equality; she tells the Black law professor she meets:

> Law school is dry and disconnected with the reality of the real world, and it's overly reliant on appellate court opinions that once reflected real problems but now are preserved as legal precedent to be dissected and analyzed, like mummies in a tomb. They serve to justify preservation of the status quo while tending to bar social reform.[13]

This story connects to a series of real-life concerns: (1) the failure of law and appellate decisions to protect civil rights as seen in actual civil rights law; (2) the concern over the use of guns and violence for self-defense as used by real activists, such as John Brown or the Black Panther Party; (3) the role of Whites in challenging racism as seen with White abolitionists during plantation slavery, White bus boycotters during the Civil Rights Movement, and contemporary White participation in antiracism organizations and marches; and (4) the recognition that racism is a permanent part of society, even if it appears it has subsided.

Chapter 6: The Rules of Racial Standing

In this story, a man is delivered five "rules of racial standing." Rule One: Whenever Blacks speak about race or when Black people praise other Black persons for their accomplishments, they are considered biased. Rule Two: Blacks are not sufficient or objective witnesses to racism, so cases about racism should not have Black jurors or Black judges. Rule Three: Support of Blacks by other Blacks is disregarded, but when a Black person criticizes Black communities, that person is given "enhanced standing." Rule Four: When a Black person speaks the truth about White racism, Black people are recruited to refute that statement/action and rewarded when they do so. Rule Five: The rules of racial standing are constant, and there is a *"frustration that follows recognition that no amount of public prophecy, no matter its accuracy, can either repeal the Rules of Racial Standing or prevent their operation."*[14] This story addresses how Whites aim to control and use the messages and voices of Blacks through social and material consequences and rewards. These rules of racial standing reflect the reality that Black people are discredited when they expose racism and rewarded when they deem it nonexistent.

Chapter 7: A Law Professor's Protest

Harvard's president gathers all of Harvard's Black faculty and administrators for a meeting; during the meeting, a bomb hits the building, and everyone dies. This tragedy serves as a call to attention to the lack of racial representation on campus, as one building could hold all the faculty of color.

After the bombing, a document is found that was written by the deceased president, a Du Boisian Talented Tenth program initiative to make 10% of Harvard's faculty and staff Black, Hispanic, or Native American. This story clearly highlights the urgency to hire and retain a racially diverse workforce and to value the scholarship and contributions of people of color.

Chapter 8: Racism's Secret Bonding

On the Fourth of July, an area begins experiencing "Racial Data Storms," a "rain" of information that penetrates White minds and souls with information on racism. Whites begin receiving statistics on Black–White disparities in areas such as unemployment, education, infant mortality, and incarceration. Whites also begin to feel the hurt, frustration, anger, and despair that racism causes. The storms lead Whites finally to understand racism. After Whites lead sit-ins, marches, and reforms, the storms abate in response. This chapter connects to the reality of the range of strategies that have been used to convince Whites that racial inequality is severe and that they should participate in challenging racism. The idea that a "rain of information" finally results in Whites' empathy suggests the question of what it might take in real life for Whites to recognize racism and act to stop it.

Chapter 9: The Space Traders

"The Space Traders" is one of Bell's most famous chapters. Aliens arrive in the United States and offer much-needed resources, such as gold, chemicals to depollute the environment, and a safe, long-standing energy source, but in exchange, the United States must give the aliens every African American. The U.S. president and his cabinet debate the pros and cons of doing so, and most of White America supports the trade. The White president has one Black cabinet member, who has long supported the president's agenda, but at this point, the cabinet member pleads to Black organizations that the only way to avoid deportation is to convince Whites that Blacks are receiving an opportunity that Whites are not. The Black cabinet member argues that "a major, perhaps the principal, motivation for racism in this country is the deeply held belief that black people should not have anything that white people don't have."[15] The Black leaders and organizations reject the cabinet member's strategy and move that they would rather stick by their morals than lie to avoid deportation. In the end, the president hands all Blacks over to the aliens on Martin Luther King Jr. Day: "There was no escape, no alternative. Heads bowed, arms now linked by slender chains, black people left the New World as their forebears had arrived."[16] In this chapter, racism is motivated by Whites' need to feel superior, which is why the Black cabinet member suggests that the way to avoid deportation is to make Whites feel jealous of Blacks' opportunity to go with the aliens. Whites have long taken what they wanted from Blacks once they found it desirable, whether that be music, fashion, or areas of residence via gentrification. The Space Traders story also, of course, addresses the cruel reality that Whites have sacrificed Black bodies and souls when it has benefited them.

How to Challenge Racism

Although some may see the belief in the permanence of racism as giving up the fight on racism, CRT scholarship is written to reveal the inhumanity of racism and how to ameliorate its effects. In a book on writings that formed the foundation of CRT, Crenshaw, Gotanda, Peller, and Thomas state that one thing that unifies critical race theorists is "the desire not merely to understand the vexed bond between law and racial power but to *change* it."[17] As seen via the preceding chapter summaries, Bell uses storytelling to challenge the belief in law's race-neutrality, to center the concerns of people of color, and to emphasize the presence of racism in society. Bell closes *Faces at the Bottom of the Well* with a letter to a fictional character, Geneva; the letter confronts the oppression that Blacks continue to face. It recounts the horrors of plantation slavery to reaffirm not only the staying power of racism but the resilience and humanity of Blacks in the face of brutality. In the recognition of a long-held struggle against racism lie the inspiration and proof that resistance will continue. The epilogue reads like a call to action: "We must … fashion a philosophy that both matches the unique dangers we face, and enables us to recognize in those dangers opportunities for committed living and humane service."[18]

By the Numbers

- After the University of California banned the use of race in admissions (Affirmative Action) in 1995, the percentage of Black students at UC Berkeley fell from 6.3% to 2.9%, and Native American enrollment dropped from 1.8% to 0.4%.

- In 1 year, the U.S. Equal Employment Opportunity Commission (EEOC) received 24,600 charges of racial discrimination (32.2% of charges made).

- Although housing discrimination is illegal, 27.4% of Black applicants and 19.2% of Hispanic applicants were denied mortgages, compared to 11% of White and Asian applicants. Blacks and Hispanics are also more likely to pay a higher interest rate on mortgages in comparison to Whites and Asians.

Sources: DeSilver and Bialik (2017); U.S. Equal Employment Opportunity Commission (2019); Mello (2018).

Evaluation

Methodological Benefits

Faces at the Bottom of the Well uses the storytelling method to address the persistence of racism and to illustrate how it continues to operate in a post–Civil Rights Movement era. In just nine brief chapters, Bell is able to address a range of difficult problems, from symbolic holidays and interracial relationships to the need for a liberated homeland. Moreover, throughout the chapters, Bell provides varied perspectives by relying on different race, class, and gender positions of the characters. In "Racial Symbols," Bell positions the thoughts of a successful Black professor against that of his driver, an older Black man of lower socioeconomic status. In "The Space Traders," the White president and his mostly White cabinet conspire to pass a law that will permit them to exile all Blacks, while in "The Last Black Hero," a favorable Black leader falls in love with a White woman who is willing to forgo her White networks to be with him. By purposely varying the race, class, and gender of his characters, along with their positions on race and racism, Bell provides the reader with insight into how people of different standings view race and racism. The storytelling method encourages people to think and empathize, rather than passively read.

Another benefit is that Bell's stories, while fiction, include real historical events and people. For example, in "The Rules of Racial Standing," Bell discusses how Louis Farrakhan, leader of the Nation of Islam, is often deemed as too outrageous on racial issues, largely because he publicly castigates Whites; as a result, Blacks are recruited to denounce him. By integrating the debate over Farrakhan, Bell brings the rules of racial standing to life. In "The Space Traders," Bell reminds the reader that President Lincoln supported the emigration of Blacks both before and after slavery, and in "The Afrolantica Awakening," Bell discusses how the Black leader Marcus Garvey sought a homeland for Blacks in Africa. This use of historical events and people embedded in the fictional stories makes the debates on race(ism) tangible and has the added benefit of teaching the reader about events that are not often included in traditional Eurocentric accounts.

Methodological Limitations

CRT is often criticized for what its theorists also believe is its strong point: storytelling. The storytelling method can be seen as biased and unscientific. *Faces at the Bottom of the Well* does not have data that can be objectively analyzed or used to "prove" the existence of racism. Many of Bell's stories are in unrealistic imaginary situations, such as the island that emerges from the water or aliens who come to take all Blacks. The method of storytelling and imaginary situations make a traditional scientific criticism of Bell's book untenable, yet he wants the stories to be received as valid enough to spur activism against racism. Bell is well aware of this criticism: "I truly believe that analysis of legal developments through fiction, personal experience, and the stories of people on the bottom illustrates how race and racism continue to dominate our society" and "with what some of us are calling CRT, we are attempting to sing a new scholarly song—even if to some listeners our style is strange, our lyrics unseemly."[19]

Theoretical Benefits

The strongest theoretical stance of CRT is perhaps that racism is a permanent force in society. It doesn't allow for the idea that racism doesn't exist or that civil rights law was successful in eliminating racism. The move for people to accept this reality then creates a need for an agenda to do something about racism. As stated previously, being a critical race scholar requires that one take an activist stance.

Additional benefits are the centering of the voices of people of color and an integration of intersectionality and anti-essentialism. CRT unapologetically centers people of color and notes their unique insight into the problems of race(ism). This stance creates an opening for people of color to speak their experience and have it accepted as truth; too often, the interpretation of social problems is accepted only when told by a "White authority." In addition, the use of intersectionality and anti-essentialism in Bell's writing keeps readers from believing in one basic experience of race, which is all too often adopted when speaking of "Blacks" and "Whites" as though they are homogenous groups with homogenous experiences and views.

Theoretical Limitations

Racism as a permanent feature is a theoretical strength of CRT, but it also can be viewed as a theoretical limitation when it comes to understanding resistance. Racism is a foundation of the United States, and racism is still present, but that does not necessarily preclude it from ever disappearing. Or if one accepts that racism is permanent, what is the most efficient way to fight racism? What kinds of resistance are successful or worth investing in? These questions do not have clear answers. Critical race theorist Cheryl Harris, while lauding the book, also notes that "the full implications of what is required if reform is doomed to fail remain unstated in Bell's work. He advances an argument of struggle for its own sake that lacks the power of his earlier analysis."[20]

There is also the unanswered question of Whites' capacity to fight racism. If racism is permanent, that implies that Whites will always remain invested in being at the top of the racial hierarchy. The book opens with an epigraph that states that Blacks are at the bottom of the well as Whites look down on them, and CRT posits that Whites have a vested interest to maintain the psychological and material rewards of their position. Yet at times, Bell's stories seem to suggest that Whites could participate in racial resistance, via the love interest in "The Last Black Hero" and the White defenders in "Divining a Racial Realism Theory." Thus, it's uncertain how Whites can forgo their investment in Whiteness and to what degree they can do so.

Conclusion

CRT begins with the premise that racism not only exists but is a permanent feature of society. This premise does not leave room for disagreement, so those who approach CRT must do so with this acknowledgment. Such agreement lessens the burden on scholars to prove that racism exists and move to the next step of describing it and fostering resistance. The theory has grown rapidly since its introduction in the 1980s and has inspired race scholars across disciplines to confront reality and interrogate the structure of racism.

REFLECT AND DISCUSS

1. How is critical race theory's presumption that racism is permanent a call to action, rather than a sign of surrender?

2. How are storytelling and narrative a strategy for discussing racism and a response to the presumption of objectivity in law?

3. According to critical race theory, why do people of color have a unique and valuable perspective?

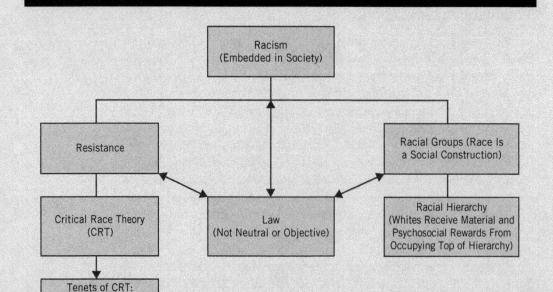

Diagram 8.1 Critical Race Theory

KEY TERMS*

Critical race theory (CRT): "Aims to reexamine the terms by which race and racism have been negotiated in American consciousness, and to recover and revitalize the radical tradition of race-consciousness among African-Americans and other peoples of color."[21]

A "radical legal movement that seeks to transform the relationship among race, racism, and power."[22]

Empathic fallacy: The "mistaken belief that sweeping social reform can be accomplished through speech and incremental victories within the system."[23]

Race: "Although race is socially constructed (the idea of biological race is 'false'), race is nonetheless 'real' in the sense that there is a material dimension and weight to the experience of being 'raced' in American society, a materiality that in significant ways has been produced and sustained by law."[24]

Racial realism: The "view that racial progress is sporadic and that people of color are doomed to experience only infrequent peaks followed by regressions."[25]

KEY PEOPLE

Derrick Bell (1930–2011): Bell became the first Black tenured law professor at Harvard University in 1971. In 1986, he led a 5-day sit-in in his office to protest Harvard University's denial of tenure to women of color who used critical race theory in their work. In 1990, he took a 2-year unpaid leave of absence to protest Harvard's lack of women of color on the faculty, and in 1992, he joined the School of Law at New York University. *Faces at the Bottom of the Well* has been cited more than 3,000 times, and though Bell passed away in 2011, a new edition of the book was published in 2018, with a foreword by Michelle Alexander (author of *The New Jim Crow*). www.professorderrickbell.com (official site)

WORKS CITED AND FURTHER READING

Bell, Derrick. 1992. *Faces at the Bottom of the Well: The Permanence of Racism.* New York: Basic Books.

Bonilla-Silva, Eduardo. 2015. "More Than Prejudice: Restatement, Reflections, and New Directions in Critical Race Theory." *Sociology of Race and Ethnicity* 1(1):73–87.

Crenshaw, Kimberlé W. 2011. "Twenty Years of Critical Race Theory: Looking Back to Move Forward." *Connecticut Law Review* 43(5): 1253–354.

Crenshaw, Kimberlé W., Neil Gotanda, Gary Peller, and Kendall Thomas, eds. 1995. *Critical Race Theory: The Key Writings That Formed the Movement.* New York: The New Press.

Delgado, Richard and Jean Stefancic. 2001. *Critical Race Theory: An Introduction.* New York: New York University Press.

DeSilver, Drew and Kristen Bialik. 2017. "Blacks and Hispanics Face Extra Challenges in Getting Home Loans." Washington, DC: Pew Research Center.

Harris, Cheryl I. 1993. "Bell's Blues: Review of *Faces at the Bottom of the Well: The Permanence of Racism* by Derrick Bell." *The University of Chicago Law Review* 60(2):783–93.

Mello, Felicia. 2018. "California's Gone without Higher Ed Affirmative Action since 1996. Black Enrollment at Top UCs Never Recovered." *NPR News*, June 10.

U.S. Equal Employment Opportunity Commission. 2019. "EEOC Releases Fiscal Year 2018 Enforcement and Litigation Data." Washington, DC: Author.

NOTES

* Because *Faces at the Bottom of the Well* is a series of stories, definitions for concepts come from other readings.
1. Delgado and Stefancic (2001).
2. Ibid. (34).
3. Ibid. (146).
4. Ibid.
5. Crenshaw et al. (1995); Delgado and Stefancic (2001).
6. Delgado and Stefancic (2001).
7. Ibid. (9).
8. Bell (1992).
9. Ibid. (21).
10. Ibid. (46).
11. Ibid. (83).
12. Ibid. (94).
13. Ibid. (99).
14. Ibid. (125, emphasis in original).
15. Ibid. (175).
16. Ibid. (194).
17. Crenshaw et al. (1995:xiii).
18. Bell (1992:195).
19. Ibid. (144).
20. Harris (1993:792).
21. Crenshaw et al. (1995:xiv).
22. Delgado and Stefancic (2001:144).
23. Ibid. (146).
24. Crenshaw et al. (1995:xxvi).
25. Delgado and Stefancic (2001:154).

From "Old Racism" to "New Racism"

Laissez-Faire Racism

*Lawrence Bobo, James Kluegel,
and Ryan Smith*

After the U.S. Civil Rights Movement, a distinct shift occurred in Whites' attitudes on racial equality, a shift away from support for segregation and toward a belief in racial integration and opportunity. Yet this attitude shift occurred without a simultaneous relief in racial discrimination. This paradox led Lawrence Bobo, James Kluegel, and Ryan Smith to propose the theory of laissez-faire racism to capture how Whites are outwardly supportive of racial equality while maintaining their belief in their racial superiority and their status at the top of the racial hierarchy. Laissez-faire racism describes persisting negative stereotyping of Blacks and the erroneous view that racial inequality is the outcome of natural market dynamics and individual choice.*

Photo 9.1 Lawrence Bobo

Source: https://alumni.lmu.
edu/connect/featuredalumni/
alumnifeatures/lawrencebobo/.

---

*Photos of Kluegel and Smith not available.

Why This Theory

The successes of U.S. Civil Rights Movement–era organizations led to a growing number of people showing support for racial equality. Surveys used to measure attitudes on racial issues indicate an increase in this trend over the years. For example, in 1942, 68% of White Americans favored segregated schools, compared to only 7% in 1985, and in 1944, 55% of White Americans thought Whites should receive preference over Blacks in access to jobs, compared to only 3% in 1972.[1] Such egalitarian views are more prevalent in the North, in more highly educated communities, and in younger groups, but the trend is also nationwide. Bobo and Smith argue that these attitudinal trends in favor of racial equality indicate that "a fundamental transformation of social norms regarding race" has occurred.[2] This radical shift in views on race then begs the question of whether the United States is moving toward a genuine color-blind society or whether the country still remains one polarized by race.

Lawrence Bobo, James Kluegel, and Ryan Smith propose the theory of laissez-faire racism "to bring greater theoretical coherence to the hotly debated question of whether the racial attitudes of white Americans reflect less racism now than was evident 40—or even 20—years ago."[3] They propose that the United States is still characterized by **racism**, which they define as "an ideology of racial domination or exploitation that (1) incorporates beliefs in a particular race's cultural and or inherent biological inferiority and (2) uses such beliefs to justify and prescribe inferior treatment for that group."[4] They specifically propose that racism has shifted from an overt Jim Crow racism to a "laissez-faire racism," wherein Whites loosely support ideals of racial equality but still believe in the inferiority of Blacks. In continuing this work, Bobo defines the new ideology of **laissez-faire racism** as one that

> incorporates negative stereotypes of Blacks; a preference for individualistic, and rejection of structural, accounts of racial inequality; and an unwillingness to see government actively work to dismantle racial inequality. This new pattern of belief is more subtle and covert than its predecessor, making it more difficult to directly confront; it is also more amenable to the more fluid and permeable set of racial divisions in the social order."[5]

The term *laissez-faire* refers to the practice of or preference for not intervening in government affairs; thus, *laissez-faire racism* refers to Whites' bias against policies or practices intended to address racism. Overall, this theory accounts for Whites' expression of more racially inclusive attitudes and at the same time their desire to maintain their position at the top of the racial hierarchy.

The theory of laissez-faire racism is also partially a response to the theory of symbolic racism as proposed by Kinders and Sears. Symbolic racism also seeks to explain why racism persists after the fall of Jim Crow and despite antidiscrimination laws. Similar to the theory of laissez-faire racism, Kinders and Sears suggest that Whites will reject blatantly anti-Black sentiments while concurrently opposing racial amelioration policies, such as school busing. They suggest that Whites develop these attitudes in relation to early childhood socialization messages that predispose them to hold anti-Black attitudes. Kinders and Sears focus on racism at the level of individual bias, which is depicted as running on a continuum from tolerant to prejudiced (see Chapter 1 on prejudice).[6] Bobo, Kluegel, and Smith propose that their theory of laissez-faire racism accounts for the gaps they perceive in symbolic racism. They outline three differences: (1) Symbolic racism does not provide an explanation for the decline in overt racism, while laissez-faire racism describes why Jim Crow racism ended; (2) symbolic racism sees prejudice as rooted in individual, psychological attitudes that emerge during childhood socialization, while laissez-faire racism explains prejudice as rooted in group position; and (3) symbolic racism analyzes attitudes of particular individuals, while laissez-faire racism focuses on macro-level patterns of racism in society.[7] These three points form the foundation of Bobo, Kluegel, and Smith's explanation of laissez-faire racism.

Description of the Theory

The theory of laissez-faire racism examines Whites' positive attitudes toward principles of racial equality within the ongoing context of a society where racism persists.[8] Laissez-faire racism explains this contradiction through three primary factors: (1) providing an analysis of why Jim Crow racism faded, (2) conceiving of prejudice as group position, and (3) identifying the persistence of widespread racist beliefs.

The Fall of Jim Crow Racism

During the Jim Crow era, surveys revealed that most Whites unashamedly believed in the practice of racial segregation, but shortly after the Civil Rights Movement, surveys indicated that Whites' attitudes shifted toward racial equality. Indeed, by 1972, just a few years after the 1964 Civil Rights Act, 97% of Whites supported the principle of equal access to jobs.[9] Such shifts in attitudes are often explained by a cohort replacement effect, personal change among individuals, or a combination of these two. Cohort replacement is the idea that biased ideologies fade as those who held them die, and a younger, more liberal cohort of people embrace egalitarian views. The personal change explanation suggests that individuals may develop new values due to soul searching, discomfort or guilt, or exposure to new evidence. Yet these "explanations" are more descriptions of trends rather than a distinct examination of why the racial ideologies of the Jim Crow era faded. The theory of laissez-faire racism centers much of its data on **racial attitudes**, which "capture aspects of the preferred group positions and those patterns of belief and feeling that undergird, justify, and make understandable a preference for relatively little group differentiation and inequality under some social conditions, or for a great deal of differentiation and inequality among others."[10]

Bobo, Kluegel, and Smith account for the fall in Jim Crow racism by explaining the connection between changes in economics and politics to changes in individual attitudes. They argue that

> there are inevitable connections between economic and political structures, on the one hand, and patterns of individual thought and action, on the other. As the structural basis of longstanding group relations undergoes change, there is a corresponding potential for change in the ways of thinking, feeling, and behaving that had previously been commonplace.[11]

In this conceptualization, for one to understand the shift in individual attitudes, the analysis must begin with the economic and political structures that supported Jim Crow.

Jim Crow racism was intimately tied to Southern agricultural Black labor, but a shift in labor needs occurred with the onset of synthetic fibers and the declining centrality of cotton. Agricultural labor in the South moved to factory labor in the North, with demand in the North particularly increasing after World War I, when there were fewer immigrant laborers available from Europe. The "great migration" of Blacks from the South to the North led to significant numbers of Black church congregations, NAACP chapters, and Black college students. The diminution of Southern agricultural life, combined with greater power in Black communities (via churches, colleges, and organizations) and Black leaders articulating goals for freedom, culminated in the successful social protests of the Civil Rights Movement. When the economic and political structures supporting Jim Crow fell, the overt racial attitudes of segregation no longer made sense because "the attitudes held by individuals must be linked to the organized modes of living in which people are embedded."[12] In other words, Whites' racial attitudes had to change to meet the new economic and political conditions.

While Whites' attitudes toward racial integration became increasingly positive, their belief in their fundamental racial superiority did not diminish. Whites had to find other pathways to and ideologies for justifying and holding onto their dominant group position. The end of Jim Crow racism did not result in a "thoroughly antiracist popular ideology based on an embracing and democratic vision of the common humanity, worth, dignity, and place in the polity for blacks alongside whites."[13] Instead, Bobo, Kluegel, and Smith propose that

> in the wake of the collapse of Jim Crow social arrangements and ideology, the new ideology of laissez-faire racism began to take shape. The new ideology concedes basic citizenship rights to African Americans; however, it takes as legitimate extant patterns of black-white socioeconomic inequality and residential segregation, viewing these conditions, as it does, not as the deliberate products of racial discrimination, but as outcomes of a free-market, race-neutral

state apparatus, and the freely taken actions of African Americans themselves.[14]

In this new era of laissez-faire racism, Whites ignore the existence of or their participation in racism and blame Blacks for their lack of mobility. Bobo, Kluegel, and Smith explain this evolution through the concept of prejudice as rooted in group position.

Prejudice as Group Position

Prejudice is often understood as an individual, psychological issue (see Chapter 1), but laissez-faire racism is premised on Herbert Blumer's theory of prejudice as group position. Blumer contends that groups come to understand that they are placed in relation to one another on a hierarchy and then treat each other accordingly based on their understanding of respective status positions. Bobo, Kluegel, and Smith use Blumer's description of **prejudice as group position** because it "places a subjective, interactively and socially created, and historically emergent set of ideas about appropriate status relations between groups at the center of any analysis of racial attitudes."[15] Thus, the traditional understanding of the racial group as the object of prejudice is erroneous; instead, the object of prejudice is the belief about proper status relations between groups.[16] For example, prejudice as an individual, psychological attitude would posit that Whites hate Blacks, but the theory of group position explains that prejudice derives from Whites' belief in a hierarchy wherein Blacks belong below them; in this sense, even if the degree of hate decreased, the belief in the position of Blacks below Whites would remain. Bobo, Kluegel, and Smith clarify that "this attitude of sense of group position is historically and culturally rooted, socially learned, and modifiable in response to new information, events, or structural conditions, as long as these factors contribute to or shape contexts for social interaction among members of different groups."[17] Group position, then, is a complex dynamic that is learned through social interactions, and a group's position may move in relation to changing social conditions, such as political and economic structures, as explained earlier.

Prejudice as group position is operationalized by three tenets: (1) Members of the dominant group sense a claim or entitlement to greater resources and status, (2) members of the dominant group perceive that there is a threat posed by subordinate racial group members to those entitlements, and (3) the dominant group's sense of entitlement and threat "become dynamic social forces" that are then used to defend and maintain their privilege.[18] Bobo, Kluegel, and Smith posit that this understanding of entitlement and threat provides "the greatest theoretical leverage in accounting for changes in whites' racial attitudes in the United States" because varying degrees of entitlement and threat felt by Whites relate to how strongly they feel they must defend their group position, which then translates into racial attitudes.[19]

Laissez-faire racism utilizes the theory of group position to make the connection between structure and individual attitudes. Using this framework,

Whites' shift in attitudes was not a spontaneous change in individual psychological or affective morality but evolved in relation to the fall of the Jim Crow structure—attitudes shifted in relation to the shift in group positioning. Bobo, Kluegel, and Smith also explain that a "key link" in articulating the change in group positioning is the presence of "significant social actors"[20] who argue for the interests and resources of a group, so that the "direction and tenor of change is shaped in the larger public sphere of clashes, debate, political mobilization, and struggle."[21] In the case of the Civil Rights Movement, leaders such as Martin Luther King and Ella Baker aided in the ideological departure from Jim Crow as they argued for the needs and interests of Blacks.

The theory of group position also aids in understanding why Whites' attitudes toward racial equality are increasingly positive, while their support for racial policies is not. Bobo, Kluegel, and Smith examine this difference through the distinction between principle questions, implementation questions, and social distance questions: **Principle questions** ask about beliefs for racial equality, such as support for racial integration; **implementation questions** ask about support for racial policies and practices; and **social distance questions** ask about relative willingness to be in spaces that range from predominantly White to predominantly Black. These three types of questions illuminate important differences; for example, attitude questions show that the majority of Whites support the idea of racially integrated schools, but Whites do not support government intervention to make integration happen and do not desire to be in spaces where there are "too many" Blacks. Principle questions reveal Whites' declining insistence on racial segregation, but implementation and social distance questions reveal Whites' continuing belief in their dominant group position.[22]

The Persistence of Widespread Racism

Laissez-faire racism is predicated on the understanding that racial inequality still exists and that *racism* continues to be the accurate term to describe contemporary racialized conditions. Basic indicators of inequality represent the continuing disparities between Whites and people of color: The unemployment gap, the pay gap, the wealth gap, residential segregation, and incarceration rates all indicate a "system of racial domination."[23] Persistent use of racial stereotypes also contributes to alienation of Black communities. **Racial stereotyping** is "projecting assumptions or expectations about the likely capacities and behaviors of members of a racial or ethnic group onto members of that group."[24] Stereotypes include assuming that Blacks and Latinxs are less intelligent, are more likely to live off welfare, and are difficult to get along with. Whites, when outwardly asked, will often say they do not believe or subscribe to such stereotypes, but research indicates that such stereotypes still affect Whites' interactions with people of color, including their willingness to be in proximity to or have relationships with people of color.[25] The lack of ameliorative policies, combined with beliefs in the cultural inferiority of Blacks, maintains severe racial inequality.

Blacks and Whites neither see nor understand this racial discrimination in the same manner. Blacks are more likely to see discrimination when Whites do not and are more likely to understand discrimination as an institutional problem. When Whites see racism, they view it as a problem of an individual instance, whereas Blacks are more likely to understand racism as reflected in the broad patterns of inequality. Blacks are also more likely than Whites to feel racial discrimination as personally important and emotionally pressing.[26] Thus, even the difference in how racism is comprehended and felt indicates the pressing problem of racism.

Laissez-Faire Racism

Laissez-faire racism does not maintain that racism is the only factor that constricts opportunities or is the central issue for Blacks (or other communities of color), but it does identify racism as a persistent and widespread problem. The historical analysis shows how changes in structure, combined with the liberatory push by Black Civil Rights Movement leaders and organizers, led to the collapse of Jim Crow but not the destruction of racism. Using Blumer's theoretical approach of prejudice as group position, laissez-faire racism shows that Whites still understand their group position as superior and therefore neither want nor will support government policies to create status equality with Blacks. Bobo maintains that racism is a "deeply, deeply rooted feature of US culture, the fashioning of our most basic institutions, of how we conceive of many, many things including what we regard as sources of truth versus falsehood, ugliness versus beauty, purity versus pollution and debasement."[27] In other words, racism still characterizes U.S. society.

In this new era, Black communities are dispersed residentially and economically so that racial gaps aren't easily seen as consequences of segregation but instead are viewed as natural outcomes of a capitalist market and the lack of good decisions by Black communities to uplift themselves. Bobo, Kluegel, and Smith describe **laissez-faire racism** as a new ideology that

> concedes basic citizenship rights to African Americans; however, it takes as legitimate extant patterns of black-white socioeconomic inequality and residential segregation, viewing these conditions, as it does, not as the deliberate products of racial discrimination, but as outcomes of a free-market, race-neutral state apparatus and the freely taken actions of African Americans themselves.[28]

In this new era, Whites now rationalize inequality based on their view of Blacks as culturally inferior. For example, the contemporary pay gap or employment gap is now seen as a result of companies hiring and paying the "best people" and best correlates with White employees. Laissez-faire theory explains how Whites can openly support statements of racial equality while helping sustain and ignore racism; in essence, "many Americans have become comfortable with as much racial segregation and inequality as a putatively nondiscriminatory polity and free-market economy can produce … enormous racial inequalities thus persist and are rendered culturally palatable by the new laissez-faire racism."[29]

How to Challenge Racism

A pathway to challenging racism is embedded in this theory's analysis of the shift from Jim Crow racism to laissez-faire racism. This theory posits that Jim Crow racism ended in relation to changes in economic and political structures; thus, another similar structural shift would be necessary to challenge contemporary laissez-faire racism. Specifically, Bobo and Smith state that change is possible if three factors are present: (1) The economic conditions have to favor chances for redistribution; (2) there must be widespread change in opinions and attitudes that reflect sympathy for the status of Blacks, at least by cultural elites; and (3) innovative organizing and resources emerge, along with leaders and movements to sustain the change.[30] If these economic conditions, outlooks among elites, and political strategies align, a coordinated government change that challenges racism is possible. Yet Bobo and Smith recognize that even if all the conditions are met, it's still possible that race and racism will be reconfigured in a way that sustains racial inequality. They argue that "only if racial identities, racialized social conditions (e.g., segregation), and the commitment to group position that such identities and conditions foster are directly reshaped would we avoid merely reconstituting racial inequality in a fashion that parallels the shift from Jim Crow racism to laissez-faire racism."[31] Therefore, only with a significant restructuring, along with a dedication to egalitarian group positions, would a serious challenge to racism exist.

By the Numbers

- Among those who say that being Black hurts people's ability to get ahead, 54% of Whites say that racial discrimination is a major reason, compared to 84% of Blacks.

- Sixteen percent of Whites and 54% of Blacks say that Blacks are treated less fairly than Whites on the job or at work, and 16% of Whites and 44% of Blacks say that Blacks are treated less fairly than Whites in stores or restaurants.

- Forty-three percent of Whites say that the federal government should take additional steps to reduce school segregation, compared to 78% of Blacks and 76% of Hispanics.

Sources: Drake (2014); Horowitz, Brown, and Cox (2019); McCarthy (2019).

Evaluation

Methodological Benefits

The theory of laissez-faire racism relies on two main types of data: historical data and survey data. The historical analysis is a synthesis of research conducted by Aldon Morris, Doug McAdam, and Jack Bloom and brings to the fore important details, such as the rise of synthetic fiber, which lowered the demand for cotton plantations, and the increase in NAACP chapters and Black college students, which led to more movement activists. These historical data provide valuable insight into the political and economic interests of the Jim Crow system and why those interests altered. The second main type of data is derived from surveys that inquire into racial attitudes. Much of these data are derived from the General Social Survey, a survey relied on by numerous social researchers, as "it is the only full-probability, personal-interview survey designed to monitor changes in both social characteristics and attitudes currently being conducted in the United States."[32] Data also come from the 1985 book *Racial Attitudes in America: Trends and Interpretations* by Howard Schuman, Charlotte Steeh, and Lawrence Bobo. This book was highly praised for its sophisticated analysis and testing of survey data drawn from three major organizations: Gallup, the National Opinion Research Center, and the Institute for Social Research. Both historical data and survey data are used in a methodologically rigorous manner to illuminate the complexities of contemporary White racial attitudes and beliefs.

Methodological Limitations

In the presentation and analysis of survey data, the differences in attitudes between people living in Northern versus Southern regions, educated versus less educated, and younger versus older Whites are acknowledged. This disparity is largely set aside with the provision that although there are regional, educational, and age differences, there is also a widespread pattern in survey results that generally characterizes Whites. Although this widespread pattern is apparent, choosing not to include in detail regional, educational, and age differences potentially obfuscates important distinctions among Whites, such as those who are willing to support racial parity or those who still hold overtly racist attitudes and beliefs.

A second limitation is a reliance on surveys to indicate Whites' sentiments on racism. Surveys can be unreliable, as people may feel pressure to provide socially conditioned answers, and there is the potential problem of attitudes not aligning with action. Bobo, Kluegel, and Smith are aware of this criticism and admit the limitation of attitudinal surveys while arguing that racial attitudes still capture a pivotal measure of preferred group positioning. In this vein, it is important to acknowledge that surveys of attitudes have limitations in what they can assess, while also recognizing that survey responses can reveal important patterns.

Theoretical Benefits

The theory of laissez-faire racism is built on three interconnected areas of analysis: the fall of Jim Crow, prejudice as group position, and survey data. The theoretical integration of these areas provides a robust analysis that leads to the conclusion that an era of laissez-faire racism has arrived. In particular, the historical material analysis provides a strong theoretical assessment of why Jim Crow racism fell and how this change in structure then resulted in a change in individual attitudes. Other theories of racism do not assess as clearly or directly why the ideological racism of Jim Crow greatly faded.

This theory also provides a novel assessment of Whites' survey answers. Bobo, Kluegel, and Smith provide the theoretical distinction between survey questions on attitude versus survey questions on implementation (e.g., policy, practice) or social distance (proximity to or intimacy with other racial groups). Whites show support for principle questions but relatively little support for racial policies or desire for proximity to Blacks. Identification of this pattern helps resolve the conundrum over the gap between Whites' increasingly positive responses to attitude questions existing alongside persistent racism.

Theoretical Limitations

This theory largely speaks to anti-Black sentiment and the ideological move from seeing Blacks as biologically inferior to viewing Blacks as culturally inferior. Other communities of color, however, are only briefly touched on. This theory does not speak in any significant degree to non-Black communities of color. This omission is notable, considering the particular attention paid to the Civil Rights Movement era when other communities of color, such as Native Americans and Latinxs, also led movements for freedom. These other racial movements also affected political and economic structures, as well as Whites' attitudes. To examine Whites' racial attitudes of Blacks isolated from analysis of other communities of color limits insights into how attitudes toward Blacks are shaped and affected by the relative group positioning of all races within the racial hierarchy.

Another limitation is in relation to the focus on prejudice; laissez-faire racism aims to move away from the analytical focus on individual psychological disposition through the focus on prejudice as rooted in group position. Yet Eduardo Bonilla-Silva (see Chapter 11 on color-blind racism) still critiques laissez-faire racism for "retaining the notion of prejudice and its psychological baggage rooted in interracial hostility." Bonilla-Silva argues that laissez-faire racism pays too much attention to individual emotion and affect, noting that the existence of White animosity toward people of color does not affect the persistence of systemic White privilege.[33]

Conclusion

Laissez-faire racism explains the transition from a Jim Crow racism, characterized by strict, widespread segregation and beliefs of biological inferiority, to a post–Jim Crow era, characterized by antidiscrimination laws and a nationally dispersed Black population existing alongside persistent beliefs in the cultural inferiority of Blacks. Rather than racism disappearing with the collapse of Jim Crow, racism evolved to meet the new structural and institutional arrangements of society and the ideology of a capitalist, free-market system. Bobo continues to depict the contemporary era as one of laissez-faire racism, "where longstanding values of meritocracy, individualism, majority rule and competition in a free marketplace weave together as rationalization for persistent inequality in a putatively anti-discrimination, race-neutral democratic state."[34]

REFLECT AND DISCUSS

1. How can one support racial equality yet at the same time feel that their group is threatened?

2. Describe the connection between shifts in economic and political structures with shifts in attitudes.

3. Explain the difference between a principle question and an implementation question.

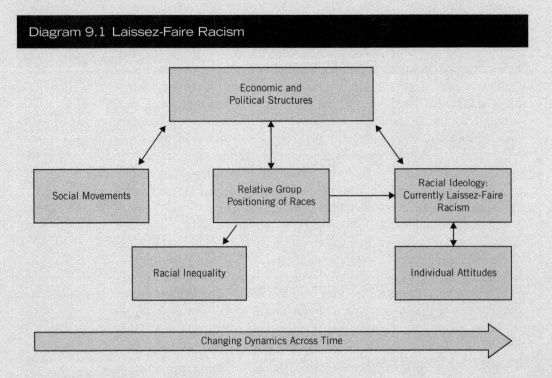

Diagram 9.1 Laissez-Faire Racism

KEY TERMS

Implementation questions: "What actions, usually by government (and, especially, the federal government), ought to be taken to bring about integration, to prevent discrimination, and to achieve greater equality."[35]

Laissez-faire racism: "This new ideology concedes basic citizenship rights to African Americans; however, it takes as legitimate extant patterns of black-white socioeconomic inequality and residential segregation, viewing these conditions, as it does, not as the deliberate products of racial discrimination, but as outcomes of a free-market, race-neutral state apparatus, and the freely taken actions of African Americans themselves."[36]

Prejudice as group position: "Places a subjective, interactively and socially created, and historically emergent set of ideas about appropriate status relations between groups at the center of any analysis of racial attitudes … a sense among members of the dominant racial group of proprietary claim or entitlement to greater resources and status and, second, a perception of threat posed by subordinate racial group members to those entitlements."[37]

Principle questions: "Whether U.S. society should be integrated or segregated and engage in equal treatment of individuals without regard to race."[38]

Racial attitudes: "Aspects of the preferred group positions and those patterns of belief and feeling that undergird, justify, and make understandable a preference for relatively little group differentiation and inequality under some social conditions, or for a great deal of differentiation and inequality among others."[39]

Racial stereotyping: "Projecting assumptions or expectations about the likely capacities and behaviors of members of a racial or ethnic group onto members of that group."[40]

Racism: "An ideology of racial domination or exploitation that (1) incorporates beliefs in a particular race's cultural and or inherent biological inferiority and (2) uses such beliefs to justify and prescribe inferior treatment for that group."[41]

Social distance questions: "The individual's willingness to personally enter hypothetical contact settings in schools or neighborhoods where the proportions of blacks to whites vary from virtually all white to heavily black."[42]

KEY PEOPLE

Lawrence Bobo (1958–): Bobo is the W. E. B. Du Bois Professor of the Social Sciences at Harvard University in Boston. He is a founding editor of the top journal *Du Bois Review: Social Science Research on Race*. Among several elite recognitions, Bobo is a member of the National Academy of Science and a Guggenheim Fellow. Twitter @lawrence_bobo

James Kluegel (1947–): Kluegel is Emeritus Professor of Sociology at the University of Illinois at Urbana–Champaign, where he was also Chair of the department for 15 years. He

is known for his work on surveying views on social stratification and is the coauthor or coeditor of five books.

Ryan Smith (1962–): Smith is Associate Professor in the Austin W. Marxe School of Public and International Affairs of Baruch College in New York City; from 2012 to 2015, he was the Lillie and Nathan Ackerman Chair of Social Justice. He is widely recognized for his research lectures on workplace stratification and racial attitudes in America.

WORKS CITED AND FURTHER READING

Bobo, Lawrence. 1983. "Whites' Opposition to Busing: Symbolic Racism or Realistic Group Conflict?" *Journal of Personality and Social Psychology* 45(6):1196–210.

Bobo, Lawrence. 2001. "Racial Attitudes and Relations at the Close of the Twentieth Century." Pp. 264–301 in *America Becoming: Racial Trends and Their Consequences,* vol. 1, edited by N. J. Smelser, W. J. Wilson, and F. Mitchell. Washington, DC: National Academies Press.

Bobo, Lawrence D. 2017. "Racism in Trump's America: Reflections on Culture, Sociology, and the 2016 US Presidential Election." *The British Journal of Sociology* 68(S1):S85–104.

Bobo, Lawrence, James R. Kluegel, and Ryan A. Smith. 1997. "Laissez-Faire Racism: The Crystallization of a Kinder, Gentler, Antiblack Ideology." Pp. 15–42 in *Racial Attitudes in the 1990s: Continuity and Change,* edited by S. A. Tuch and J. K. Martin. Westport, CT: Praeger.

Bobo, Lawrence and Ryan Smith. 1998. "From Jim Crow Racism to Laissez Faire Racism: The Transformation of Racial Attitudes." Pp. 182–220 in *Beyond Pluralism: The Conception of Groups and Group Identities in America,* edited

by W. F. Katkin, N. Landsman, and A. Tyree. Urbana: University of Illinois Press.

Bonilla-Silva, Eduardo. 2003. *Racism Without Racists: Color-Blind Racism and the Persistence of Racial Inequality in America.* Lanham, MD: Rowman and Littlefield.

Drake, Bruce. 2014. "The Civil Rights Act at 50: Racial Divides Persist on How Much Progress Has Been Made." *Fact Tank*, April 9. Washington, DC: Pew Research Center.

Horowitz, Juliana Menasce, Anna Brown, and Kiana Cox. 2019. "Race in America 2019." Washington, DC: Pew Research Center.

Kinder, Donald R. and David O. Sears. 1981. "Prejudice and Politics: Symbolic Racism versus Racial Threats to the Good Life." *Journal of Personality and Social Psychology* 40(3):414–31.

McCarthy, Justin. 2019. "Most Americans Say Segregation in Schools a Serious Problem." Washington, DC: Gallup Poll.

NORC at the University of Chicago. 2016. "About the General Social Survey." Retrieved February 25, 2020 (https://gss.norc.org/About-The-GSS).

NOTES

1. Bobo and Smith (1998).
2. Ibid. (123).
3. Bobo, Kluegel, and Smith (1997:16).
4. Ibid. (17)
5. Bobo (2001:292).
6. Kinder and Sears (1981).
7. Bobo et al. (1997); Bobo and Smith (1998).
8. Bobo et al. (1997).
9. Ibid.
10. Ibid. (38–39).
11. Ibid. (31).
12. Ibid. (39).
13. Ibid. (16).
14. Ibid. (38).
15. Ibid. (22).
16. Ibid. (38).
17. Ibid. (38).
18. Ibid. (22).
19. Ibid. (22).
20. Ibid. (39).
21. Bobo and Smith (1998:211).
22. Bobo et al. (1997:39–41).
23. Bobo and Smith (1998:190).

24. Bobo (2001:275).
25. Bobo (2001:275); Bobo and Smith (1998).
26. Bobo (2001:284–85).
27. Bobo (2017:S89).
28. Bobo et al. (1997:38).
29. Bobo and Smith (1998:213).
30. Ibid. (214).
31. Ibid.
32. NORC at the University of Chicago (2016).
33. Bonilla-Silva (2003:7–8).
34. Bobo (2017:S91).
35. Bobo et al. (1997:23).
36. Ibid. (38).
37. Ibid. (22).
38. Ibid. (23).
39. Ibid. (38–39).
40. Bobo (2001:275).
41. Bobo, Kluegel, and Smith's definition of *racism* is taken from William Julius Wilson's 1973 book *Power, Racism, and Privilege: Race Relations in Theoretical and Sociohistorical Perspectives* (Bobo et al. 1997:17).
42. Bobo et al. (1997:23).

Structure and Culture

William Julius Wilson

Social scientific analyses of racism often focus on structural barriers or how institutions are arranged in ways that result in oppression of people of color. The role of how culture, as it is formed in relation to micro-communities that are racially segregated, has not received as much attention. This chapter relies on William Julius Wilson's perspective in *More Than Just Race,* where he proposes that a structure *and* culture framework should be used in examining racial inequality. Wilson particularly analyzes how low-income, inner-city Black communities have some distinctive cultural frameworks and traits that shape responses to structural barriers and therefore affect their social mobility, or lack thereof.*

---

*Photo of Wilson unavailable.

Why This Theory

At the turn of the 20th century, the social problems that people of color experienced, such as lower employment, income, and education, were predominantly seen by social scientists as the consequences of their own inferiority. Racist narratives about the superiority of Whites deemed people of color as biologically and culturally inferior. Yet scholars of racism, particularly scholars of color, knew that unequal racialized outcomes were not because people of color were inferior but because they were oppressed by inferior structural conditions. Social institutions such as education, employment, health, and housing were arranged so that people of color had few, if any, opportunities for social mobility. As the 20th century progressed, this perspective became more predominant among social scientists, and bio-cultural explanations for racial inequality faded as the reality of structural constraints became clear. People who continued to use cultural explanations were seen as "blaming the victim" for their own plight, and liberal analyses and policies avoided using culture as an explanatory variable. In fact, in 1965, when sociologist and politician Daniel Patrick Moynihan wrote a report on racial inequality that suggested Black families have a dysfunctional culture, there was an immediate and severe backlash against Moynihan for his use of culture as an explanatory variable.[1] Since then, racial inequality studies that implicate people of color for having flawed cultural values have largely been dismissed by liberals as bordering racist ideals.

In the 1980s and 1990s, sociologist William Julius Wilson published a series of books on studies of impoverished African American communities that were stuck in persistent poverty. In these books, he emphasizes racial and economic structural conditions that constrain low-income Blacks but argues that in the contemporary era, classism is more important than racism as the primary determinant in the oppression of poor Black communities. This emphasis on class over race received both considerable attention and criticism. Then in 2010, Wilson published *More Than Just Race: Being Black and Poor in the Inner City*, which continues the focus on oppressive racial and economic structures but adds a component on the role of culture in sustaining the status of poor Black communities. In earlier research, Wilson had described culture as a byproduct of structural conditions, while in this work, he aims to show how culture has some autonomous effect. In publishing this book, Wilson knew he was going to face some condemnation for analyzing the culture of low-income Black communities as an important variable; he writes:

> This book will likely generate controversy because I dare to take culture seriously as one of the explanatory variables in the study of race and urban poverty—a topic that is typically considered off-limits in academic discourse because of a fear that such analysis can be construed as "blaming the victim."[2]

Aware of this tension, Wilson aims for a nuanced perspective on culture by emphasizing structural explanations but showing where culture, as he says, "mediates" structure. Wilson suggests that culture should be considered in policy proposals that address Black poverty in order to "further our understanding of the complex and interrelated factors that continue to contribute to racial inequality."[3]

Description of the Theory

Wilson's argument on structure and culture focuses on impoverished Black communities with the aim to understand why intergenerational inner-city Black poverty is so persistent. In particular, he hones in on inner-city neighborhood conditions; the challenges faced by inner-city, low-income Black men; and single-parent, Black families. As stated earlier, Wilson uses a racial and class analysis; however, the primary contribution in *More Than Just Race* is the proposal of how culture plays an important role. He examines how culture mediates people's responses to the structure they experience and how sometimes these cultural responses are detrimental to their upward mobility. To show this role of culture, Wilson reviews structural conditions that restrict opportunities, followed by an analysis of culture that emerges from these conditions to show the interaction of structure and culture. However, Wilson takes a careful, balanced approach to this analysis; he writes: "In terms of major effects on immediate group social outcomes and racial stratification, structure trumps culture. Nevertheless, I firmly believe that to apply these explanations totally separately, without any attempt to show how they interact, is indeed a mistake."[4]

Structure

Social scientists who study structural racism look to any number of social institutions that are arranged in ways that afford opportunities to Whites and deny opportunities to people of color. Wilson defines **social structure** as "the way social positions, social roles, and networks of social relationships are arranged in our institutions, such as the economy, polity, education, and organization of the family," and an example is a "labor market that offers financial incentives and threatens financial punishments."[5] Within this analysis of structure, there are two types of "structural forces" that affect racial inequality: (1) social acts and (2) social processes. **Social acts** occur when individuals or groups use their power to deny equality, status, or opportunity to people of color. An example of a social act can be stereotyping or more active discrimination, such as denying a job or school admission. **Social processes** are "the 'machinery' of society that exists to promote ongoing relations among members of the larger group."[6] Examples of social processes are laws and policies that restrict people of color, such as residential segregation, or more covert practices, such as school tracking and racial profiling. Ideologies that sustain belief in the differences in racial groups are embedded in these social acts and social processes. Wilson analyzes social acts and social processes that are explicitly racist, those that are partly imbued with racial motives, and those that appear to be nonracial on the surface but in reality have direct negative consequences for people of color. He examines all three types because he points out how policies that appear nonracial on the surface are often overlooked, even though they have more racial consequences than presumed. In this analysis, Wilson looks at two main areas: (1) the conditions of inner-city neighborhoods and (2) the issues that low-skilled Black men encounter.

Poor inner-city neighborhoods tend to sustain intergenerational poverty due to specific institutional arrangements and the consequences of state and federal policies. For example, policies on road infrastructure, though they appear to be nonracial, as highways are a part of city growth, can have severe racialized consequences. When decisions are made to construct highways through Black neighborhoods, the results include a loss of neighborhood networks and employment opportunities and an increase in racial segregation, as roads operate as neighborhood barriers. Another example Wilson uses is the reduction of federal aid to cities with large Black populations; the loss of federal funds results in dire conditions, as seen in the detrimental living conditions in city public housing.

The second area Wilson focuses on are the problems facing unemployed Black men. This demographic is usually counted by using the U.S. Census unemployment rate as defined by those who are actively seeking a job, but Wilson expands the definition of unemployment to include those who are unemployed *and* to those who are jobless because they have left the labor market for any number of reasons. For example, in 2008, "the official unemployment rate among men of ages twenty-five to fifty-four was 4.1 percent, but the jobless rate was 13.1 percent. This larger number includes millions of adult males who are not recorded in official U.S. labor market statistics, either because they are not looking for a job or because they are incarcerated."[7] Wilson explains this jobless rate is shaped by structural forces such as decreased demand for low-skilled labor spurred by use of computers, a decreasing manufacturing sector, an increase in globalization and outsourcing of jobs, and an increase in service industries. All these changes have consequences for the opportunities of inner-city Black men. For example, working-class Black communities historically relied on manufacturing jobs and unions for stable jobs and pay, but the move of manufacturing plants abroad and increased reliance on computers have drastically decreased these entry-level, low-skill jobs. Other practices and policies, such as school tracking that keeps Black students in lower-performing classes and racial profiling by police, limit the opportunities for Black men.

Culture

In a traditional use of culture, conservatives cling to a cultural explanation of outcomes because it emphasizes the decisions that individuals make rather than the structural forces that create unequal conditions. For example, conservatives often say that communities develop a culture that supports dropping out of high school instead of understanding that low-income high schools do not provide the resources needed for a successful education. Contrary to this narrow view of culture, Wilson makes a more nuanced examination, as he does not depict culture as independent of structure, nor does he see it as more important than structural forces. Instead, Wilson analyzes how inner-city Black culture shapes responses to racism and poverty and how these responses sometimes hinder upward mobility.

Culture is often studied by analyzing a group's norms, values, and attitudes, but Wilson expands the definition of **culture** to the

> sharing of outlooks and modes of behavior among individuals who face similar place-based circumstances (such as poor segregated neighborhoods) or have the same social networks (as when members of particular racial or ethnic groups share a particular way of understanding social life and cultural scripts that guide their behavior).[8]

Wilson further expands this definition by outlining two types of **cultural forces**: (1) "national views and beliefs on race" and (2) "cultural traits—shared outlooks, modes of behavior, traditions, belief systems, worldviews, skills, preferences, styles of self-presentation, etiquette, and linguistic patterns—that emerge from patterns of intragroup interaction in settings created by discrimination and segregation and that reflect collective experiences within those settings."[9]

In the first case, national views and beliefs on race are described as the ways that negative, biased beliefs about people of color become dominant and widely held, to the point that it leads to discriminatory actions. Whites hold cultural beliefs about the inferiority of Blacks because racism has been and continues to be a major cultural frame of the United States. **Racism** is

> an ideology of racial domination with two key features: 1) beliefs that one race is either biologically or culturally inferior to another and 2) the use of such beliefs to rationalize or prescribe the way that the "inferior" race should be treated in this society, as well as to explain its social position as a group and its collective accomplishments.[10]

When Whites subscribe to this cultural frame, that is, racism, ideologies about the inferiority of people of color and racial discrimination are perpetuated. For example, with the case of inner-city neighborhoods, racist cultural beliefs depict residents as lazy and living off welfare. Despite the structural barriers in low-income neighborhoods, racist cultural frames still depict the neighborhoods as having the basic ingredients for success, such as schools and housing, so lack of mobility is blamed on the individual rather than on structural oppression. In the case of unemployed Black men, racist ideologies purport that inner-city Black men are dishonest and lazy, which is why they are less likely to be hired or promoted. Wilson cites a study that his research team conducted in the late 1980s that found that the majority of employers felt that inner-city Black men were "uneducated, uncooperative, unstable, or dishonest."[11]

The second type of cultural force, cultural traits, seeks to capture the ways in which racial groups, in this case low-income Black communities, may cultivate a cultural frame that emerges from the micro society they occupy. Wilson refers to this cultural force as

> shared outlooks, traditions, belief systems, worldviews, preferences, manners, linguistic patterns, clothing styles, and modes of behavior in the inner-city ghetto. These traits are embodied in the micro-level processes of meaning making and decision making—that is, the way individuals in segregated communities develop an understanding of how the world works and make decisions and choices that reflect that understanding.[12]

This definition of culture includes "processes of meaning making and decision making" that are relative to particular segregated communities and is a point that Wilson emphasizes; it is this understanding of culture that lays the foundation for Wilson's argument that culture plays a role in sustaining inequality. For example, if a community cultivates a shared cultural belief that Whites are dishonest, when opportunities arise sponsored by a White organization, they may be turned down.

In analyzing neighborhoods and unemployment among Black men, Wilson uses the example of a "code of the streets," which includes cultivating cultural strategies such as avoiding eye contact and being skeptical of people. These strategies can be logical when living in an unsafe neighborhood but may not help when trying to get a job. Thus, Wilson explains that a culture that developed as a source of protection from an oppressive environment may then end up perpetuating one's social position. Wilson posits that "even though these codes emerge under conditions of poverty and racial segregation, once developed they display a degree of autonomy in the regulation of behavior. The behavior generated by these autonomous cultural forces often reinforces the very conditions that have emerged from structural inequities."[13] Another example Wilson uses to exhibit how cultural frames are used to assign meaning and make decisions is through his summary of Sandra Smith's findings in her book *Lone Pursuit*. Her study reveals that inner-city Black men were less likely to rely on their informal network and personal referrals to get a job for two reasons: (1) The men didn't give referrals, for fear it would go awry, or (2) men did not seek referrals from friends, to avoid the potential shaming of being unemployed. Referrals and networks are important ways of finding and getting jobs, so this culture of non-referral can have a significant effect on Black unemployment. In both of these cases, Wilson explains that structural conditions led to poor neighborhood conditions and unemployment, which then led to cultural worldviews that then shaped decisions in how to respond to the structural inequality; in this manner, there is a feedback loop between structure and culture wherein culture develops a role in this process. This autonomy of culture is why Wilson argues that culture should be recognized as a variable in explaining persistent inequality.

Structure Plus Culture

Wilson repeatedly states that structure has a greater effect on inequality than does culture but also maintains that it is vital to understand the important ways in which culture is part of persistent Black poverty. In considering culture as a significant variable in analyzing social inequality, Wilson states that an

> exploration of the cultural dimension must do three things: 1) provide a compelling reason for including cultural factors in a comprehensive discussion of race and poverty, 2) show the relationship between cultural analysis and structural analysis, and 3) determine the extent to which cultural factors operate independently to contribute to or reinforce poverty and racial inequality.[14]

Wilson exemplifies his consideration of culture within a structural analysis in a chapter on Black families. Traditional structural analyses of the barriers facing Black families emphasize institutional conditions, such as poorly performing schools, little access to quality healthcare, and economically-racially segregated neighborhoods that provide few opportunities for jobs. A traditional culture argument, on the other hand, emphasizes familial or neighborhood values that permit teenage sexual activity, low rates of parental involvement in schooling, and little value on marriage or stable relationships. Wilson's structure-culture approach integrates these two arguments and more accurately shows how cultural values are used to respond to structural forces faced by low-income Black families.

Wilson applies his structure-culture approach to analyze why low-income Black families continue to have relatively high rates of single motherhood, high rates of teenage pregnancy, and low rates of marriage. It is a structure-culture interaction: Having few job opportunities results in economic instability, which is connected to fewer marriages; then the lack of financial stability and marriages can lead to a culture that doesn't place a high value on marriage and condones having children outside of marriage. Wilson explains this relationship as follows: "Discouraging economic conditions tend to reinforce any tolerance for having children without marriage or even partnering. The weaker the norms are against premarital sex, out-of-wedlock pregnancy, and nonmarital parenthood, the more economic considerations affect decisions to marry."[15] In this manner, the structural conditions lead to cultural values that are rooted in the experiences of this structural inequality; these cultural values then continue to shape responses to the structural inequality that Black families encounter.

Wilson provides another example of this structure-culture relationship by looking at the perpetuation of Black child poverty in single-Black-mother households. Given the economic conditions of the neighborhoods, Black women may develop a cultural belief that it isn't necessary to have a permanent partner in order to have children. This decision to be a single mother then inadvertently increases the chances of children remaining in poverty because single-parent children often do not have resources equal to those of two-parent households. In showing how culture shapes responses to structure, Wilson reveals that there is an iterative effect between structure and culture, where culture can end up reinforcing structural conditions. By highlighting this iterative process, Wilson explains some of the persistent patterns among low-income Black families.

How to Challenge Racism

Wilson positions his theoretical analysis between liberals who emphasize structure over culture and conservatives who emphasize culture over structure; his integration of structure and culture is with the specific purpose of providing a more holistic analysis for policy makers to use when addressing issues affecting inner-city Black communities. Yet Wilson is aware that cultural arguments are more seductive to policy makers and the public alike, as they put the burden of change on the individuals facing the barriers, rather than on society and policy. In his closing chapter, Wilson explicitly recognizes this challenge:

> Beliefs that attribute joblessness and poverty to individual short-comings do not engender strong support for social programs to end inequality. But in addressing the problem of structural inequities, it would not be wise to leave the impression in public discussions that cultural problems do not matter. Indeed, proposals to address racial inequality should reflect awareness of the inextricable link between aspects of structure and culture.[16]

Thus, Wilson urges academics and policy makers to be careful with cultural explanations while moving forward with an *integration* of culture into proposals that address structural barriers. In addition to this call to use structure and culture in policy, Wilson states that lawmakers should also directly address unique racial and class struggles, rather than solely relying on a one-size-fits-all approach. This suggestion to create policies that are specific to racial and economic circumstances is contrary to popular beliefs that policies should be color-blind; indeed, this recommendation by Wilson reveals a shift in his own thinking, as he previously recommended general uplift policies, and therefore is an important factor in his perspective on how to challenge racism.

- Forty-seven percent of Black children live with a single mom, and 23% of Hispanic, 13% of White, and 7% of Asian children do so.

- Between 2007 and 2017 in Shreveport, Louisiana, there were 726 arrests for illegal saggy pants, and 96% of those arrested were Black men.

- Blacks are the largest racial group of extremely low-income renter households, at 35%, followed by Hispanics at 29%, Asians at 24%, and Whites at 21%.

Sources: Livingston (2018); MacNeil (2019); National Low Income Housing Coalition (2018).

Evaluation

Methodological Benefits

Wilson synthesizes research from the past few decades with some of his own research that he conducted in the 1980s. He does not use primary data collection to test his theory; rather, by reviewing previous studies, he makes the argument that research reveals that there are both structural and cultural forces at play in producing racial inequality. Within this useful and tailored review of work, Wilson makes sure to highlight specific data rather than over-generalizations of findings. He provides detailed data from studies by leading scholars such as Elijah Anderson, Jennifer Hochschild, Devah Pager, Robert Sampson, Bruce Western, and Alford Young Jr. He also combines the data from these studies with historical policies and practices that have contributed to contemporary racial inequality. For instance, he notes the Wagner-Steagall Housing Act of 1937, which affected the availability of public housing; the $4 billion of state aid that New York City lost from 1980 to 1989; the change in how many workers used a computer on the job in 1984 compared to 2003; and the decline in industry, which led to the end of the Second Great Migration from the South to the North. The synthesis of research and historical context is supplemented by current statistics on important indicators such as unemployment, college degree attainment, and income levels. Wilson provides accessible and meaningful integration of data from his previous research, other leading studies, historical policies, and contemporary statistics.

Methodological Limitations

Wilson touches on many studies that analyze these institutions, but, perhaps given the length of the text, there are many significant structural barriers that are not addressed or not addressed in detail, such as research on incarceration, public housing, schools, transportation, health access, and more. However, a greater limitation is the inclusion of a narrow number of studies that support a cultural argument. Because (liberal) academic discourse has avoided cultural arguments, there is not the same amount, in quantity or quality, of research that can be used to support Wilson's description of cultural forces. Although this point is not the fault of Wilson, making a strong argument for the inclusion of culture requires a rigorous method and data to support it. It is difficult to make a strong argument on how inner-city Black communities have a particular culture that mediates their structure without more research that confirms this perspective. The reliance on other studies' findings that do not have Wilson's exact theoretical approach in mind makes the methodology less substantial.

Theoretical Benefits

This theory brings together the interactive effects that structure and culture have on one another in a fair and balanced manner. As noted earlier, it can be difficult to study culture without seemingly "blaming the victim" for the inequality that people of color experience. Wilson largely avoids this potential misstep by emphasizing two points: (1) that structure is the larger, more determining force and (2) that culture serves as mediator, rather than a singular, driving factor. To the first point, Wilson recounts the numerous structural barriers that Black communities face and that must be addressed before racial equality can be attained. To the second point, culture has a broad definition, including shared outlooks and worldviews that shape meaning making. In this sense, culture serves as a framework that people use to make sense of their micro social world and helps them make decisions that align with that perspective. Thus, rather than seeing culture as a force that unilaterally dictates outcomes, this theory illuminates how culture is in an iterative relationship with structure. Through this use of structure and culture, this theory reveals how culture can be an important factor to consider in assessing and addressing inequality.

Theoretical Limitations

Wilson's two main goals are to explain how culture operates in persistent Black poverty and why it should be considered in policy analysis. Wilson does provide a theoretical explanation as to how culture operates, but his judgment of culture is just that—a judgment. He comments on how poor Black inner-city men have sexual relationships with women and have children without marriage, but in a review of this book, Deirdre Royster points out that this culture of encouraging men to have multiple sexual partners without commitment is common to American culture, not just that of inner-city Black men. Royster points to sexual relationships on college campuses as just one example of where men also have a culture of sex without commitment.[17] In this sense, Wilson does not recognize how hegemonic masculinity is embedded in the U.S. culture, not just in inner-city Black communities. Moreover, he does not recognize how this same culture has harsher consequences for those who occupy low statuses on racial and class hierarchies than those who occupy statuses at the top of social hierarchies. For example, Black men and White men can make the same exact choices, but consequences for these choices are often much more severe for Black men. In addition, Wilson's evaluation of sex and marriage doesn't account for changing mores and values that are not necessarily negative; marriage is a confining institution for many women, and national marriage rates are on the decline. Rather than evaluating the negative consequences of not marrying, one might suggest modifying policies so that people are not penalized for having children outside of marriage.

Wilson's second goal is to create a structure and culture framework that would be accessible for and persuasive to policy makers. Yet while he shows a relationship between structure and culture, he doesn't make clear how policy makers should address culture. Recognizing that there are ways in which inner-city Black communities' culture mediates structure is a significant contribution, but what to do with that information is ambiguous. He also has relatively little analysis on how Whites have a culture of racism, which greatly affects Blacks' opportunities for employment, education, health, politics, and more.

Conclusion

Wilson embarks on a difficult path in his argument to include culture in examinations and explanations of persistent Black poverty. He expands on classic definitions of culture, he challenges long-held liberal hesitations to include culture as a variable, he engages with the problem of addressing culture while not feeding into conservative conversations that blame individuals, and he aims to engage policy makers in his theory of structure-culture interaction. Wilson balances these tensions and addresses these problems to provide a meaningful theoretical perspective on the interaction of structure and culture. While this work is focused on inner-city, low-income Black communities, this theoretical perspective pushes the dialogue forward on how to address the vexing intricacies of contemporary racism among any racial group.

REFLECT AND DISCUSS

1. Explain the interaction between structure and culture.

2. How can an analysis of culture lead to placing blame on the individual?

3. How can racial and class segregation result in the development of distinct cultural worldviews?

Diagram 10.1 Structure Plus Culture

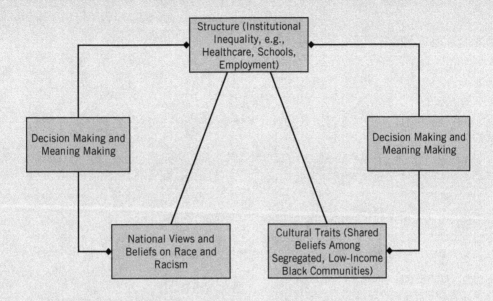

KEY TERMS

Cultural forces: (1) "National views and beliefs on race" and (2) "cultural traits—shared outlooks, modes of behavior, traditions, belief systems, worldviews, skills, preferences, styles of self-presentation, etiquette, and linguistic patterns—that emerge from patterns of intragroup interaction in settings created by discrimination and segregation and that reflect collective experiences within those settings."[18]

Culture: "Sharing of outlooks and modes of behavior among individuals who face similar place-based circumstances (such as poor segregated neighborhoods) or have the same social networks (as when members of particular racial or ethnic groups share a particular way of understanding social life and cultural scripts that guide their behavior)."[19]

Racism: "An ideology of racial domination with two key features: 1) beliefs that one race is either biologically or culturally inferior to another and 2) the use of such beliefs to rationalize or prescribe the way that the 'inferior' race should be treated in this society, as well as to explain its social position as a group and its collective accomplishments."[20]

Social acts: "The behavior of individuals within society."[21]

Social processes: "The 'machinery' of society that exists to promote ongoing relations among members of the larger group."[22]

Social structure: "The way social positions, social roles, and networks of social relationships are arranged in our institutions, such as the economy, polity, education, and organization of the family."[23]

KEY PEOPLE

William Julius Wilson (1935–): Wilson is the Lewis P. and Linda L. Geyser University Professor at Harvard University and previously led the Center for the Study of Urban Inequality at the

University of Chicago. Wilson is well known for his many award-winning books on race and class. He became a MacArthur Fellow in 1987, was named president of the American Sociological Association in 1990, served as a member of President Clinton's Commission on White House Fellowships from 1994 to 2001, and was awarded the National Medal of Science in 1998.

Wilsons' the Joblessness and Urban Poverty Research Program: https://jup.hks.harvard.edu/about

WORKS CITED AND FURTHER READING ——————

Livingston, Gretchen. 2018. "About One-Third of US Children Are Living with an Unmarried Parent." Washington, DC: Pew Research Center.

MacNeil, Sarah. 2019. "After Shooting of Black Man, Louisiana City Votes to End Sagging Pants Law." *Shreveport Times*, June 12.

National Low Income Housing Coalition. 2018. "The Gap: A Shortage of Affordable Homes." Washington, DC: Author.

Royster, Deirdre. 2010. "Review: More Than Just Race: If We're Going to Study Culture, Let's Get It Right." *Sociological Forum* 25(2):386–90.

Small, Mario L., David J. Harding, and Michèle Lamont. 2010. "Reconsidering Culture and Poverty." *The ANNALS of the American Academy of Political and Social Science* 629(1):6–27.

Wilson, William Julius. 2009. *More Than Just Race: Being Black and Poor in the Inner City.* New York: W. W. Norton and Company.

Wilson, William Julius. 2010. "Why Both Structure and Culture Matter in a Holistic Analysis of Inner-City Poverty." *The ANNALS of the American Academy of Political and Social Science* 629(1):200–219.

Wilson, William Julius. 2012. *The Truly Disadvantaged: The Inner City, the Underclass, and Public Policy.* 2nd ed. Chicago: University of Chicago Press.

See also Book Review Symposium on *More Than Just Race* by William Julius Wilson. 2010. *Sociological Forum* 25(2):375–94.

NOTES ——————

1. Wilson (2009).
2. Ibid. (3).
3. Ibid.
4. Ibid. (21).
5. Ibid. (4).
6. Ibid. (5).
7. Ibid. (65).
8. Ibid. (4).
9. Ibid. (14–15).
10. Ibid. (15).
11. Ibid. (73).
12. Ibid. (148).
13. Ibid. (134).
14. Ibid. (79).
15. Ibid. (116).
16. Ibid. (136).
17. Royster (2010).
18. Wilson (2009:14–15).
19. Ibid. (4).
20. Ibid. (15).
21. Ibid. (5).
22. Ibid.
23. Ibid. (4).

CHAPTER

11

Color-Blind Racism

Eduardo Bonilla-Silva

Today, when questioned about issues of race and racism, Whites often espouse a "color-blind" stance, a claim that race is not an important or driving factor in society. Eduardo Bonilla-Silva, in his book *Racism Without Racists* (now in its fifth edition, published in 2018), explains how Whites frame their language not to sound racist, even though they, knowingly or not, still defend their status at the top of the racial hierarchy. Bonilla-Silva refers to this racial ideology adopted by Whites as *color-blind racism* and shows how Whites' position at the top of the racial hierarchy informs their racial ideology and their day-to-day actions and beliefs.

Photo 11.1 Eduardo Bonilla-Silva

Source: https://sociology.duke.edu/ people/eduardo-bonilla-silva.

Why This Theory

Eduardo Bonilla-Silva proposes a theory of a "racialized social system," wherein a racial ideology is one facet of this system.[1] He refers to the contemporary racial ideology that Whites hold as "color-blind racism"; in his book *Racism Without Racists,* he analyzes how Whites openly endorse ideals of racial equality but continue to support White superiority.[2] The concept of color-blind racism is in response to three interrelated conversations: (1) a response to the dominant focus on racism as an individual psychological problem, (2) a response to perceived gaps in the theories of symbolic racism and laissez-faire racism, and (3) a response to the question of how to conceive of the shift from "old racism" to "new racism."

Bonilla-Silva responds to a dominant perspective on racism that emphasizes a psychological framework and that defines racism as a set of ideas or beliefs. Instead, Bonilla-Silva suggests a materialist and structural approach to the study of racism. His theory is that of a "racialized social system," which refers to "societies in which economic, political, social, and ideological levels are partially structured by the placement of actors in racial categories or races," so that "in all racialized social systems the placement of people in racial categories involves some form of hierarchy that produces definite social relations between the races."[3] Thus, society is structured by a racial hierarchy wherein Whites benefit from occupying the top of this hierarchy and where the racial ideology they hold reflects this material reality.

Bonilla-Silva's theory is also partially a response to two other major theories on contemporary racism: symbolic racism and laissez-faire racism. Sears and Kinder's theory of symbolic racism focuses on how Whites blame Blacks for their lack of upward mobility and how an anti-Black affect is central to contemporary racism. Laissez-faire racism, put forth by Bobo, Kluegel, and Smith, centers on Whites' dominant perception of Blacks as inferior and Whites' characterization of racial inequality as a problem of Blacks' deficient culture (see Chapter 9 on laissez-faire racism). Bonilla-Silva sees these two contemporary theories of racism as too rooted in "*individual psychological* dispositions" and therefore too caught up with individual prejudice, rather than an analysis of the system.[4] In contrast to these theories, Bonilla-Silva's theory of a "racialized social system" moves the analysis away from one of psychological dysfunction to an analysis of how people's views are tied to their placement in the system; he explains that "those at the bottom of the racial barrel tend to hold oppositional views and those who received the manifold wages of whiteness tend to hold views in support of the racial status quo."[5] This theoretical approach to racism aims not to criticize people who say racist things but rather to criticize the system that places people in different positions on the racial hierarchy; it is this position in the system that shapes their ideology on race and racism. As Whites occupy the top of the racial hierarchy and receive the material benefits of that position, they adhere to racist ideologies that support their status.

The third conversation contextualizing the emergence of this theory is understanding the shift from "old racism" to "new racism." Old racism is characterized by overt, blatant racism, as seen with malevolent laws and practices such as slavery, theft of tribal lands, segregation, and anti-immigration laws. New racism, of the contemporary era, exists within a society that has antiracism laws and a rhetoric of equality but manifests through unequal institutional arrangements and covert racial beliefs and practices. People of color continue to face significant racial inequality in areas such as pay, educational attainment, housing, and political representation. Bonilla-Silva thus asks: "How is it possible to have this tremendous degree of racial inequality in a country where most whites claim that race is no longer relevant? More important, how do whites explain the apparent contradiction between their professed color blindness and the United States' color-coded inequality?"[6] He suggests that the ideology that characterizes and explains how this "new racism" operates is that of **color-blind racism**. Color-blind racism "explains contemporary racial inequality as the outcome of nonracial dynamics … whites rationalize minorities' contemporary status as the product of market dynamics, naturally occurring phenomena, and blacks' imputed cultural limitations."[7] Color-blind racism thereby explains how Whites can claim "not to see color" but still support a racialized system wherein Whites are at the top of the racial hierarchy.

This chapter is on color-blind racism because it is commonly used in contemporary scholarship as a theory of racism. However, it is important to note that Bonilla-Silva's theory is that of the racialized social system, and color-blind racism, identified as the contemporary racial ideology, is only one facet of that theory.

Description of the Theory

The conceptualization of color-blind racism relies on Bonilla-Silva's specific definitions of racial structure, race, and racial ideology. *Racial structure*, or a *racialized social system*, is "*the totality of the social relations and practices that reinforce white privilege.*"[8] This social system formed with European colonialization and imperialism and the creation of "White" people and "non-White" people, the result of which was Whites being given systemic privileges. *Race*, then, is a social construction without any biological reality but with a definite social reality. Belonging to the "White" race means that one receives benefits and resources that those who are "non-White" do not receive. To continue receiving these benefits, Whites develop a racial ideology to defend their interests. A **racial ideology** is "*the racially based frameworks used by actors to explain and justify* (dominant race) or *challenge* (subordinate race or races) *the racial status quo.*"[9] Color-blind racism is the ideology that Whites currently use to justify their status and rationalize racial inequality.

Color-Blind Racism

Color-blind racism, as an ideology, consists of several elements: (1) frames, (2) styles, and (3) stories. **Frames** are the "*set paths for interpreting information*";[10] **styles** are "*the linguistic manners and rhetorical strategies (or race talk)*, to the technical tools that allow users to articulate its [the ideology's] frames and story lines";[11] and, **stories** "narrate status ... biases ... and beliefs about the social order ... and are important because they help us reinforce our arguments."[12] Each component of the ideology of color-blind racism works with the others to create a seamless racial ideology that is easily utilized by Whites.

Frames

Frames, as "*set paths for interpreting information*," help Whites filter information and aid them in rationalizing away racism. Bonilla-Silva identifies four frames: (1) abstract liberalism, (2) naturalization, (3) cultural racism, and (4) minimization of racism. **Abstract liberalism** points to how people use ideas of liberalism, such as equality of opportunity and freedom of choice, to explain their rejection of governmental policies intended to address racial inequality. For example, one rejects the use of Affirmative Action because racial preferences should not exist, or one opposes school busing because it denies families freedom of choice. This frame ignores the historical and contemporary racist conditions that led to current racial inequality and focuses on the idea that any policy that recognizes race is inherently unequal. In this vein, Whites can rely on a rhetoric of equality, such as "freedom of choice," to rationalize the existence of racially segregated schools.

The **naturalization** frame implies that racialized outcomes such as residential racial segregation or homogenous friendship groups are merely a result of an innate inclination for similar people to group together, not a consequence of racial forces. In reality, racial segregation is an outcome of policies and norms such as higher-interest rates on mortgages and steering practices by real estate agents, which push people of color out of communities. People of color also respond to racial discrimination by self-segregating into safe spaces. However, Whites use the naturalization frame to explain the existence of segregation through beliefs that people like to socialize with those who have common interests.

The third frame, **cultural racism**, relies on the idea that racial groups create and cultivate different norms and values, which is how Whites explain the lower social status of people of color. This frame is used to blame social outcomes such as low educational attainment, poor health, or high incarceration rates on non-Whites' "bad culture." For example, Whites say that Latinxs have families that are too large or that Blacks are more prone to violence. This frame places the blame on communities of color for their low socioeconomic status, instead of paying attention to racially biased structures that lead to these outcomes.

The fourth frame is **minimization of racism**, which, as it sounds, detracts from the extent to which racism is a problem. Rather than recognizing racism as a pressing issue, people who espouse this frame believe that there is a small amount of racism in society but nothing that cannot be overcome by individual hard work and merit. The minimization frame often includes the dismissal of people who discuss racism by suggesting that they are "playing the race card" or injecting race into conversations where it is irrelevant. These four frames are often used in conjunction with one another and are flexibly applied.

Styles

Styles comprise a second component of the color-blind ideology. *Style* references how people use linguistic manners and strategies to relate a message that otherwise might come across as racially offensive. Whites who are socialized to use color-blind racism may learn how to maneuver racial conversations without being aware of doing so, but this behavior still has identifiable patterns. There are four specific styles: (1) avoidance of direct language, (2) semantic moves, (3) projection, and (4) the role of diminutives. The first, avoidance of direct language, describes the ways in which Whites are sure to use certain labels and terms in public; in other words, they use racist terminology only in private circles, but in public, they know to use politically correct terms.

The second style, semantic moves, includes the ways in which Whites rely on common phrases to reduce the apparent racist nature of a statement. For example, the phrases "some of my best friends are Black" and "yes and no, but" are used to cloak an opinion on how Blacks are lazy or on how Blacks shouldn't be given special treatment when it comes to schools or jobs. The use of these semantic moves couches statements in such a way that Whites are seemingly giving neutral or nonjudgmental statements, even though a highly racialized logic underlies them.

Likewise, projection is another style used toward this end. Rather than analyzing society or taking responsibility for a worldview that they have, Whites criticize Blacks for believing in the significance of race. Whites will project an opinion onto Blacks, such as "If I were Black, I wouldn't want to accept Affirmative Action because it wouldn't be based on merit." Thus, like the other styles, this language maneuver manipulates the message so that a rather explicit racial message appears to be nonracial.

The last style is the role of diminutives, or how Whites use descriptions such as "a little," "a bit more," or "some"; for example, "I might be a little concerned about multiracial children" or "I think some Black men are violent." These characterizations make it appear that Whites are not generalizing about a whole group of people or stereotyping; they are broad statements but with an embedded disclaimer.

Like the four frames, these styles can also be used together in creative ways to relay a racial message, and they are also often complemented by "total incoherence." Incoherence is the injection of utterances and extra words into sentences, including "uh," "you know," "I, I, I" and "I mean." These words make it difficult for the listener to comprehend exactly what the speaker intends and muddles the conversation, thereby making it harder to identify when someone is using a racialized argument. All these linguistic styles provide a way for people to deliver their thoughts without being called racist; it allows them to appear to be color-blind, even though they are not.

Stories

Color-blindness is also implemented through storytelling, as narration itself is an ideological practice; all events can be told with a particular preference for how the story unfolds. There are two kinds of stories: (1) story lines and (2) testimonies. Story lines are the *"socially shared tales that are fable-like and incorporate a common scheme and wording."*[13] Testimonies are *"accounts in which the narrator is a central participant in the story or is close to the characters in the story."*[14] Story lines are particularly useful tools, as they are narratives that appear to be common sense and are easily grasped. Common story lines for today's color-blind ideology are "the past is the past," "I didn't own any slaves," and "if Jews, Italians, and Irish have made it, how come Blacks have not?" These stories support the notion that races have equal opportunities based on oversimplistic narratives of history that ignore Whites' role in racial inequality. More to the point, these story lines support the ideological standpoint that Whites are not responsible for any current inequalities.

A second type of story is testimony. Testimonies seem to be more truthful than story lines, as they include a personal experience or that of a close friend, but like story lines, they are descriptions of events that blame people of color for their position and depict Whites as nonbiased. For example, a testimony might explain someone's fear of Black people because they heard someone was robbed by a Black man in the neighborhood. Or a positive testimony might be given to explain that one couldn't possibly be racist, as "There's a black member who married into my family," or "I had a Black friend who talked to me about prejudice in college." Such testimonies appear to be more neutral and real, yet they are still strategies used to deflect any possible accusations of racism. Storytelling as a common language tool makes color-blind racism more consumable.

White Habitus

Bonilla-Silva's analysis of color-blind racism is buttressed by the existence of what he calls a **white habitus**, or "a racialized, uninterrupted socialization process that *conditions* and *creates* whites' racial taste, perceptions, feelings, and emotions and their views on racial matters."[15] The identification of a habitus is akin to other frameworks that analyze how isolated groups develop a distinctive culture relative to their experience (see Chapter 10 on

structure and culture). Bonilla-Silva argues that because of racial segregation, Whites develop a positive sense of themselves as the "in-group" and a
negative perception of people of color as the "out-group" (for more information on in-groups and out-groups, see Chapter 1 on prejudice). A White
habitus is characterized by three general traits: (1) racial segregation and
isolation while growing up, (2) an interpretation of this isolation as normal,
and (3) a lack of interracial unions. Whites tend to grow up in predominantly White areas and attend predominantly White schools. Yet Whites
tend to see this isolation as normal and *not* an outcome of racial dynamics.
And although Whites abstractly support the idea of "love is love," Whites
are not likely to support interracial unions or be in one. Thus, Whites' close
ties with other Whites create a supportive environment, so that "the universe
of whiteness navigated on an everyday basis by most whites fosters a high
degree of homogeneity of racial views and even of the manners in which
whites express these views."[16]

Is Color-Blind Racism Universal?

Color-blind racism is an ideology that largely belongs to Whites, and
most Whites subscribe to it. However, there are Whites who do not subscribe to color-blindness; usually these people are women, are of a lower or
working class, and are those who have had close, significant relationships
with people of color. Their experiences allow them some insight into social
inequality and understanding for people of color. Bonilla-Silva also addresses
how Blacks might subscribe to color-blindness, but Bonilla-Silva finds that
Blacks—by and large—do not follow the frames, styles, and storytelling of
color-blind racism. The power of color-blind racism, however, does frame
the vocabulary and conversations around race and racism and therefore can
limit Blacks' resistance efforts.[17] This ideology makes it exceedingly difficult
to foster conversations around race and racism, conversations that are necessary to move toward a just society.

How to Challenge Racism
• •

The identification of color-blind racism dynamics helps people see how
covert racism operates and to see how race is still a central factor in society.
Racism Without Racists closes with real and practical applications that propose how to address racism, including a call to Whites to recognize color-
blind racism, to form coalitions with "vulnerable Whites" (e.g., Whites who
are oppressed based on class, gender, and/or sexuality) to contest racism,
and to create a new movement to address racism in institutions and policies.
These suggestions are expanded upon in the fifth edition, where Bonilla-
Silva engages Whites on what they can specifically do to change on the individual level and to cultivate change at a macro level; Bonilla-Silva notes that
a goal of his book is "to influence many young white readers; to try to change

- Black–White racial segregation, as measured by the index of dissimilarity, is at 60 or higher in most major metropolitan areas, which means that 60% of White people would have to move to attain even racial distribution.

- Sixty-two percent of Whites, 47% of Hispanics, and 28% of Blacks say that students should go to schools in their local community, even if it means the school will *not* be racially or ethnically mixed.

- Seventy-five percent of Whites say that it is very good or somewhat good that the United States is composed of people of many different races and ethnicities, but only 21% of Whites say that when it comes to decisions about hiring and promotions, companies and organizations should take a person's race and ethnicity into account, in addition to qualifications, in order to increase diversity.

Sources: Frey (2018); Horowitz (2019); Ibid.

their views and move them to be part of the movement to advance racial justice in our nation."[18]

Evaluation

Methodological Benefits

Bonilla-Silva's findings are based on data from surveys and interviews with two main population sets: (1) Whites and Blacks from the general Detroit population and (2) Whites and Blacks who are currently enrolled in college. The college data are comprised of 627 surveys and 41 interviews, and the Detroit data provide 400 surveys and 84 interviews. Between the two sites, there are a total of 1,027 surveys and 125 respondents who completed in-depth interviews—a significant sample size. The survey data are helpful, but the in-depth quotes from the interviewees provide the data that are perhaps the clearest and most convincing.

Bonilla-Silva made several strategic methodological choices regarding his sample: (1) The sample is large; (2) the college students were from three regions of the United States: the South, the Midwest, and the West Coast; (3) and the choice of college students, who should have more recognition of racial diversity and racism both via people and via intellectual conversation, provides a data source that is not biased toward proving his theory. Thus, the strategic sample choice, coupled with surveys and in-depth interviews, makes a solid foundation for the strong theoretical inferences that support the presence of color-blind racism.

Methodological Limitations

One of the methodological benefits of the sample can also be a limitation. The data purposefully draw on both college students from a range of regions and the general population in Detroit. On the one hand, this sample allows solid inferences that color-blindness is widespread. Yet conclusions may also be limited, as the sample size from any one area is small, and comparisons are difficult. The college data consist of surveys and interviews from three schools that are in three regions of the United States, a total of 627 surveys and 41 interviews. Thus, the interviews, presupposing an even division, include 13 students from each school/region—a very small population size from which to draw conclusions. The limitations of this sample can be observed in a look at Chapter 2 (first edition), "The Central Frames of Color-Blind Racism." This chapter uses quotes from 12 college students and 13 from the Detroit sample; of the college students, six are from the South, three are from the Midwest, and three are from the West Coast. The responses could indicate how college students from the South, a region traditionally known for moving more slowly in racial progress, are more likely to espouse color-blind views. Likewise, the quotes from Detroit interviewees are from people mostly in their 40s or older, and research shows that older populations in comparison to younger populations are less likely to show signs of racial progress. In addition, overall, most of the respondents' answers are framed in relation to views of Black communities, and interviewers could have done more to ascertain how color-blind racism also applies to views of other communities of color.

Theoretical Benefits

The identification of the frames, styles, and stories that compose color-blind racism reveals how Whites effectively do not sound racist while still espousing a racial ideology that supports racism. This revelation shows how old racism has evolved into a new racism wherein Whites have learned how to navigate social norms and expectations around racial equality while maintaining their status at the top of the racial hierarchy. Moreover, the conceptualization of a White habitus illuminates how Whites are inculcated into racial views, intentionally or not. This leads to the second strong theoretical benefit of this theory: the focus on the racial structure and racial ideology, rather than on individual prejudice, for as Bonilla-Silva says, "the purpose of this book is not to demonize whites or label them 'racist.'"[19] Through this analytical focus on the system and ideology, it becomes clear how everyone can participate in *or* choose to challenge racism. The deconstruction and clear identification of the components of color-blind racism can help people reflect on how their own views and actions might align with aspects of color-blind racism.

Theoretical Limitations

Racism Without Racists is now in its fifth edition. A limitation of early editions is the absence of an explanation for how color-blind racism emerged within a broader historical analysis of society and its connection to the racial hierarchy. This limitation is later addressed in the fourth edition of the book in Chapters 2 and 9; Chapter 2 addresses the historical evolution of new racism and explains how Blacks continue to occupy the bottom of the racial structure, while Chapter 9 addresses projections for a new racial hierarchy of the United States.

A second limitation is how the presence of color-blind racism competes with two other contemporary racial developments: the election of President Obama as the first Black president and the emergence of overt racism. The election of President Obama as the first Black president appears to contradict the persistence of racism, while blunt racism and the election of Trump contradict the "undercover" nature of color-blind racism. The fourth and fifth editions address these issues. Bonilla-Silva argues that Obama is not a racial progressive; therefore, his election does not disturb or contradict the presence of persisting racism. In regard to the rise of overt racism and President Trump's racist rhetoric, Bonilla-Silva argues that color-blind racism is still the dominant ideology espoused by most people, and even Trump feels the need to call himself "the least racist person."[20] Bonilla-Silva also suggests that "the hegemony of one form of racial ideology does not mean that at certain historical junctures a secondary form cannot be heightened," thereby suggesting that another ideology of overt racism may also be at work.[21]

Conclusion

The central tenet driving a color-blind perspective is "the idea that race has all but disappeared as a factor shaping the life chances of all Americans."[22] The persistence of racism, however, indicates the contrary, and the practice of color-blind racism reveals how Whites continue to align their interests with the maintenance of the racial hierarchy. This research illuminates how Whites have learned and adopted frames, styles, and stories that they, knowingly or not, use not to sound racist while still maintaining their superior racial status. Thus, Bonilla-Silva details how color-blind racism is an ideology that supports the racialized structure and exposes how this ideology is used and practiced in everyday life.

REFLECT AND DISCUSS

1. How does the theory of color-blind racism help us understand that people espouse racist ideologies without seeing themselves as racist?

2. How do stories and style complement the four frames?

3. Explain the connections between race, racial ideology, and racial structure.

Diagram 11.1 Color-Blind Racism

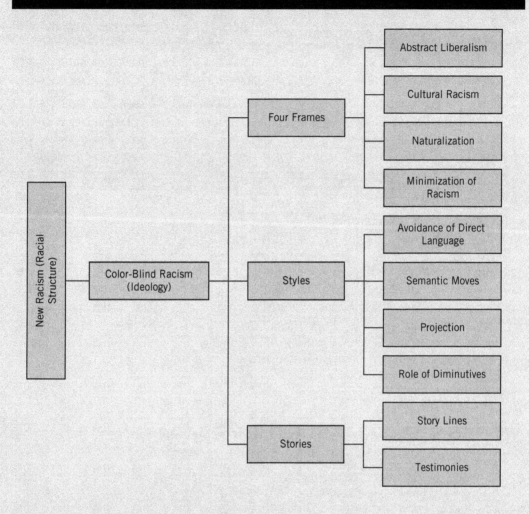

KEY TERMS

Abstract liberalism: "Using ideas associated with political liberalism (e.g., 'equal opportunity,' the idea that force should not be used to achieve social policy) and economic liberalism (e.g., choice, individualism) in an abstract manner to explain racial matters."[23]

Color-blind racism: "Explains contemporary racial inequality as the outcome of nonracial dynamics ... whites rationalize minorities' contemporary status as the product of market dynamics, naturally occurring phenomena, and blacks' imputed cultural limitations."[24]

Cultural racism: "Relies on culturally based arguments such as 'Mexicans do not put much emphasis on education' or 'blacks have too many babies' to explain the standing of minorities in society."[25]

Frames: "Set paths for interpreting information."[26]

Minimization of racism: "Suggests discrimination is no longer a central factor affecting minorities' life chances ('It's better now than in the past' or 'There is discrimination, but there are plenty of jobs out there')."[27]

Naturalization: "Allows whites to explain away racial phenomena by suggesting they are natural outcomes."[28]

Racial ideology: "The racially based frameworks used by actors to explain and justify (dominant race) or challenge (subordinate race or races) the racial status quo."[29]

Stories: "Narrate status ('When we were at the Gold Golf Club ...'), biases ('This guy, who was not even a member of the GG Club ...'), and beliefs about the social order ('... had the audacity of asking me out, even though he just drives a Cavalier'.)"[30]

Styles: "Linguistics manners and rhetorical strategies (or race talk), to the technical tools that allow users to articulate its [the ideology's] frames and story lines."[31]

White habitus: "A racialized, uninterrupted socialization process that conditions and creates whites' racial taste, perceptions, feelings, and emotions and their views on racial matters."[32]

KEY PEOPLE

Eduardo Bonilla-Silva (1962–): Bonilla-Silva is James B. Duke Distinguished Professor of Sociology at Duke University in Durham, North Carolina. He is widely known for his research on racism, theory, race and methodology, and Whiteness. He has been president of the American Sociological Association (2018) and president of the Southern Sociological Society (2017–2018). Bonilla-Silva has written numerous articles and books but perhaps is most well known for *Racism Without Racists*, which has sold more than 50,000 copies and is in its fifth edition.

WORKS CITED AND FURTHER READING

Bonilla-Silva, Eduardo. 1997. "Rethinking Racism: Toward a Structural Interpretation." *American Journal of Sociology* 62(3):465–80.

Bonilla-Silva, Eduardo. 2001. *White Supremacy and Racism in the Post-Civil Rights Era*. Boulder, CO: Lynne Rienner Publishers.

Bonilla-Silva, Eduardo. 2003. *Racism without Racists: Color-Blind Racism and the Persistence of Racial Inequality in America*. Lanham, MD: Rowman and Littlefield.

Bonilla-Silva, Eduardo. 2006. *Racism without Racists: Color-Blind Racism and the Persistence of Racial Inequality in America*. 2nd ed. Lanham, MD: Rowman and Littlefield.

Bonilla-Silva, Eduardo. 2010. *Racism without Racists: Color-Blind Racism and the Persistence of Racial Inequality in America*. 3rd ed. Lanham, MD: Rowman and Littlefield.

Bonilla-Silva, Eduardo. 2012. "The Invisible Weight of Whiteness: The Racial Grammar of Everyday Life in America." *Ethnic and Racial Studies* 34(12):173–94.

Bonilla-Silva, Eduardo. 2014. *Racism Without Racists: Color-Blind Racism and the Persistence of Racial Inequality in America*. 4th ed. Lanham, MD: Rowman and Littlefield.

Bonilla-Silva, Eduardo. 2018. *Racism without Racists: Color-Blind Racism and the Persistence of Racial Inequality in America*. 5th ed. Lanham, MD: Rowman and Littlefield.

Bonilla-Silva, Eduardo and Ashley W. Doane, eds. 2003. *White Out: The Continuing Significance of Racism.* New York: Routledge.

Frey, William H. 2018. "Black-White Segregation Edges Downward since 2000, Census Shows." Washington, DC: The Brookings Institution.

Horowitz, Juliana Menasce. 2019. "Americans See Advantages and Challenges in Country's Growing Racial and Ethnic Diversity." Washington, DC: Pew Research Center.

NOTES

1. Bonilla-Silva (1997).
2. Bonilla-Silva (2003).
3. Bonilla-Silva (1997:469).
4. Bonilla-Silva (2003:7, emphasis in original).
5. Ibid. (8).
6. Ibid. (2).
7. Ibid. (2).
8. Ibid. (9, emphasis in original).
9. Ibid.
10. Ibid. (26, emphasis in original).
11. Ibid. (53, emphasis in original).
12. Ibid. (75, emphasis in original).
13. Ibid. (76, emphasis in original).
14. Ibid. (76, emphasis in original).
15. Ibid. (104, emphasis in original).
16. Ibid. (125).
17. Bonilla-Silva (2014).
18. Bonilla-Silva (2018:240).
19. Bonilla-Silva (2003:15).
20. Bonilla-Silva (2018:222).
21. Ibid. (223).
22. Bonilla-Silva (2003:178).
23. Ibid. (28).
24. Ibid. (2).
25. Ibid. (28).
26. Ibid. (26).
27. Ibid. (29).
28. Ibid. (28).
29. Ibid. (9).
30. Ibid. (75).
31. Ibid. (53).
32. Ibid. (104).

More Than Race

Colorism

Evelyn Nakano Glenn | Ronald Hall |
Margaret Hunter | Kimberly Norwood

Colorism, also known as skin-tone stratification, is discrimination against those with dark(er) complexions and preferential bias toward those with light(er) complexions. This preference for lightness is largely rooted in early European control, which established White/light complexion and features as superior. Theoretical explanations of colorism, however, are relatively recent and move beyond analysis of intergroup racism to a focus on how skin complexion discrimination occurs intraracially, or within racial groups. There is no one central theory of colorism, and the scholarship of it is vast, so this chapter is a synthesis of multiple works, with a reliance on the work by Evelyn Nakano Glenn, Ronald Hall, Margaret Hunter, and Kimberly Norwood.

Photo 12.1 Evelyn Nakano Glenn

Source: http://ethnicstudies.berkeley. edu/faculty-profile/evelyn-nakano-glenn-1.

Photo 12.2 Ronald Hall

Source: https://socialwork.msu.edu/ About-Us/Faculty-Staff/Ronald-E-Hall.

Photo 12.3 Margaret Hunter

Source: https://www.mills.edu/faculty/ margaret-hunter.php.

Photo 12.4 Kimberly Norwood

Source: https://source.wustl.edu/ experts/kimberly-norwood/.

Why This Theory

Racism is rooted in a racial hierarchy wherein Whites, who occupy the top of the hierarchy, participate in discrimination against people of color. This discrimination includes the perception of physical traits deemed "non-White" as undesirable and inferior. Yet people of color also participate in such discrimination and show favor toward a White Westernized phenotype, including light skin tone, straight hair, narrow nose, and round eyes. This discrimination against people with dark(er) complexions has been in effect since early colonization and enslavement, but a distinct analysis of it under the theoretical framework of colorism is relatively recent. In 1982, Alice Walker coined the term *colorism* to refer to the light-skin privilege among Black communities.[1] Colorism, like racism, is rooted in White superiority, but colorism distinctly explains how discrimination operates along the skin-tone spectrum and how this discrimination manifests within and across racial groups. This chapter brings together work by a multitude of scholars to frame a theory of colorism; it particularly relies on the scholarship of Evelyn Nakano Glenn, Ronald Hall, Margaret Hunter, and Kimberly Norwood.

Description of the Theory

Colorism, or *skin tone stratification*, is defined by Glenn as "the preference for lighter skin and social hierarchy based on skin tone,"[2] by Herring as "the discriminatory treatment of individuals falling within the same 'racial' group on the basis of skin color,"[3] or by Russell-Cole, Wilson, and Hall as **color-class hierarchies**, or the "social, economic, and political societal framework that allows skin-color differences, such that along a continuum of possible shades, those with the lightest skin color enjoy the highest social standing, and those with the darkest skin color are among the poorest."[4] Colorism operates both on the individual level, where personal bias exists, and on a structural level, where there is a systemic valuing of light complexions.[5]

Evidence of colorism is documented through the preferential treatment of those who have light skin-tone complexions and/or typical Westernized features, such as small nose, round eyes, thinner lips, and straight hair.[6] Labeling of "light skin" and features as "round" or "thin," however, clearly depends on perception. One person's label of "light brown" can be another person's "medium brown," or lips can be seen as "thin" by one person but not by another. Moreover, perception of complexion and features can be mediated by other factors, such as age, class status, occupational status, nationality, gender, or even dress and fashion.[7] A stark example of the relative perception of skin tone is how some American-born, White women who wear a hijab are then read as potentially Arab, due to the ways in which

Islam is associated with non-White and non-American communities.[8] Perception also varies by racial group and region of the world; "dark" is not the same in African American communities as it is within Filipino communities, and colorism does not operate the same in the United States as it does in the Philippines. Furthermore, while colorism often focuses on the discrimination those with darker skin tones receive, sometimes those with light complexions are discriminated against out of a disdain for the cultural valuing of light complexions.

Akin to the understanding that races are not real but racism is, colorism is also not based in any biological reality but is based on social assignment of meaning to phenotype. There is no biological connection between a light skin tone and ability, ethics, or personality. The variation in skin-tone pigmentation originated in an evolutionary adaptation. People who lived closer to the equator, such as in Africa, had dark complexions because melanin, which gives the skin pigment, serves as protection from the sun. Yet the sun also provides vitamin D, necessary for bone support. Thus, those who migrated north and away from the sun's strongest rays experienced an evolutionary adaptation for their melanin to decrease (lighter skin) so that more of the sun's benefits could be absorbed. Primary differences in skin tone, therefore, are an adaptation to the environment. With the onset of sophisticated clothes and shelter, however, the natural evolutionary response to sun was no longer necessary.[9] The vast majority of skin-tone variation we now see is due to population migration and procreation, both voluntary and forced. Today's preference for light skin is because of a social assignment, not a biological one.

The problem of colorism has been studied from a range of angles by many scholars, so this chapter relies on a synthesis of that research. By highlighting commonalities and particular contributions, the main theoretical facets of colorism are identified as (1) the historical origins of light-skin valorization; (2) delineating interracial versus intraracial colorism; (3) the gendered aspect of colorism and light skin as beauty; (4) the relationship between multiraciality and colorism; (5) definitions and measurements of colorism; and (6) the institutional effects and consequences of colorism in areas such as income, housing, family, and criminality.

Historical Origins of Light-Skin Valorization

Prior to widespread colonization, a relationship between skin tone and class status existed in agrarian communities, as darker skin complexions were associated with lower socioeconomic workers who did manual labor outdoors.[10] However, while there was a precedent of associating darker skin tones with a low-class status, colorism largely originated with European imperialism and an emergence of mixed-race populations. This expansion has been global in nature, as there are few places in the world untouched by European and American colonization.

A few examples in specific nations offer some insight into the historical nature of colorism. In the Philippines, a Western ideology was first supported by the Spanish colonizers and then later by the United States.[11] Since colonization of this land more than 400 years ago, interracial contact between indigenous communities, Spanish colonizers, and Chinese settlers resulted in a mixed-race population. Mixed populations with lighter complexions were given more respect and higher social status; this valuation remains today, as is evident with an estimated 50% of Filipina women using a skin-lightening product.[12] In India, prior to British colonization, there was already some attention paid to skin tone, but with the advent of British imperialism, the skin-tone hierarchy was amplified. British colonization supported a caste system where Brahmins who had light complexions occupied the top of the caste system and thereby received the highest status and most respect. In Central and South America, the mixed population came to be known as *mestizaje, mestizo,* or *mulatto.* These terms referred to people of mixed European and African descent, mixed European and indigenous descent, mixed African and indigenous descent, and the offspring of these groups.[13] Mexico encouraged a *mestizaje* population by encouraging Whitening as a national project "with the goal of raising the status of Mexico in the eyes of Europe, despite its significant indigenous and African populations."[14] Brazil had a similar goal to lighten the population, a goal that led to a complex color hierarchy, rather than racial hierarchy, with categories such as *moreno* and *pardo* to denote gradations in skin tone; "one's color in Brazil commonly carries connotations about one's value in accordance with general Western racial ideology that valorizes lightness and denigrates darkness."[15]

In the United States, the color hierarchy largely emerged from practices during plantation slavery. White masters used sex with enslaved Black women as a tool of terror, control, and reproduction. In order to maximize control over Black communities and profits of the slavery system, plantation owners relied on the "one-drop rule," which stated that any person who was perceived to have any Black ancestry, no matter how small and no matter the color of one's skin, was considered Black and therefore could be enslaved.[16] However, everyday practice in society often meant the multiracial offspring of these White men received better treatment on the plantation through jobs in the house instead of the field, through opportunities to learn to read and write, and sometimes even through eventual granting of freedom. Such plantation practices were buttressed by religious and scientific beliefs that said those with "White blood" were smarter, kinder, and more capable. Darker complexions became synonymous with savagery, irrationality, and ugliness, while lighter complexions were associated with beauty, intelligence, and refinement.[17] These beliefs encouraged the valuing of mixed-race people with light skin complexions, resulting in a "mulatto class." This group was more likely to be educated, to have good jobs, and to have higher incomes. This "mulatto elite" practiced social exclusion from other communities of color. For instance, those who had darker skin complexions were often denied entry into organizations, clubs, schools, and churches. Norwood explains that "the elevation in success and status based on white blood was so clear and unequivocal that the mulatto group almost always socialized and married people whose skin tone matched their own or was lighter."[18] Evidence of that persistent light-skin privilege can be seen in the predominance of contemporary celebrities who have light complexions.[19]

Although colorism is rooted in the racism of White colonization and enslavement, it now exists as a phenomenon outside the connections to historic White domination. Colorism is intimately related to racism, but it is not reducible to it. Harvey, Banks, and Tennial state that "while connected in their origin, racism and colorism are not dependent upon each other for their modern existence. Thus, a decrease or even annihilation of racism does not preclude the existence of a colorism problem, since colorism can exist independent of an intergroup context."[20] Colorism has evolved and developed since its historic origins and has resulted in a contemporary skin-tone hierarchy with its own particular dynamics.

Interracial and Intraracial Colorism

Colorism is a preferential bias toward people who have light complexions and Westernized features. This bias can occur both *inter*racially, between groups, and *intra*racially, within a racial group.

Interracial Colorism

Interracial colorism is most often exhibited by Whites who show a preference for people of color with a light skin tone, either within a racial group or across other racial groups. For example, Whites show preferences for Blacks with lighter complexions over Blacks with darker complexions, but they also exhibit a preference for Asians with light(er) skin tones over Blacks. This preference for light skin tone is evident in how Whites are more likely to intermarry with Asians and Latinxs, who have lighter complexions. Interracial colorism can also be seen between communities of color, such as some Asians or Latinxs who discriminate against Blacks or Latinxs with dark(er) complexions.[21] While colorism is evident on an interracial level, it is most often studied as an intraracial phenomenon.

Intraracial Colorism

Within racial groups, there is skin-tone stratification wherein those of light complexion receive better treatment. This bias for light(er) skin is evident in the assignment of light skin to a higher social status, the judgment of light skin as more beautiful, and higher marriage rates among those with light skin. Studies on colorism often also report family preference for their children to marry someone with a light complexion, so that they may have children with a light complexion.[22] Russell-Cole, Wilson, and Hall note that people of color learn the importance of skin color in stages. First, young children become aware of race and racism. Second, around puberty, they become aware of beauty standards and the association of light skin with beauty and femininity and dark skin with masculinity. Third, as adults, people of color recognize that having a light complexion means one will be seen as more beautiful, will be preferred as a partner, and will be given more opportunities.

The desire for a light complexion is imposed on people of color by people of color, but the pressure to attain this lightness comes from internalizing a White ideology that deems Whiteness as superior. The status that comes with light skin can be so valued that many women "try to alter their appearance through skin bleaching creams, make-up application, use of colored contact lenses, dieting, hair straightening and hair extensions, and even cosmetic surgery."[23] Hall calls this internalization of White/light superiority by people of color the "bleaching syndrome." He writes that "the effort on the part of people of color to assimilate and simultaneously bring about a reduction in psychological pain is made possible by their obsession with the 'bleached' ideal, which is manifested in their perception of preferred white norms and rootedness in white culture."[24] Hall explains that people of color reach for this light ideal to conform to society's standards in an effort to feel welcomed and valued. The bleaching syndrome reveals the oppressive power of Whiteness to infiltrate, affect, and shape the minds of people of color, so much so that lightness becomes a goal.

Colorism is rooted in the preference for light complexions, but there is also discriminatory backlash against those who are perceived as having light complexions. The obvious preferential treatment for those with light complexions can result in envy, angst, and/or anger from those with darker complexions. It is also often assumed that those with light complexions believe in their light-is-better status, so they are ridiculed for being snobby and for having a superiority complex. Women with light complexions are particularly targeted with labels that are intended to demean their status; one such label is "high yellow."[25] Norwood addresses how Blacks with light complexions face discrimination via **blackthink**, which is the way in which light skin is idolized while simultaneously criticized as not "Black enough." For example, if one is perceived as too light, s/he/zie is seen as not living a "real" Black experience because encounters with discrimination are not the same or because somehow light skin tone prevents connection with Black culture and communities in an authentic manner.[26] Thus, although intraracial colorism is usually a problem of discrimination against those with dark complexions, it can also manifest as discrimination against those with light complexions.

Gendered Colorism

Gendered colorism references how colorism particularly affects women because of the sexist emphasis on beauty, as well as the relationship between beauty assignment and light complexions. Glenn uses the term *symbolic capital* and Hunter uses *social capital* to reference how light skin is marketed and used as an asset to increase one's upward mobility. Hunter argues for the idea of **beauty and lightness as social capital**: "Light skin tone is interpreted as beauty, and beauty operates as social capital for women. Women who possess this form of capital (beauty) are able to convert it into economic capital, educational capital, or another form of social capital."[27] Women who wish to attain this capital but have darker complexions are targeted with "beauty regimens," often via skin creams that whiten the skin. These creams are a global industry and are present in areas such as the Philippines, India, Japan, Korea, Latin America, Europe, and the United States, yet "the market for skin lighteners, although global in scope, is also highly decentralized and segmented along socioeconomic, age, national, ethnic, racial, and cultural lines."[28] Much effort is put into tailored marketing of these beauty products, which have product names such as Whitening Cream Enzyme Q-10 in the Philippines, White Lucent in Japan and Korea, White Secrete in Latin America, and Ultra Glow in the United States. Although these lightening/whitening creams have been shown to be very dangerous because of their ingredients, they are a multibillion-dollar industry and an integral part of beauty marketing.[29] In addition to lightening skin tone, women are encouraged to have surgery on their eyelids, lips, nose, and breasts in order to look more "normal," aka Westernized.[30] Another facet of gendered colorism is a focus on hair, as natural hair, permed hair, weaves, and wigs mediate skin tone, and having straight hair is associated with White/light features.[31] This urge to attain light and Westernized features manifests in what Hunter calls the **beauty queue**, which "is a rank ordering of women from lightest to darkest where the lightest get the most perks and rewards, dates for example, and the darkest women get the least."[32] Norwood and Foreman, likewise, note that girls are highly sensitive to gradations in skin tone so that "incremental shades of light matter, and lighter is always better."[33]

Gendered colorism has long been present in African American communities, where there is a message that light equals beautiful, intelligent, and desirable. Wilder proposes the term **everyday colorism** to encapsulate how colorism operates through the language, internal scripts, and external practices of Black women. Language is the "everyday vocabulary and system of meaning attached to skin tone," such as "yellow" or "redbone," which conceptually support the hierarchy attached to light skin. Internal scripts are the "socially constructed ideas, expectations, emotions, and beliefs women carry with them about skin tone," such as a light complexion correlates with beauty, intelligence, and desirability. External practices are the "everyday behaviors and actions enacted by women toward themselves and others based upon their internalized views about skin color," such as using skin-bleaching creams, staying out of the sun, and straightening hair.[34] Colorism persists through the use of everyday language, scripts, and practices.

While most studies of gendered colorism focus on women, initial studies indicate that Black men with light complexions do not receive similar treatment in the dating sphere. In fact, Black men with *darker* complexions tend to be seen as more masculine and more sexually desirable on an interpersonal, romantic level.[35] Thakore points out that a similar phenomenon exists in South Asia, where South Asian women experience immense pressure to have light complexions, but South Asian men do not face the equivalent.[36] Yet there is research that indicates that men with darker complexions in the United States are seen as less intelligent, more violent, and more corrupt, and their sexuality is connected to historical stereotypes of Black men as hypersexual and deviant.[37] Thus, although men with darker complexions may not be greatly affected by colorism on an individual, romantic level, they do not escape its other social consequences.

Colorism and Multiraciality

Historically, colorism developed in relation to the emergence of mixed-race populations; those of part-White mixed-race descent became more favored if they had lighter skin tones and narrower features. Today, there continues to be a relationship between colorism and multiracials, the contemporary term to refer to people of mixed-race descent. As more people of mixed-race descent choose to identify as multiracial, a cultural awareness of and fascination with multiraciality has grown. For example, marketing of multiraciality as particularly attractive and exotic is seen in advertisements, movies, and fashion.[38] Multiracials fare better in online dating and are perceived as being more unique and attractive.[39] This embrace of multiraciality has led to the widespread assumption that people of color with a light skin tone are often multiracial, whether they are or not. Thus, in some manner, contemporary colorism supports the exoticization of multiraciality, and contemporary multiraciality associated with lightness supports colorism.

Measuring Colorism

A significant problem with evaluating colorism is the difficulty in gauging what constitutes "light," "medium," and "dark" skin tone. It's possible that on each end of the spectrum, there may be general agreement about what constitutes light and dark complexion, but largely these labels are in the eye of the beholder. This relative perception of a light-to-dark scale makes it difficult to document cases of colorism and establish when colorism has occurred. Research on the effects of skin tone discrimination often uses a general color continuum scale, with labels such as "very dark," "dark," "medium," "light," and "very light."[40] Two such specific scales that have been used in national research are the New Immigrant Survey and the Project on Race and Ethnicity in Latin America Color Palette, both of which identify people based on 11 gradations in skin tone.[41] Implicit bias tests have also been used to measure people's discrimination based on skin tone (see Chapter 4 on implicit bias). These scales of measurement are useful but are constrained to individual perception and reception of skin-tone gradations.

Harvey, Banks, and Tennial suggest two colorism scales that aim to move beyond a single perception by evaluating the degree to which people assign significance and meaning to skin tone gradients on a series of factors.[42] They suggest that there are four areas in which colorism holds significance: (1) self-concept, which is how skin tone affects the self-esteem of an individual; (2) impression formation, which is how skin tone affects how others assign a positive or negative status to a person; (3) attraction and affiliation, which is how skin tone affects one's opportunities in romantic relationships and memberships in organizations; and (4) upward mobility, which is how skin tone affects one's opportunities in social and economic standings. These four areas are used as the basis for two colorism scales: an In-Group Colorism Scale to measure intraracial colorism and an Out-Group Colorism Scale to measure interracial colorism. The **In-Group Colorism Scale** has statements associated with the areas of self-concept, impression formation, attraction and affiliation, and upward mobility. Each area has four statements that are evaluated with a seven-point Likert scale, from "strongly agree" to "strongly disagree." Examples from this scale are "My skin tone is an important part of my self-concept" and "Blacks with lighter skin tone tend to be more pleasant people to deal with."[43] The **Out-Group Colorism Scale** operates in a similar manner, with three to four statements also evaluated with a Likert scale in the areas of impression formation, upward mobility, attraction, and affiliation. These two scales are useful for evaluating different facets of significance assigned to skin tone. Although they were written in relation to Black communities, the scales could be modified to reflect other communities of color.

The Effects of Colorism on a Macro Level

The effects of colorism are often studied on an individual level where preferential treatment is evident; however, the effects of colorism also exist on a macro level. People with dark complexions have on average lower incomes, lower educational attainment, lower marital rates, and, when applicable, longer criminal sentences. Norwood and Foreman note a series of differences for Blacks with light complexions; they are more likely to be employable and employed, they are more prevalent in all forms of advertising, they are often better educated, they have a higher occupation status, they have more money, and they are more likely to be married.[44] Similar effects are seen in other communities of color; Ryabov's study of Asian Americans and Hispanic Americans reveals a strong connection between high educational attainment and a light complexion,[45] and Hersch shows that in the United States, there is wage discrimination against Asian and Latin American immigrants who have darker complexions.[46] Another example is a study by Messing, Jabon, and Plaut that shows how colorism was injected into the U.S. 2008 presidential race through political ad campaigns that darkened Obama's image to convey negative emotions and a sense of criminality.[47]

Bonilla-Silva moves the conversation on colorism one more step through the suggestion that the current U.S. hierarchy based on race could change to one based on color.[48] He proposes that the United States may be moving toward a color-based tri-racial hierarchy, more akin to the hierarchies that characterize Latin America; he refers to this projection as the Latin Americanization of U.S. race relations. The tri-racial hierarchy consists of Whites at the top, an intermediary group of Honorary Whites, and Collective Blacks at the bottom. The White group includes Whites, assimilated White Latinxs, and multiracials and Asians who are phenotypically light. Honorary Whites include those who have lighter skin tones, such as Japanese Americans and Korean Americans, Latinxs with lighter complexions, and most multiracials. Collective Blacks, at the bottom of the hierarchy, are those with dark complexions, such as Filipinos, Laotians, Latinxs with dark complexions, Blacks, and West Indian and African immigrants. The proposed ranking of these groups is based on a pigmentocracy, a ranking based on a *group's general skin tone*. Within this tri-racial hierarchy, "categorical porosity" can still exist; this porosity allows for certain individuals, regardless of group affiliation, to move up (or down) the hierarchy based on *individual skin tone*. There is already some evidence of this color-based hierarchy coming to fruition based on indicators such as income differentials, racial identity, intermarriage, and racial attitudes: White Latinxs have a higher income compared to darker Latinxs, Latinxs with White complexions are likely to identify as White on the Census, Whites are more likely to intermarry with Latinxs and Asians who have light complexions, and Asians often hold anti-Black attitudes. It is yet to be seen if the United States will develop a color-based hierarchy, but there is evidence that suggests the significance attached to complexion is increasing.

How to Challenge Racism

Depending on their vantage point, scholars suggest challenging colorism on an individual basis or at the system level. On the micro level, individuals can learn to recognize when they are participating in colorism to prevent further discrimination. Families can become aware of their internalized biases and stop encouraging a preference for light complexions and Western features while also actively socializing their children not to discriminate against those with darker complexions. At the meso and macro level, the skin-bleaching industry can be targeted in its mass marketing of a beauty that relies on Whitening. There are also efforts to push private and public policies to acknowledge colorism as a unique form of discrimination, a form that cannot be subsumed under typical antiracism policies. Scales or other

By the Numbers

- Seventy-seven percent of women in Nigeria and 40% of women in China use skin-lightening products; 61% of the dermatological market in India consists of skin-lightening products.

- Sixty-four percent of Hispanics with darker skin report experiencing discrimination, compared to 50% of Hispanics with lighter skin.

- Blacks with darker complexions receive harsher criminal sentences than Blacks with lighter complexions, and Whites with Afrocentric features receive harsher punishment than Whites without such features.

Sources: Gonzalez-Barrera (2019); King and Johnson (2016); World Health Organization (2011).

measuring guides for evaluating colorism will aid in this effort, as will education campaigns acknowledging that skin-tone stratification does exist.

Evaluation

Methodological Benefits

Colorism has been studied with various methodological approaches, including quantitative analysis of data sets, surveys, in-depth interviews, content analysis, and historical research. There is also a valuable range of ways to ask about color gradation, such as using a given color-gradation scale, developing open-ended questions that allow the respondent to identify phenotype, or developing a new measurement tool catered to the study. Due to the relative nature of skin-tone complexion, a multimethod approach has served well to identify and explain the different facets of the colorism problem.

Methodological Limitations

The limitation to studying and documenting colorism is discerning a clear and agreed-on method for doing so. The line between "medium" and "light," for example, is one that can be clear or obscure depending on any manner of factors, such as context, class status, gender, and age, to name a few. This problem is not new to the area of racial research, as the issue is similar when determining racial identities; people often mistakenly assume the incorrect racial identity of others they encounter. Yet color gradations are another level of complexity, particularly when trying to classify who specifically receives what preferential (or discriminatory) treatment. As the research on colorism grows, the methodology used to evaluate skin tone and colorism will have to become more sophisticated.

Theoretical Benefits

Colorism moves beyond the analysis of interracial discrimination to theorize the ways in which skin tone, in addition to race, affects people differently, *between* and *within* racial groups. For example, analyses of colorism permit insight into how Blacks with light complexions fare better both in inter- and intraracial dynamics. Although all people of color face racism, colorism provides a theoretical insight into understanding the additional layer of severity that is encountered in relation to how dark or light one is. In addition, colorism brings attention to the ways in which White superiority has been internalized—so much so that some people of color now stratify themselves based on skin tone.

Theoretical Limitations

The limitation of colorism is the potential to lose sight of broader structural racial hierarchies that are shaping the meanings associated with skin tone. In many countries, darker complexions are not valued because they are associated with an African lineage, one that is understood as belonging to "the Black race." People who receive negative discrimination based on their darker complexions may get this treatment because they are understood as "more Black," and people with lighter skin tones are preferred because they are seen as "more White"; in this vein, racial classification and hierarchies are still at the root of skin-tone bias. Specifically, in the United States, suggesting the emergence of a new hierarchy based on skin tone discounts the persistent power of racial categorization. For example, although Bonilla-Silva suggests that Latinxs with light complexions could be Honorary Whites, Latinxs of all skin tones encounter racism due to contention over immigration. It is important to recognize the unique significance of colorism that is distinct from racism, but a limited focus on colorism can possibly obscure its roots in structural racism.

Conclusion

Racial analysis that relies only on racial group divisions misses the significant ways in which color shapes racial experiences. The theory of colorism pushes both racial analysis and intragroup dialogue forward to question the ways in which Whiteness/lightness is governing structural opportunities and individual bias. New insights are being gained into areas such as interracial color-based discrimination, intraracial internalization of light bias, and the effects of a skin-tone hierarchy on the racial hierarchy.

REFLECT AND DISCUSS

1. How is colorism historically rooted in racism but not solely dependent on it today?

2. Compare and contrast interracial colorism and intraracial colorism.

3. How does the beauty industry reinforce colorism?

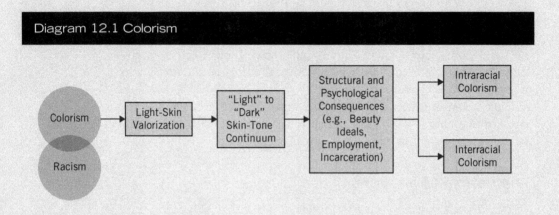

Diagram 12.1 Colorism

KEY TERMS

Beauty and lightness as social capital: "Light skin tone is interpreted as beauty, and beauty operates as social capital for women. Women who possess this form of capital (beauty) are able to convert it into economic capital, educational capital, or another form of social capital."[49]

Beauty queue: "A rank ordering of women from lightest to darkest where the lightest get the most perks and rewards, dates for example, and the darkest women get the least."[50]

Blackthink: "An attempt to determine who is really black and who is not black enough, and it makes these determinations based on certain criteria … as defined by the guardians of black identity."[51]

Color-class hierarchies: "Social, economic, and political societal framework that allows skin-color differences, such that along a continuum of possible shades, those with the lightest skin color enjoy the highest social standing, and those with the darkest skin color are among the poorest."[52]

Colorism: "The preference for lighter skin and social hierarchy based on skin tone"[53] or "the discriminatory treatment of individuals falling within the same 'racial' group on the basis of skin color."[54]

Everyday colorism: "A system of language, beliefs, and practices that govern the everyday interactions and experiences of black women as it relates to skin tone."[55]

In-Group Colorism Scale: A scale "developed to assess the significance and meaning of skin color variations on the part of those inside a community of color" and comprised of five subscales of self-concept, impression formation, affiliation and attraction, and upward mobility.[56]

Out-Group Colorism Scale: A scale "developed to assess the significance and meaning of skin color variations on the part of those outside of the focal community of color" and comprised of four subscales of impression formation, attraction, affiliation, and upward mobility.[57]

KEY PEOPLE

Evelyn Nakano Glenn (1940–): Glenn is Professor Emeritus in the Department of Ethnic Studies at University of California, Berkeley and the founding director of the University's Center for Race and Gender. She was president of the American Sociological Association for the 2009 to 2010 term.

Ronald Hall: Hall is a Professor in the School of Social Work at Michigan State University. He has written extensively on the effects of colorism and has provided expert testimony on the subject in federal courts and in Congress.

Margaret Hunter (1972–): Hunter is Professor of Sociology at Mills College in Oakland, California. She is known for her research on colorism and gender and was featured in the documentary *Light Girls*.

Kimberly Norwood (1960–): Norwood is the Henry H. Oberschelp Professor of Law at Washington University in St. Louis, Missouri. She has lectured at schools across the world and organized the first international colorism conference in the United States.

WORKS CITED AND FURTHER READING

Bonilla-Silva, Eduardo. 2004. "From Bi-racial to Tri-racial: Towards a New System of Racial Stratification in the USA." *Ethnic and Racial Studies* 27(6):931–50.

Curington, Celeste V., Ken-Hou Lin, and Jennifer H. Lundquist. 2015. "Positioning Multiraciality in Cyberspace: Treatment of Multiracial Daters in an Online Dating Website." *American Sociological Review* 80(4):764–88.

DaCosta, Kimberly M. 2007. *Making Multiracials: State, Family, and Market in the Redrawing of the Color Line*. Stanford, CA: Stanford University Press.

Dixon, Angela R. and Edward E. Telles. 2017. "Skin Color and Colorism: Global Research, Concepts, and Measurement." *Annual Review of Sociology* 43:405–24.

Glenn, Evelyn Nakano. 2009. "Consuming Lightness: Segmented Markets and Global Capital in the Skin-Whitening Trade." Pp. 166–87 in *Shades of Difference: Why Skin Color Matters*, edited by E. N. Glenn. Stanford, CA: Stanford University Press.

Gonzalez-Barrera, Ana. 2019. "Hispanics with Darker Skin Are More Likely to Experience Discrimination Than Those with Lighter Skin." Washington, DC: Pew Research Center.

Hall, Ronald E. 2008. "Manifestations of Racism in the 21st Century." Pp. 25–44 in *Racism in the 21st Century: An Empirical Analysis of Skin Color*, edited by R. E. Hall. New York: Springer.

Hall, Ronald E., ed. 2013. *The Melanin Millennium: Skin Color as 21st Century International Discourse*. New York: Springer.

Harvey, Richard D., Kira Hudson Banks, and Rachel E. Tennial. 2014. "A New Way Forward: The Development and Preliminary Validation of Two Colorism Scales." Pp. 198–217 in *Color Matters: Skin Tone Bias and the Myth of a Post-Racial America*, edited by K. J. Norwood. New York: Routledge.

Herring, Cedric. 2004. "Skin Deep: Race and Complexion in the 'Color-Blind' Era." Pp. 1–21 in *Skin Deep: How Race and Complexion Matter in the "Color-Blind" Era*, edited by C. Herring, V. Keith, and H. D. Horton. Chicago: University of Illinois Press.

Hersch, Joni. 2008. "Skin Color, Immigrant Wages, and Discrimination." Pp. 77–90 in *Racism in the 21st Century: An Empirical Analysis* of *Skin Color,* edited by R. E. Hall. New York: Springer.

Hunter, Margaret L. 2005. *Race, Gender, and the Politics of Skin Tone.* New York: Routledge.

Jablonski, Nina G. and George Chaplin. 2010. "Human Skin Pigmentation as an Adaptation to UV Radiation." *Proceedings of the National Academy of Sciences of the United States of America* 107(2):8962–68.

Keith, Verna M. 2009. "A Colorstruck World: Skin Tone, Achievement, and Self-Esteem Among African American Women." Pp. 24–39 in *Shades of Difference: Why Skin Color Matters,* edited by E. N. Glenn. Stanford, CA: Stanford University Press.

King, Ryan D. and Brian D. Johnson. 2016. "A Punishing Look: Skin Tone and Afrocentric Features in the Halls of Justice." *American Journal of Sociology* 122(1): 90–124.

Martin, Lori Latrice, Hayward Derrick Horton, Cedric Herring, Verna M. Keith, and Melvin Thomas, eds. 2017. *Color Struck: How Race and Complexion Matter in the "Color-Blind" Era.* Rotterdam, The Netherlands: Sense Publishers.

Messing, Solomon, Maria Jabon, and Ethan Plaut. 2016. "Bias in the Flesh: Skin Complexion and Stereotype Consistency in Political Campaigns." *Public Opinion Quarterly* 80(1):44–65.

Norwood, Kimberly Jade. 2014a. "Colorism and Blackthink: A Modern Augmentation of Double Consciousness." Pp. 158–81 in *Color Matters: Skin Tone Bias and the Myth of a Post-Racial America,* edited by K. J. Norwood. New York: Routledge.

Norwood, Kimberly Jade, ed. 2014b. *Color Matters: Skin Tone Bias and the Myth of a Post-Racial America.* New York: Routledge.

Norwood, Kimberly Jade and Violete Solonova Foreman. 2014. "The Ubiquitousness of

Colorism: Then and Now." Pp. 9–28 in *Color Matters: Skin Tone Bias and the Myth of a Post-Racial America,* edited by K. J. Norwood. New York: Routledge.

Rondilla, Joanne L. and Paul Spickard. 2007. *Is Lighter Better? Skin-Tone Discrimination among Asian Americans.* Lanham, MD: Rowman and Littlefield.

Russell-Cole, Kathy, Midge Wilson, and Ronald E. Hall. 2013. *The Color Complex: The Politics of Skin Color in a New Millennium.* New York: Anchor Books.

Ryabov, Igor. 2016. "Educational Outcomes of Asian and Hispanic Americans: The Significance of Skin Color." *Research in Social Stratification and Mobility* 44:1–9.

Selod, Saher. 2018. *Forever Suspect: Racialized Surveillance of Muslim Americans in the War on Terror.* New Brunswick, NJ: Rutgers University Press.

Sims, Jennifer P. 2012. "Beautiful Stereotypes: The Relationship between Physical Attractiveness and Mixed Race Identity." *Identities* 19(1): 61–80.

Telles, Edward. 2009. "The Social Consequences of Skin Color in Brazil." Pp. 9–24 in *Shades of Difference: Why Skin Color Matters,* edited by E. N. Glenn. Stanford, CA: Stanford University Press.

Thakore, Bhoomi. 2016. *South Asians on the U.S. Screen: Just Like Everyone Else?* Lanham, MD: Lexington Books.

Wilder, JeffriAnne. 2015. *Color Stories: Black Women and Colorism in the 21st Century.* Santa Barbara, CA: ABC-CLIO.

World Health Organization. 2011. "Mercury in Skin Lightening Products." Geneva, Switzerland: Author.

NOTES

*   Birth year is not available.
1. Norwood and Foreman (2014).
2. Glenn (2009:166).
3. Herring (2004:3).
4. Russell-Cole, Wilson, and Hall (2013:27).
5. Glenn (2009); Russell-Cole et al. (2013).
6. Glenn (2009).
7. Ibid.
8. Selod (2018).
9. Jablonski and Chaplin (2010).
10. Hunter (2005); Russell-Cole et al. (2013).
11. Glenn (2009).
12. Russell-Cole et al. (2013).
13. Glenn (2009); Russell-Cole et al. (2013).
14. Hunter (2005:23).
15. Telles (2009:10).
16. Hunter (2005).
17. Hunter (2005); Keith (2009); Russell-Cole et al. (2013); Wilder (2015).
18. Norwood (2014a:160).
19. Glenn (2009); Hunter (2005); Russell-Cole et al. (2013).
20. Harvey, Banks, and Tennial (2014:201).
21. Bonilla-Silva (2004); Dixon and Telles (2017).
22. Hunter (2005); Wilder (2015).
23. Hunter (2005:3).
24. Hall (2008:39).
25. Hunter (2005); Norwood (2014a); Wilder (2015).
26. Norwood (2014a).
27. Hunter (2005:37).
28. Glenn (2009:168).
29. Glenn (2009); Hunter (2005).
30. Hunter (2005).
31. Wilder (2015).
32. Hunter (2005:65).
33. Norwood and Foreman (2014:19).
34. Wilder (2015:58).
35. Wilder (2015).
36. Thakore (2016).
37. Hunter (2005); Norwood and Foreman (2014); Russell-Cole et al. (2013).
38. DaCosta (2007).
39. Curington, Lin, and Lundquist (2015); Sims (2012).
40. Hunter (2005).
41. Dixon and Telles (2017).
42. Harvey et al. (2014:199).
43. Ibid. (204).
44. Norwood and Foreman (2014:16).
45. Ryabov (2016).
46. Hersch (2008:89).
47. Messing, Jabon, and Plaut (2016).
48. Bonilla-Silva (2004).
49. Hunter (2005:37).
50. Ibid. (69).
51. Norwood (2014a:163).
52. Russell-Cole et al. (2013:27).
53. Glenn (2009:166).
54. Herring (2004:3).
55. Wilder (2015:16).
56. Harvey et al. (2014:202–3).
57. Ibid. (203–5).

Intersectionality

Kimberlé Crenshaw

Intersectionality, also known as intersectional analysis, examines how discrimination operates at the intersection of multiple structures of oppression. Intersectionality is a response to the gap in traditional forms of analyses that focus on a single axis of discrimination, for example, how racism affects Black communities or how sexism affects women, neither of which analyzes the effect of the intersection of racism and sexism on women of color. Intersectionality aims to reveal and uncover the power dynamics at these structural intersections so that intervention and activism can be more effective in communities that experience two or more axes of subordination. Kimberlé Crenshaw, also a founder of critical race theory, coined the term *intersectionality* in the 1980s; her work is the focus of this chapter.

Photo 13.1 Kimberlé Crenshaw

Source: https://commons.wikimedia. org/wiki/File:Kimberl%C3%A9_ Crenshaw_(40901215153).jpg.

Why This Theory

Intersectionality was born of Critical Legal Studies and Black feminism, both of which challenged traditional approaches to social problems. Critical Legal Studies scholars found the antidiscrimination laws of the Civil Rights Movement to be insufficient in addressing persistent discrimination and thus aimed to reveal the ways in which legal language masked entrenched power differentials. Black feminism also addressed the limitations in law, policy, and social movements to meet the needs and concerns of Black women. Black women were put in a difficult bind of either choosing to align themselves with Black, antiracist movements that centered on Black men and often had a patriarchal approach or choosing feminist movements that centered on the needs of White women. Kimberlé Crenshaw, whose work this chapter is based on, framed this problem: "The failure of feminism to interrogate race means that the resistance strategies of feminism will often replicate and reinforce the subordination of people of color, and the failure of antiracism to interrogate patriarchy means that antiracism will frequently reproduce the subordination of women."[1] Crenshaw proposed the theory of intersectionality as an answer to this conundrum and squarely and unapologetically placed Black women's experiences at the center of the discussion, rather than at the margins:

> With Black women as the starting point, it becomes more apparent how dominant conceptions of discrimination condition us to think about subordination as disadvantage occurring along a single categorical axis. I want to suggest further that this single-axis framework erases Black women in the conceptualization, identification and remediation of race and sex discrimination by limiting inquiry to the experiences of otherwise-privileged members of the group.[2]

Intersectionality explains how addressing only one aspect of one's identity (e.g., race or gender) that correlates to only one aspect of a social hierarchy (e.g., racism or sexism) is insufficient; instead, the interlocking aspects of one's identity and the correlating interlocking hierarchies need to be at the center of analysis. In this manner, intersectionality seeks to focus on those who experience multiple axes of oppression and expose the hidden power structures of movements and agendas, even ones that intend to be liberatory.

Description of the Theory

Intersectionality was introduced and coined by Kimberlé Crenshaw in her 1989 article "Demarginalizing the Intersection of Race and Sex: A Black Feminist Critique of Antidiscrimination Doctrine, Feminist Theory and Antiracist Politics" and in her 1991 article "Mapping the Margins: Intersectionality,

Identity Politics, and Violence Against Women of Color." To communicate the necessity and utility of intersectional analysis, Crenshaw first had to expose the limitations of the single-axis approach.

As noted in the title of the 1989 article, Crenshaw offers a Black feminist critique of the then-prevailing antidiscrimination policies, feminist theory, and Black politics. In analyzing antidiscrimination policies, Crenshaw chooses a few key court decisions to reveal the failure in their ability to address how Black women differently experience discrimination. For example, in *DeGraffenried v. General Motors*, Black women sued General Motors for disproportionately targeting Black women during a company layoff, but because White women had been hired, their case was denied, and the company was deemed not sexist. The Black women were subsequently told that they should fold their complaint in with another case filed by Black men if they wanted to claim discrimination based on race. The problem was that Black women could "receive protection only to the extent that their experiences are recognizably similar to those whose experiences tend to be reflected in antidiscrimination doctrine."[3] The court did not see the Black women's claims as a clear gender issue *or* a clear race issue, and the court refused the idea that Black women constituted a new class of minorities that could claim discrimination as a distinct group. The discrimination that the Black women experienced was, in fact, due to the *intersection* of racism and sexism, but the court did not recognize it as such.

In exposing the need for intersectionality, Crenshaw also analyzes the ways in which feminist and antiracist agendas obscure the voices of Black women. In critiquing feminist theory, Crenshaw notes how feminist politics attempted to speak for all women, when in fact they were representing only the experiences of White women. For example, White women addressed how rape laws were not meant to protect women but were in actuality laws encoded with a patriarchal ideology around chastity and sexual mores. Proof of rape had to come through "clear evidence," such as skin under the fingernails as a sign of struggle; otherwise, it was presumed that the woman was guilty of willingly engaging in a deviant sexual situation. Although it is evident that rape laws were meant to control White women's sexuality, the same was not true for Black women's sexuality. Rape was long used as a tool of racial terror against Black women, and Black women's bodies were seen as hypersexualized. In this vein, the feminist movement articulated the concerns and experiences of sexual violence in relation to White women, but their analyses and arguments did not speak to or offer defense for the lives of Black women. Like feminist movements that used single-axis analysis and assumed a White woman as the target, organizations that fought on the behalf of Black communities also used single-axis analysis and presumed a Black man as the victim. For example, Crenshaw notes the debate over the 1965 Moynihan Report, a famous government issued report that suggested that the "pathologies" of Black single-mother families were due to a high unemployment rate among Black men, a dysfunctional

Black culture, and a domineering culture among Black women. Black organizations, with Black men as their leaders, criticized the Moynihan Report for reproducing racist ideologies about Black families and Black men, but they did not criticize the report for being sexist in its portrayal of Black women as too domineering. In her examination of these agendas, Crenshaw shows how the "complexity of compoundedness" that Black women experience is obscured or ignored.[4] She refers to this complexity as the intersection between racism, sexism, and other salient oppressions. She likened the intersection of discrimination to a traffic intersection where traffic "may flow in one direction, and it may flow in another. If an accident happens in an intersection, it can be caused by cars traveling from any number of directions and, sometimes, from all of them."[5] Intersectionality articulates how discrimination occurs at the intersection of marginalized structures of oppression.

The Foundations of Intersectionality

Crenshaw set forth intersectionality as a paradigm for understanding how Black women were marginalized in politics, law, and social discourse. This marginalization could be addressed by paying attention to how identities are not unilaterally experienced and by analyzing those identities in relation to the reproduction of power. Crenshaw outlines three aspects or types of intersectionality: (1) structural, (2) political, and (3) representational.[6]

Structural Intersectionality

To explain **structural intersectionality**, Crenshaw studied battered women's shelters in Los Angeles. She found that women of color experienced issues getting help due to a predominantly White and middle-class approach to sexual violence. Immigrant women of color were less likely to get help for reasons such as language barriers, fear of deportation, and cultural barriers to seeking therapy. These women were facing interlocking structural barriers based on gender, race, class, and nationality, but the women's shelters were not addressing these barriers. Crenshaw explains that "women of color are differentially situated in the economic, social, and political worlds. When reform efforts undertaken on behalf of women neglect this fact, women of color are less likely to have their needs met than women who are racially privileged."[7] In the case of the women's shelters, outreach was solely focused on the structure most clearly tied to sexual violence, but without also paying attention to the intersectional structures of class, race, and nationality, the outreach efforts were failing: "The fact that minority women suffer from the effects of multiple subordination, coupled with institutional expectations based on inappropriate nonintersectional contexts, shapes and ultimately limits the opportunities for meaningful intervention on their behalf."[8] Structural intersectionality calls for the recognition of how discrimination occurs on multiple and often intersecting structural levels.

Political Intersectionality

In **political intersectionality**, the focus is how political agendas rarely address intersecting dynamics of power; instead, their agendas reflect single-axis analysis. As noted earlier, this problem is easily observable in Black social movements that focus on the discrimination faced by Black men and feminist movements that focus on the discrimination faced by White women. In analyzing the issue of sexual violence, Crenshaw points out how feminist policies and services reflect White women's needs, as shelters are often in White neighborhoods and provide English-only services. In addition, the feminist movement addressing sexual violence was centered on a campaign to emphasize how sexual violence affected White women. Crenshaw states the failure of this campaign to use political intersectionality; this feminist movement was more focused on making sure White women got services than on addressing all women's needs. Black political agendas also failed Black women by framing sexual abuse as a result of the violence and racism experienced by Black men and by focusing concerns on innocent Black men who were accused of rape. Though these two issues are warranted, the Black political agenda did not validate and address the sexual violence Black women experienced. Black political movements also implicitly suggested that Black women should prioritize the fight on racism over sexism and put aside the pain they suffered as Black women. Political intersectionality "highlights the fact that women of color are situated within at least two subordinated groups that frequently pursue conflicting political agendas" and that "the need to split one's political energies between two sometimes opposing groups is a dimension of intersectional disempowerment that men of color and white women seldom confront."[9]

Representational Intersectionality

Images in popular culture influence and shape narratives about communities; therefore, **representational intersectionality** analyzes how racist and sexist representations marginalize women of color. Crenshaw looked at the case against 2 Live Crew (a popular rap music group in the 1980s and 1990s), the first music group prosecuted for obscenity in their lyrics. Crenshaw summarizes the popular debate on the case as two main sides, for and against the group. One side pushed for the obscenity charges due to the misogynistic lyrics; however, this stance was not about the harm done to women but rather was a racist narrative about the violence in Black communities and a dismissal of Black music as culturally valuable. On another side of the debate was a defense of 2 Live Crew as a band whose music was a valid form of African American culture and whose lyrics were an attempt to resist racism and stereotypes. Crenshaw points out how both arguments left out the concerns of Black women, who were the subjects of the misogynistic lyrics; the focus was on Black men or Black communities as a whole, while the harm done to Black women was obfuscated. Thus, representational intersectionality looks at the ways in which "images are produced through a confluence of prevalent narratives of race and gender, as well as recognition of how contemporary critiques of racist and sexist representation marginalize women of color."[10]

Intersectionality and the Relationship to Identity Politics and Anti-Essentialism

Intersectionality is often interpreted as or conflated with conversations on identity politics and anti-essentialism. Intersectionality has connections to these two other principles but is also distinct from them. Anti-essentialism is the idea that no one category should be essentialized; for example, *woman* does not have one confined definition, nor does it exist *a priori*. Rather, it is understood that categories such as race and gender are social constructions wherein the meaning assigned to these categories varies and comes from society. The anti-essentialism stance has led some to argue that because categories are not biologically real, they should be erased from the lexicon and culture. Although intersectionality agrees that these categories are socially constructed, it does not advocate that the categories should be eliminated. Race and gender are not essential identities, but they do hold important significance and consequence in society, so they should not be discarded.[11]

Intersectionality also speaks to the issue of identity politics. Identity politics emphasize particular identities in activism and political agendas: for example, a movement based on queer identity or a movement based on Black identity. Intersectionality aligns with this importance of identity-based movements, but instead the focus is on the *structural power relations* that affect people with multiple marginalized identities, not *identity*. Furthermore, intersectionality suggests that identity work is better used as a tool of coalition building rather than as a basis of division. For example, people of color with a range of intersecting identities, such as women of color, queer people of color, and working communities of color, can, instead of working separately, come to see their commonalities in order to build coalitions against sexism, homophobia, and poverty. Unlike the stances of anti-essentialism or identity politics, intersectionality is not focused on the categories/identities themselves but on the power relations that are attached to these categories and the oppression that follows.[12]

The Expansion of Intersectionality

Since Crenshaw's initial articles, intersectionality has spread to multiple disciplines, including history, sociology, literature, philosophy, anthropology, feminist studies, ethnic studies, queer studies, geography, legal studies, and organizational studies.[13] The theoretical application and methods of intersectionality have evolved and manifested in various ways as its influence has grown in this wide range of disciplines. In a review of sociological articles that use intersectionality, Jones, Misra, and McCurley identify three ways in which intersectionality is applied: (1) inclusion, (2) relational, and (3) anticategorical.[14] In the inclusion/voice model, the analysis is used to center disadvantaged groups and reveal heterogeneity within a community that is often overlooked. An example is focusing on transgender women of color, to bring attention to dynamics of gender identity among women of color. In the relational/process model, intersectional analysis emphasizes the relationship between disadvantage and privilege, such as studies that compare low-income Black men to low-income White men. This mode of using intersectionality looks at how certain identities can be more or less salient in any given situation while recognizing that identities shape one another. The third model, anticategorical/systemic, approaches analysis with the presumption that no one identity is ever more salient than another and that all identities are co-constitutive of each other. In this case, an example could be analyzing how undocumented students of color, who hold a multiply marginalized identity, navigate their status with different authority groups, such as teachers, classmates, friends, or legal officials. Each approach utilizes intersectionality in a slightly different manner, but each one is true to intersectionality's goal of centering multiple, intersecting subordinations.

Crenshaw and coauthors Cho and McCall analyze intersectionality's evolution and growth in order to propose a field of intersectionality studies.[15] In their analysis, they point out that the use of intersectionality varies by application, whether it is in research and teaching, theory and methods, or political intervention. They also explain how intersectionality has morphed through different disciplinary frameworks, sometimes even losing its original intent as "disciplinary conventions import a range of assumptions and truth claims that sometimes contribute to the very erasures to which intersectionality draws attention."[16] Yet in framing a field of intersectionality studies, they do not aim for a narrow, unified application of intersectionality; in fact, they note that "it is important to consider the intersectional project a communal one, one undertaken not in academic silos but in conjunction with fellow travelers with shared insights, approaches, and commitments, guiding critique and collaboration for communal gain."[17] As intersectionality evolves, the larger aims of intersectionality remain rooted in the initial framing of structural intersectionality (analyzing structures of domination and power dynamics), political intersectionality (applied praxis), and intersectional knowledge production (using the theory to challenge the social reproduction of power). Cho, Crenshaw, and McCall summarize the call of intersectionality:

> What makes an analysis intersectional … is its adoption of an intersectional way of thinking about the problem of sameness and difference and its relation to power. This framing—conceiving of

categories not as distinct but as always permeated by other categories, fluid and changing, always in the process of creating and being created by dynamics of power—emphasizes what intersectionality does rather than what intersectionality is.[18]

How to Challenge Racism

Intersectionality is a theory of intervention as much as it is a theory of explanation and examination. Crenshaw uses intersectionality to uncover how marginalized communities are overlooked, even by well-intentioned social welfare agencies. For example, Crenshaw uses intersectionality to show how battered women's shelters' policies were constructed for the experiences of White women, thereby not accounting for how intersecting oppressions such as racism, classism, and nativism present barriers to help for abused women of color. The identification of these barriers can lead to shelters reforming their practices to serve multiple communities' needs. Intersectionality reveals that a one-size-fits-all approach to social problems is ineffective, particularly when the "one size" is predicated on a privileged status (e.g., Whiteness in relation to White women or patriarchy in relation to Black men). Intersectionality is more than a theoretical approach; it's about defining the problem in a way that allows intervention to be more effective. Cho, Crenshaw, and McCall state that

> the trajectory of intersectionality as part of a larger critique of rights and legal institutions reveals how the intersectional lens looked beyond the more narrowly circumscribed demands for inclusion within the logics of sameness and difference. Instead, it addressed the larger ideological structures in which subjects, problems, and solutions were framed.[19]

Likewise Thornton and Zambrana outline **intersectional scholarship** as a call to action:

> (1) Reformulate the world of ideas so that it incorporates the many contradictory and overlapping ways that human life is experienced; (2) convey this knowledge by rethinking curricula and promoting institutional change in higher education institutions; (3) apply the knowledge in an effort to create a society in which all voices are heard; and (4) advocate for public policies that are responsive to multiple voices.[20]

Crenshaw has continued the work of intersectionality in the 30 years since she introduced it and cofounded the African American Policy Forum (AAPF) in 1996. In an interview celebrating 20 years of AAPF and the utility of intersectionality, Crenshaw notes that the theory's import is still rooted in community action: "We try to take ideas and make them into hands-on tools that advocates and communities can use."[21]

- The median weekly earnings of Black women are 65.3% of White men's earnings and 89% of Black men's earnings; Asian women's earnings are 93.5% of White men's earnings and 75.5% of Asian men's earnings.

- Among all full-time assistant professors in degree-granting postsecondary institutions, 38% are White women, 34% are White men, 7% are Asian men, 6% are Asian Women, 4% are Black women, 3% are Black men, 3% are Hispanic men, and 3% are Hispanic women.

- Twelve percent of Black girls are suspended from school, compared to 2% of White girls, which means that Black girls are suspended at six times the rate of White girls.

Sources: Crenshaw, Ocen, and Nanda (2015); Hegewisch and Hartmann (2019); National Center for Education Statistics (2018).

Evaluation

Methodological Benefits

Crenshaw merges the theoretical approach of intersectionality with a methodological imperative by intentionally choosing data from marginalized voices. Crenshaw often looks at the cases of Black women (or other women of color), whether that is through the unsuccessful discrimination suits filed by Black women or the shelters for battered women. The methodological goal of intersectionality is to broaden the understanding of marginalized communities; this insight can be accomplished by comparing and contrasting communities that share an axis of discrimination, by analyzing multiple types of structural discrimination, and/or by exposing a hidden axis of privilege. In the first case of compare and contrast, intersectional methods call for data where comparisons of power can be made, such as comparing men and women of color to analyze the differential effects of patriarchy or comparing White women and women of color to analyze the differential effects of racism. In the second case of bringing in multiple types of structural discrimination, Crenshaw accomplishes this by bringing citizenship status and language into the race-gender analysis of battered women's shelters. The third way intersectionality can direct methodology is by exposing an axis of privilege; for example, Carbado uses a gender discrimination case where the presumption of womanness defined by Whiteness is ignored.[22] Carbado calls this "color-blind intersectionality," which "refers to instances in which whiteness helps to produce and is part of a cognizable social category but is invisible or unarticulated as an intersectional subject position."[23] As intersectionality has evolved, so has its methodological imperatives, always with the benefit of using intersectionality as a means of uncovering hidden power and increasing the voices of marginalized communities.

Methodological Limitations

Crenshaw, as a legal scholar, rooted her early work in analysis of legal decisions that obfuscated the needs of women of color; she dissected these cases to show how single-axis analyses of power obscured the discrimination that women of color experienced. Crenshaw notes that she chose cases where an intersectional analysis can be usefully employed to reveal the short-sightedness in court decisions, but this means that cases were picked to meet the theory, instead of showing how the theory can be applied in any number of cases. Though Crenshaw is clear in why she used these cases, choosing data to fit a theory's framework can be seen as a methodological sidestep. Yet a greater question is how to define the methods of intersectionality. Intersectionality is a theory, but on some level, as mentioned previously, it also implies a methodological approach via the choice of data. However, the methods that correlate with or fit intersectionality are unclear: Which data are best suited, which identities should be prioritized, and how many intersecting identities should one pay attention to—is there a minimum or limit? This last question points to one of the more common criticisms of intersectionality, the methodological feasibility of studying multiple intersecting identities or structures. For example, if one studies the effects of racism and sexism, classism, homophobia, and ableism are left out. There isn't clear direction for methodologically accounting for multiple interacting constitutive discriminating structures.

Theoretical Benefits

A primary theoretical benefit of intersectionality is providing a means to escape the harm of single-axis analysis. With intersectionality, Crenshaw can simultaneously argue against the racism that Black men experience *while also showing* how Black patriarchy harms Black women or support the fight of White women against sexism *while also criticizing* the racism in White feminism; she dispels the notion of an either/or political alignment by providing a theory that questions a rhetorical inclusion in favor of an analysis of power. Intersectionality speaks to the validity and value in identity politics but emphasizes that the focus needs to be on how *structures intersect*. This attention to the intersections of hierarchies is at the heart of the theory's contribution; for example, no other theory clearly articulates how race/racism and gender/sexism interact. Moreover, the theory has been broadened to study any number of other intersecting structures, such as sexuality, class, age, religion, and disability. This uncovering of the intersecting dimensions of power offers unique theoretical insight.

Overall, intersectionality brings marginalized voices to the forefront in an intentional, unapologetic manner. The ability of the framework to bring these voices to the center of conversation and analysis is perhaps the theory's greatest benefit. As Risman says about the import of intersectionality: "There is now considerable consensus growing that one must always take into consideration multiple axes of oppression; to do otherwise presumes the whiteness of women, the maleness of people of color, and the heterosexuality of everyone."[24] The theoretical intersectional imperative is now felt in virtually all major analyses of oppression.

Theoretical Limitations

Intersectionality reveals the dynamics of power at the intersection of oppressions, which is the unique contribution of this theory. Yet at times it can be unclear how intersectional discrimination operates. Crenshaw explains how Black women can experience gendered discrimination similar to White women; they can experience racial discrimination similar to Black men; they can experience double discrimination, which is the additive effect of racial discrimination plus gender discrimination; and/or Black women can experience discrimination not as double discrimination but distinctly as occupying the intersection of Black woman.[25] In this sense, it's difficult to decide if, or when, discrimination and identities are additive, constitutive, or intersecting. Recent intersectional work tends to reject the double/additive model and instead likens intersectionality to an intersection in the road, a matrix, or a birdcage. Another theoretical limitation is a lack of attention to how people use their agency to deploy their identities in various manners and contexts. Intersectionality notes the relationship between structure and individuals, but the emphasis is on the intersecting structural oppressions that shape multiple subordinated communities, without as much attention to how people use individual agency to navigate intersectional discrimination.

Conclusion

The analytical insight into how discrimination works at the intersection of multiple structures reveals a limitation in all other studies of inequality; an analysis that doesn't take intersectionality into account is most likely omitting a (sub)community from its analysis. The theory of intersectionality has encouraged scholars of inequality to step back and interrogate whether they are properly analyzing the salient dimensions of inequality or if a story of marginalization is not being told for lack of an intersectional approach. The term *intersectionality* was coined by Crenshaw, but a community of scholars from a range of disciplines has published and continues to work on the best practices for intersectionality's theory, methods, and application.

REFLECT AND DISCUSS

1. How does intersectionality show that single-axis analysis limits the voices of marginalized communities?

2. How does intersectionality challenge the ideal of inclusion as a solution?

3. How can Crenshaw's original focus on women of color be used as a model for applying intersectionality to other communities who are multiply marginalized?

Diagram 13.1 Intersectionality

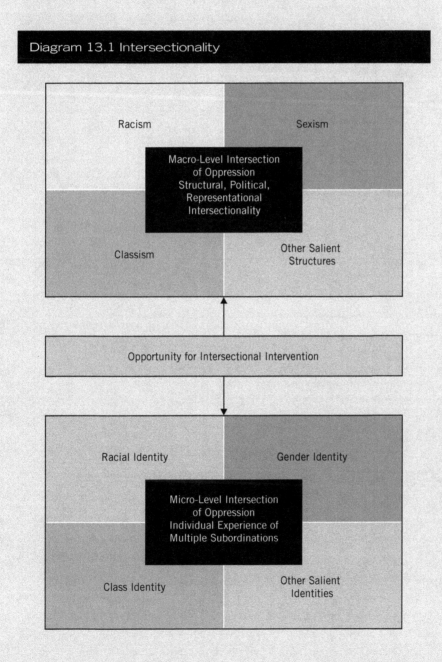

KEY TERMS

Intersectionality: "What makes an analysis intersectional … is its adoption of an intersectional way of thinking about the problem of sameness and difference and its relation to power. This framing—conceiving of categories not as distinct but as always permeated by other categories, fluid and changing, always in the process of creating and being created by dynamics of power—emphasizes what intersectionality does rather than what intersectionality is."[26]

Intersectional scholarship: "(1) Reformulate the world of ideas so that it incorporates the many contradictory and overlapping ways that human life is experienced; (2) convey this knowledge by rethinking curricula and promoting institutional change in higher education institutions; (3) apply the knowledge in an effort to create a society in which all voices are heard; and (4) advocate for public policies that are responsive to multiple voices."[27]

Political intersectionality: "Highlights the fact that women of color are situated within at least two subordinated groups that frequently pursue conflicting political agendas."[28]

Representational intersectionality: "Images are produced through a confluence of prevalent narratives of race and gender, as well as recognition of how contemporary critiques of racist and sexist representation marginalize women of color."[29]

Structural intersectionality: "The multilayered and routinized forms of domination."[30]

KEY PEOPLE

Kimberlé Crenshaw (1959–): Crenshaw is Professor of Law at the University of California, Los Angeles and Columbia Law School, as well as the director of the Center for Intersectionality and Social Policy Studies at Columbia Law School. She is known for her foundational work with critical race theory and intersectionality. In 1996 she cofounded the African American Policy Forum, which is known for initiatives such as Say Her Name and Black Girls Matter. In 2016, Crenshaw received the Fellows Outstanding Scholar award from the American Bar Foundation.
Podcast: aapf.org/podcast
Twitter @sandylocks

WORKS CITED AND FURTHER READING

Carbado, Devon W. 2013. "Colorblind Intersectionality." *Signs: Journal of Women in Culture and Society* 38(4):811–45.

Cho, Sumi, Kimberlé W. Crenshaw, and Leslie McCall. 2013. "Toward a Field of Intersectionality Studies: Theory, Application, and Praxis." *Signs: Journal of Women in Culture and Society* 38(4):785–810.

Collins, Patricia Hill. 2000. *Black Feminist Thought: Knowledge, Consciousness, and the Politics of Empowerment.* New York: Routledge.

Crenshaw, Kimberlé W. 1989. "Demarginalizing the Intersection of Race and Sex: A Black Feminist Critique of Antidiscrimination Doctrine, Feminist Theory and Antiracist Politics." *University of Chicago Legal Forum* 1(8):139–67.

Crenshaw, Kimberlé W. 1991. "Mapping the Margins: Intersectionality, Identity Politics, and Violence against Women of Color." *Stanford Law Review* 43(6):1241–99.

Crenshaw, Kimberlé W. 2014. "The Structural and Political Dimensions of Intersectional Oppression." Pp. 16–22 in *Intersectionality: A Foundations and Frontiers Reader,* edited by P. R. Grzanka. Boulder, CO: Westview Press.

Crenshaw, Kimberlé W. 2017. "Interview: Kimberlé Crenshaw on Intersectionality, More Than Two Decades Later." Columbia Law School, June 8. Retrieved June 1, 2019 (https://www.law.columbia.edu/pt-br/news/2017/06/kimberle-crenshaw-intersectionality).

Crenshaw, Kimberlé W., Priscilla Ocen, and Jyoti Nanda. 2015. "Black Girls Matter: Pushed Out, Overpoliced and Underprotected." New York: African American Policy Forum and Center for Intersectionality and Social Policy Studies.

Dill, Bonnie Thornton and Ruth Enid Zambrana, eds. 2009. *Emerging Intersections: Race, Class, and Gender in Theory, Policy, and Practice.* Piscataway, NJ: Rutgers University Press.

Grzanka, Patrick R., ed. 2014. *Intersectionality: A Foundations and Frontiers Reader.* Boulder, CO: Westview Press.

Hegewisch, Ariane and Heidi Hartmann. 2019. "The Gender Wage Gap: 2018 Earnings Differences by Race and Ethnicity." Washington, DC: Institute for Women's Policy Research.

Jones, Katherine C., Joya Misra, and K. McCurley. 2013. "Intersectionality in Sociology." Lawrence, KS: Sociologists for Women in Society. Retrieved June 1, 2019 (http://www.socwomen.org/wp-content/uploads/swsfactsheet_intersectionality.pdf).

National Center for Education Statistics. 2018. "Race/Ethnicity of College Faculty." Washington, DC: U.S. Department of Education.

Risman, Barbara. 2004. "Gender as a Social Structure: Theory Wrestling with Activism." *Gender and Society* 18(4): 429–50.

See also the entire special thematic issue of *Signs* (2013), Volume 38, Issue 4.

NOTES

1. Crenshaw (1991:1252).
2. Crenshaw (1989:140).
3. Ibid. (152).
4. Ibid. (166).
5. Ibid. (149).
6. Crenshaw (1991).
7. Ibid. (1250).
8. Ibid. (1251).
9. Ibid. (1252).
10. Ibid. (1283).
11. Crenshaw (1991).
12. Ibid.
13. Cho, Crenshaw, and McCall (2013).
14. Jones, Misra, and McCurley (2013).
15. Cho et al. (2013).
16. Ibid. (793).
17. Ibid. (804).
18. Ibid. (795).
19. Ibid. (79).
20. Dill and Zambrana (2009:2).
21. Crenshaw (2017).
22. Carbado (2013).
23. Ibid. (817).
24. Risman (2004:442).
25. Crenshaw (1989:149).
26. Cho et al. (2013:795).
27. Dill and Zambrana (2009:2).
28. Crenshaw (1991:1252).
29. Ibid. (1283).
30. Ibid. (1245).

Index